The Villa Ariadne

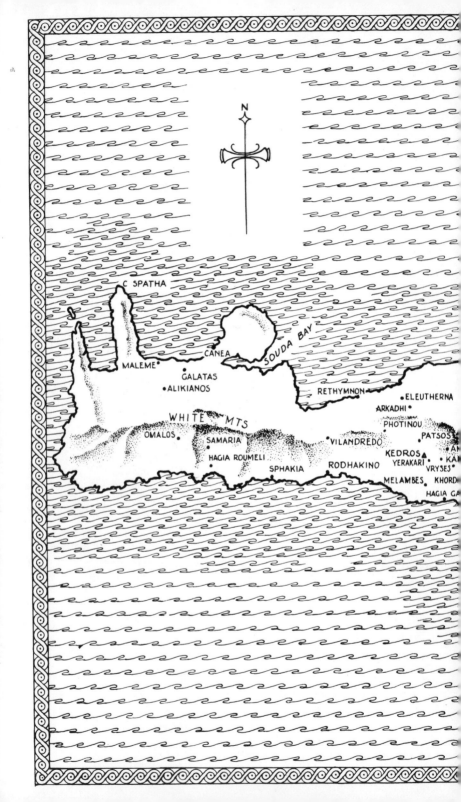

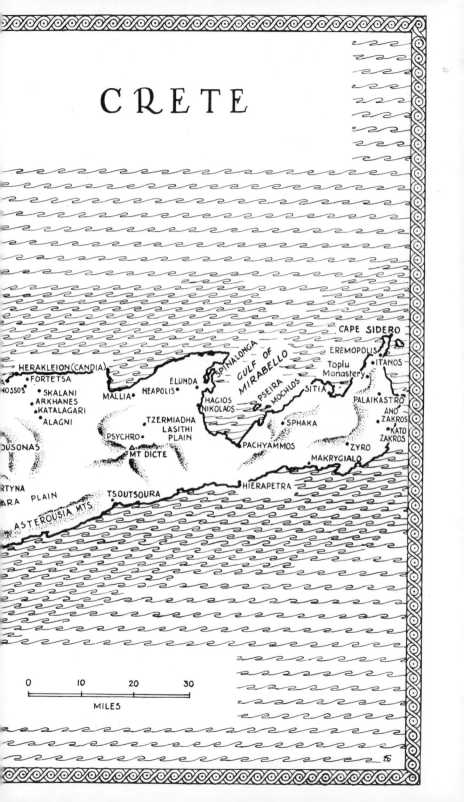

DILYS POWELL

The Villa Ariadne

◊✳◊✳◊✳◊✳◊

A COMMON READER EDITION
THE AKADINE PRESS

The Villa Ariadne

A COMMON READER EDITION published 1999
by The Akadine Press, Inc., by arrangement with Ivor Powell.

A COMMON READER EDITION and fountain colophon are trademarks
of The Akadine Press, Inc.

ISBN 1-888173-66-1

10   9   8   7   6   5   4   3   2   1

AUTHOR'S NOTE

THIS BOOK is set in Crete, and Crete is changing. Some of the changes I have lately seen, but more are coming, and the traveller may not always recognise the places I describe. My Crete is chiefly an older Crete. And the people I have known—in the light of the passing years they too change. I have tried to tell a truthful story; where I could I have sought out the witnesses; but there are some I have failed to trace. In one instance at any rate I have preferred to leave the legend, if legend it is, untouched. In writing about Patrick Leigh Fermor I have set down what the Cretans said to me. It seemed a pity to risk destroying the charm of their tales, and I have not asked him to confirm or deny; I hope he will forgive this omission.

I will not make a great show of apologising for the inconsistent spelling of Greek words and names. As a rule I have used the form familiar to me—Herakleion rather than Iraklion—or the form which retains some trace of its origin; I pronounce Ayia, but I write Hagia. My transliteration of place-names thus is erratic; I have abandoned the attempt to distinguish between the nominative and the accusative of Christian names or between the masculine and the feminine of surnames; and for readability I have left out all the accents.

I am indebted for help from many people, both British and Greek, whose names occur or whose stories are recorded in the book; I thank them all. I owe especial thanks to Dr Joan Evans, who allowed me to quote from the Evans letters and on whose book *Time and Chance* (Macmillan) I have relied in sketching Sir Arthur's early life; to the late Hilda Pendlebury, who without restriction handed over to me her husband's letters, as also to her daughter Joan Pendlebury; and to Mrs Doreen Dunbabin, who entrusted to me her husband's manuscript account of his experiences in Occupied Crete. The British School of Archaeology at Athens has generously given permission for quotations from Evans's records, published in the School Annual, of the first years of excavation at Knossos. I have referred in the text to my indebtedness to the late Stanley Moss's book *Ill Met By Moonlight* (Harrap), and I have quoted briefly from Mary Chubb's *Nefertiti Lived Here* (Geoffrey Bles). I should like to thank also Miss Edith Clay, Mrs M. J. Thornton, Miss Euphrosyne Sideropoulou, Mr John Stanley and Mr Stelio Hourmouzios.

PROLOGUE

i

FROM HERAKLEION the road, leaving the ramparts, ran southeast beside a ravine, past a straggle of shops and little houses with gardens, between vineyards and fringes of eucalyptus towards dry gradual hills. I took a ticket to Knossos, and in a quarter of an hour the bus was pulling up by a café opposite the entrance to the Palace of Minos. Then I realised that I should have got out fifty yards or so farther back. I had not seen the place since 1935, and this was 1958; you forget, in twenty-three years, the exact position of a gate.

'Where,' I said—I knew, but I asked all the same—'where is the Villa Ariadne?' The conductor was blank. 'The Villa Ariadne,' I said again, 'where the archaeologists stay, the English archaeologists?' Blank again and a shrug. As I moved to get out I tried once more. 'The Villa Ariadne, Sir Arthur Evans's house?' 'Ah, Evans's house! Wait!' He shouted down the bus. 'The lady wants Evans's house!' 'Evans's house!' the driver repeated. 'Wait!' He leaned out of the window and backed. 'There,' said the conductor, 'there is the entrance.'

I pushed open the door in the wall and went into the courtyard. A woman whom I did not know answered when I knocked at the door of the lodge. The Director, she said, had gone to Rethymnon, and since it was a Sunday the students too would probably be out for the day, but I could go up to the Villa and look for myself. Morning glory swarmed over the wall by the road; it was cool in the court-yard. But at the top of the few steps which skirted the little white-washed building everything was thin, everything thirsty. Wire netting enclosed the lodge garden. Inside its irregular triangle long grass wove a mat over the soil; a few exhausted hollyhocks struggled out of the weeds. I went through the gate in the fence and up the path towards the Villa. Pines, reeds, desiccated palms, oleanders, bougainvillea, dusty olives; long ago, fond preserving hands had set fragments of antique statuary here and there among the trees— an empty shrine, a plinth, a broken capital. Headless but majestic, a marble Hadrian posed in the shade; a turkey with her brood scratched round the base at his sandalled feet. Emaciated, the shrubbery dangled spiky branches. A pomegranate had put out a few parched flowers, but there was no sign of the hibiscus whose blossoms we used to pick on breathless July afternoons, nothing was growing in the urns on the terrace where amidst the scent of jasmine we used to dine.

But the Villa itself—that looked unchanged: the polygonal blocks of sand-coloured stone outlined in mortar, the flat roof against the background of pine trees, the dark shutters and the half-basement, the sense of suffocation, stubbornly Victorian in the Mediterranean landscape. Somewhere a dog barked furiously and rattled his chain. The front door stood open. I climbed the flight of stone steps and went in. On the right-hand wall, a replica of a relief from the Palace—the noble head of the charging bull. Beside it, a commemorative plaque: dates, names. Nothing else: floors bare, ceilings cracked, walls peeling. The passage at the end of the hall led past the long dining-room; sparse furniture, the table minimally laid with the necessary frugality of an archaeological expedition.

An unwarranted ghost, I crept downstairs to where, for coolness in the Cretan summer, the bedrooms had been contrived below ground level. Through an open door I could see the stone floor naked, the shutters drooping from their hinges, green light filtering through windows overgrown with creeper; nothing except a camp bed, a tray of sherds and a suitcase exposing a trail of shirts and socks. Time had sucked the house dry.

When I went out two young men were walking up the path from the lower house. In that arid garden they were unmistakably English. Two archaeological students from a British excavation party; simply to look at them reminded me how long I had been an alien from their society. The dog barked again frantically. He was in view now

—prickly black coat and old white muzzle—bouncing on the roof of his kennel; and a woman came from the servants' entrance behind the terrace to see what was going on. Yes, she said, she was Ourania. I asked if she remembered me: 'I think,' I said, 'I used to know your husband.' No, she said, at that time, though she was married in 1933, she did not work at Knossos but lived up at her village. But the name I gave, Payne—she knew that. And her husband? Ah, Manoli had gone to his own village, to Lasithi, for the day.

'I will come back tomorrow,' I told her. On the bank behind the Villa the pines had shed a dark slippery carpet of needles. I scrambled up and looked towards the slopes which hid Fortetsa village and Herakleion. A donkey was tethered by the tumbling stones of a broken hut, and in the field beyond it a group of women in head-scarves were cutting the corn. In the still, warm, aromatic air I could hear them calling to one another. Only the house and its garden were dying.

I walked down to the gates at the bottom of the Villa drive, but they were locked, and I went back the way I had come. Farther down the main road, cars and buses were drawn up in a car-park outside the Palace of Minos; a pavilion sold embroideries and orangeade; there was a ticket-office. I paid and went in, up the leafy approach, across the courtyard with the walled pits on the left and the trees on the right shading mysterious trenches. A maze: but I remembered not so much the involutions and the dead ends as the pall of history pressing bloodstained and heavy on summer days; and the Cretan light settling dense, like the red local wine; and the hot smell of dust in the paths; and the afternoon shadows creeping thick as tar from the walls. For me it had always been afternoon in the Palace, late afternoon, men trudging home from the dig in the cemetery behind the hill, the pines solid and gold-fringed in the dying sun, and as I clambered about the reconstructed passages something sacrificial in the air; one half-expected a roll of drums. In those days it had been comforting to escape from the deserted laby-rinth back to the company at the Villa.

But now the Palace buzzed with visitors. Tourists with cameras and handbooks; a bearded young man in shorts and a blue shirt, a peasant's straw hat on the ground beside him, sat sketching under the cypresses beyond the pits. Taking a short cut, I climbed over a wall into the complex of buildings. In the Central Court a polyglot guide was lecturing to bemused faces, English, French, German; abruptly he turned and made off, trailing his party behind him down long stairways. I waited till the footsteps had faded, then wandered without plan. Along corridors, down steps, past light-wells, under colonnades, through porticos, out to terraces—at last I stopped short on a high jagged edge. Still a maze; it was a struggle to find the way back. Here and there vegetation was reasserting itself. Liquorice plants rooted in crevices, and gold and yellow daisies rampaged over the Court. Behind the reproductions of the frescoes on the walls of the royal rooms the swallows had nested; wings flashed and whirred as they flew between the Minoan columns. But the huge restored Palace itself, the old-and-new Palace, Evans's Palace—that was still arrogantly alive. Storey upon storey, new walls propping up old, twentieth-century pillars raising roofs which might have fallen before Troy—war and the tremors of the earth had scarcely marked it. Time had made it accessible, that was all.

On my way out I stopped to look at the bust under the pine-trees near the entrance. Stirred by the wind, a branch gently brushed the back of the bronze head. 'Sir Arthur Evans', said the Greek inscription, 'The people of Herakleion in gratitude'.

ii

I never stayed at the Villa Ariadne while Sir Arthur Evans was there himself. Indeed I came to Crete late, several years after my husband Humfry Payne had begun taking me on my first novice excursions in the islands and on the mainland of Greece. At the time of those early trips Humfry was still a student at the British School of Archaeology at Athens, and I—not a student, just a student's wife with a knowledge of the classics which the most euphemistic friend could not have called as much as rudimentary—was still struggling to find my bearings in archaeological society. But the unknown Villa was already part of my background. A pale gold phantom, it presided over remote arguments. At dinner in the Athens students' hostel its name brought a touch of fable, and sitting silent over the rissoles, embarrassed by my endless ignorance, I imagined oriental splendours.

In my first spring in Athens the air seemed to me full of talk about Crete. Sites, villages, monasteries, mountains, dates, digs, sherds, seals, tablets, scripts, everything rang confusedly in my head. Even when we set out for a trip in the country Knossos went with us. Staying for a night or two at Old Corinth, where the Americans were digging, we found among our companions the English architect and draughtsman Piet de Jong, who worked sometimes for the American School of Classical Studies, sometimes for the British School, sometimes for Evans in Crete. It was from Piet that I first heard stories, already merging with legend, of feudal state at the Villa Ariadne.

'There was a train of donkeys bringing snow from Mount Ida for the sherbet,' he said, pursing his mouth and giving his subdued little laugh. The amused eyes with their spectacles beneath the prominent eyebrows, the long fine nose, the whole spare, self-contained face was happily bent on the joke, and for a moment I almost believed him.

And the names. Long before I saw the setting I was aware of the cast—Duncan Mackenzie, Evans's assistant; Gilliéron, who had been occupied in some way not clear to me with the restoration of the Palace at Knossos; Wace, the Cambridge scholar who had dug at Mycenae and was now locked with Evans in a ruthless and to me incomprehensible controversy. In 1927 John Forsdyke, later Director of the British Museum, was finishing the exploration of a Minoan necropolis, discovered a year earlier by Evans himself, on the slopes beyond the stream which bounds the Palace to the east. Humfry also was digging in the Knossos area, and when that summer I joined him in Athens for a holiday Arcadian in both the metaphorical and the geographical sense of the word, he often talked about the people at Knossos. But several years were still to pass before I saw any of the Cretan characters in the story of the Villa. In treasured visits to Greece, in breathless trains and buses, on mule-back and on foot Humfry took me travelling the width and length of the

Peloponnese. We crossed mountain ranges, we took ship to the Archipelago—but never to Crete.

Not, that is, together. In the summer of 1929 Humfry was once again digging there, this time at Eleutherna in the foothills of Mount Ida. He was appointed Director of the Athens School that year, and had the dig proved important he might have gone on working in Crete. There was indeed one rediscovery—a reliable and responsible Cretan foreman, Yanni Katsarakis, who had worked for the School long before. But the soil at Eleutherna held no great treasure. Instead, the main British excavation for some time was to be on the Greek mainland at the Heraion of Perachora. There for the next four years Yanni worked with us, and Eleutherna and Mount Ida joined Knossos, the Palace of Minos and the Villa Ariadne in the haze of gossip and legend and archaeology which for me enveloped all Crete.

Not that my grasp of the other business of the School was much firmer. In retrospect the incidents and encounters of the first season as Director's wife in Athens have meaning for me, but at the time the weeks went by unrecognised. The names of eminent American and European scholars jostled one another in my head. With the early days of temperate sun, of wild tulips and almond blossom, hordes of tourists called at the Director's house and, mistaking me for an archaeologist's mate suitably equipped, vainly questioned me about the validity of Evans's reconstructions at Knossos or the relation of the egg-and-dart motive to fertility rites. Students set off on trips to places with strange names, while with my handful of Greek words I took the tram down to the city, performed inessential shopping and made statutory requests for my residence permit. Once at the police station—though this I think must have been in some later year—I came across a young man even more disorientated than I was. Angular high cheekbones, deep brown hair, a fine dark flush of the skin and an off-hand, remote splendour of physique—in the crowd he looked lost, and hearing him speak in English I asked if I could help. He was, it turned out, a student newly arrived at the School: Tom Dunbabin, from Oxford and before that Tasmania. I directed him to the right room, supplied him with the right phrase, and went home to lunch disproportionately pleased with myself.

And Tom Dunbabin, too, was to be part of the Cretan story. But that was years later. Meanwhile as I grew familiar with the names I began little by little to know the characters in the tale. In England, where we spent part of each year, Sir Arthur Evans used occasionally to invite us to a week-end at Youlbury, his house on Boar's Hill outside Oxford. Some people, it is true, were never more to me than distant figures in a myth. Evans's lieutenant Mackenzie was one I never saw, though there was an occasion when, confusing me with the wife of some earlier Director—a woman no doubt with the qualifications for membership of archaeological society which I never managed to acquire—he wrote me a charming and gallant letter.

The stories about him merged into my picture of the Villa: Mackenzie complaining that the nightingales kept him awake and employing a boy to throw stones at them, or commenting sourly on the prevalence of romantic human attachments. Those were the days when women in the academic world were apt to be regarded as intruders; and on the news, blameless one would have thought, of an engagement between a young Cambridge archaeologist and another of the Athens students, 'Never a week passes,' Mackenzie was reported as remarking in his soft Scottish accent, 'without some fresh scandal at the British School.'

But by the time I at long last made a first trip to Crete he was no longer there. In the summer of 1929 he fell ill and was obliged to retire. His work at the Villa had been dual. Not only had he been Evans's assistant and indeed right-hand man, he had served as Curator of Knossos, a post which in some manner not at the time clear to me was under the control of the British School at Athens. Ironically enough the man elected to follow him in the job was one of those he had marked down as symbolising the decline of archaeological morals. Coincidental with Humfry Payne's appointment as Director in Athens came the appointment as Curator at Knossos of John Pendlebury, by then married to his partner in 'scandal'.

The Pendleburys and Humfry had been contemporaries as students at the School. Now they were colleagues with official as well as friendly relations. It was usual for the Director to visit Knossos to discuss the various responsibilities of the School; it was usual for the Curator to stay at the School on his way out to Crete. The Director took up residence in the autumn, the Curator not until after the New Year. When John and Hilda Pendlebury came through Athens the fresh spring afternoons were beginning to dazzle, the processionary caterpillars were spinning their cocoons in the pines, and the four of us would play vociferous games of tennis on the hard court in the School garden. Then the season's business would disperse our party. Humfry would already be planning the year's campaign at Perachora, and Hilda and John would take ship to Crete and their own enigmatic preoccupations with lustral areas and protopalatial houses.

They were established at Knossos—it was their second season—when I was taken on a first visit to Crete. It was early in the year, with the days cool, unsettled. I was not yet at ease with the Pendleburys, and the nervousness of spring tightened the nervousness I have always felt on coming to an unfamiliar house and on having to find my bearings in a strange society and strange surroundings. The talk, the questions to be settled, everything was foreign to me; in an obscure disquiet I listened while around me echoed phrases about the tenancy of vineyards, the evasiveness of lawyers, the incidence of earthquakes and the friable nature of archaeological remains.

As Curator John Pendlebury lived in the small house, the lodge, always known as the Taverna, at the lower end of the garden where the road from Herakleion ran past the high wall. But we all had meals together in the big house, the Villa; and again the position was far from clear to me, for it appeared that the School had the responsibility for both houses but that the Villa was still at the disposal of Sir Arthur Evans when he arrived to carry out further excavations or further studies. Indeed his invisible presence seemed to me that spring to command the house and the dark-foliaged garden. Faint traces of his autocratic scholarly comfort still clung about the place. Denuded though the rooms were, here and there a carpet, a curtain, a sofa recalled the welcome of a Victorian country week-end. The

Villa Ariadne was still an enclosed, self-contained little world from which one made forays into a countryside so far tamed by few roads and fewer buses.

We made one such expedition ourselves. Humfry wanted to show me the site of Eleutherna, and in a hired car we were driven off into a landscape which I recall as lowering and claustrophobic. One of the house servants, Kosti the steward, was in attendance, and spread wild flowers round the rug on which we sat to eat our picnic lunch. After it we left the car and the road and walked under a cloudy sky. There was a hill and a moist, luxuriant canopy of trees and it began to rain; on this at least memory is explicit. I was wearing shoes with crepe rubber soles; as we scrambled back towards the car my feet slid on the streaming path, and Kosti tugged me up the inclines. The precipice road was covered with rich mustard-coloured mud, and the driver expressed alarm lest the car should slide. We were thankful to get back to the Villa and drag off our soaking clothes in the basement bedroom. There was even the chance of hot baths. Suddenly, in Hilda's attentions, I recognised the face of genuine friendship.

Twice more I stayed at Knossos. Humfry's close friend Alan Blakeway, tutor in ancient history at Corpus Christi College, had raised in Oxford funds for the excavation of an ancient cemetery, and in 1933 we set off with him for Crete. It was high summer. The School session was over, everybody except the servants had left, and we had the Villa to ourselves. Humfry and I slept under mosquito nets on the terrace roof beneath moonlight which seemed to generate heat; at sunrise we woke to the wild rusty screech of the first cicadas. In 1935 the three of us were back at Knossos, joined this time by our friend James Brock, a student of the School who later was to be responsible for the splendid publication of the finds.

Spellbound, I watched the two seasons drifting past me. Once we took time off to drive westward along the coast and through Rethymnon. When we passed Souda Bay there were warships in the huge natural harbour, and somebody remarked that it had been used by Allied shipping in the Great War. But 1914 was more remote to us than the Minoan age. Our lives revolved round the Villa, and though our drive had taken us as far as Canea, capital of the island, though the names of great Minoan sites—Phaistos, Mallia, Hagia Triadha—

were constantly in the day's talk, to me Crete was Knossos. The slopes where Evans's restorations, the jag-ended roofs and interrupted colonnades, hung conjecturally in the fiery air; the bleached hills across the valley; and the Villa garden with its rich integument of shade and flowers, pomegranates, plumbago, hibiscus—that was Crete; that and midday with lunch in the long cool dining-room; shadows thickening, and dinner on the terrace with its hoods of jasmine.

Alone in the house during the day, I struggled to write. Then as the afternoon swam on I would throw down my work and stroll out towards the village of Fortetsa and the fields and olive groves and vineyards where, hollowed in the banked earth, the ancient cemetery was giving up its painted burial jars. The little boys of the village looked at me with curiosity as I went by, and once, I remember, I rescued a toad with which they had been amusing themselves. For the rest my exchanges with the Cretans were confined to the minimal daily greetings.

All the same I was learning to fit faces and voices to some of the names which for so long had rung in my head. Kosti I had met on my first visit, Kosti the steward with the flowing, light brown moustache, eyes of a mad bright blue, and a disposition wheedling but obstinate. He was the hero of an abduction, not an uncommon event in the Crete of the 1920s. The young man who served at table was Manoli Markoyannakis, a good-looking boy, quiet-voiced, deferential. Sometimes a woman muffled in black was seen emerging stealthily from the kitchen quarters or sweeping with a vague tentative broom the stone floors in the bedrooms; this was Maria, widowed Maria, like Kosti a relic from the great days of the Evans régime. And when I wandered out to the dig there was Manolaki the foreman—Manolis Akoumianakis, who had long worked for Evans in the excavation of the Palace and who now was serving a season with our party; one of his sons, Micky—a boy like the other village children but graver, more observant—ran industriously about the site, carrying messages.

The sun swung across the screen of pine trees round the Villa garden, the cicadas filled the air with a sound as thick as silence, and a handful of Cretan names were added to my stock of characters.

Occasionally an incident, absurd or tragic, broke the routine of the week. There was an invitation to lunch in Herakleion with the British Vice-Consul, a friendly Cretan citizen given to what I am sure he regarded as high-life English persiflage; at any rate he trapped me into desperate apologies for damaging an armchair by upsetting a bottle of ink—which turned out to be a joke-bottle with rubber ink-pool attached. Once at midday, sitting in the dining-room in the Villa, we could hear in the distance long painful cries. It was some time before we discovered that they were cries of uncontrollable mourning; Yanni Katsarakis, our foreman at Perachora, had come over from his home in the east of the island with the news that his wife had died. The loss was calamitous from the practical as well as the emotional point of view. She had been, we knew, an ideally capable woman, good at the management of her household, good at spinning and dyeing and weaving—I still possess a tough, bright-patterned bedspread which she sent me as a present. And all that day Yanni, his face blotched with tears, sat in the kitchen rocking back and forth in his chair and howling with grief and despair.

Meanwhile in the pale crumbling soil beyond the sultana vines the cluster of tombs was being methodically opened and cleared. Sometimes a south wind brought dust and mosquitoes and lassitude; but at the noon-time break in the work, or at night when we dined on the terrace, the archaeologists still wrangled with happy obstinacy. I began to take life in the Villa for granted. We should pick it up again next summer; that seemed as natural as midday.

But next summer Humfry was dead; and a few months after him Alan Blakeway, best of friends, was gone too. Three years later the War broke my remaining ties with Crete.

iii

Or so I had thought at the time. Now I found that the passage of twenty-three years had left nearly everything clear in my mind. As I loitered about the courts and stairways of Knossos I felt as if I had never been away. There was even, to remind me of Evans's massive reconstructions, some restoration in progress—only this time it was the restorations which were being restored. Workmen were cleaning the Palace, brushing soil from the pavements, mending the cement in the walls. And like those shreds of coloured paper which, dropped into water, swell and branch into waving flowers, the stones blossomed in my mind. I remembered lost days: an evening on the beach beyond Herakleion, Alan bringing out a bottle of Greek champagne, unpalatably warm from the late sun, to drink after our swim, and the three of us squabbling about the best way of keeping the bubbles in while pouring; night in the Villa and Alan again, flown with Cretan wine, lingering on the stairs to pursue some archaeological argument before he clattered down to his subterranean bedroom—the room, it struck me now, in which Humfry and I had slept on that cool, initiatory spring visit.

The long interval between then and now suddenly contracted, and as if in some non-temporal time the days were telescoped. In the same moment Evans was walking across the garden of the British School to lecture to an Athenian audience; and Kosti was writing to me from his village to tell me that he had put flowers on Humfry's grave at Mycenae; and in some war-time office in London I was reading news of the Battle of Crete and the story of John Pendlebury.

In the summers of 1933 and 1935, with the excavation of the cemetery taking up the days from early morning to late afternoon, to go into Herakleion, no more than three miles away, seemed an expedition. I scarcely knew the place. And in that I echoed the ignorance of a good many foreigners. Travellers came to Greece to see the monuments and the museums. Even visitors who were sensible of the charm of the villages were indifferent to the life of urban Greece. Athens they might enjoy. But a provincial town was something which had to be endured, a mere stage in the journey to the collection of sculpture, or the ancient theatre, or the fragmentary temple. My impression of Herakleion—which for years I inclined to call by its old Italian name of Candia—was of sun, market stalls and harbour walls on which with the image of the Lion of St Mark the Venetians had left occasional traces of their former occupation. Once or twice I sat in a café. But I had never really looked.

Now in 1958 with the new, comfortable Hotel Astir to stay in, there was a chance to explore. I took to strolling about the market. One of the streets, I noticed, was called ὁδός ᾽Εβαυς: Evans Street. Seventeen years since Evans had died; twenty-three years since he had last visited Crete; twenty-seven years since he had last undertaken any serious excavation of the Palace. In the interval, the Second War; and Greece is a country much given to the political game of renaming its streets. But there in the company of high patriotic tributes (a road a few yards away is called, after the date of a famous bid for Cretan independence, 1866 Street) was the name of the foreign archaeologist; war and Occupation and a temporary coolness between Greece and Britain over Cyprus had not erased it. Interesting, I reflected, to discover the local views. In England many people were still living who had been colleagues of Arthur Evans, and reminiscences had been published by friends and family. But nobody so far as I knew had enquired from the Cretans. Already it might be too late. Those who knew him at the beginning of the excavation of Knossos were long since dead. And the war had made a great crack in the life of the island. Some of the men who had worked on the site in the twenties and thirties had been killed in battle; a younger generation might recall nothing.

Without much hope I began to ask the people I met what they remembered of the great Evans. A few remembered him well—a Greek archaeologist; an Englishwoman who before the war had been an archaeological student and had worked with Evans. Yet this was not quite the kind of opinion I was after. Rather I wanted strictly local memories, and once or twice I found them. There were still Cretans who had dug at Knossos and Cretans who had been servants at the Villa Ariadne. Occasionally from some unexpected quarter—a taxi-driver perhaps—there would be a scrap of reminiscence.

But now there was an interruption. When asked what he remembered of Evans, sometimes a man would break off to talk of another name: Blebbery. At first I could not make it out. Who on earth was Blebbery? Then on a trip eastward I had a flash of recognition. Ashamed of my ignorance of Crete outside Knossos, I was using my time in visiting some of the places which I knew only by name, on this occasion Mallia, a Minoan palace excavated by French archaeologists. A few colossal pithoi, storage jars each of which could have accommodated a couple of Ali Baba's thieves—for the rest little more than the foundations remained, and bemused by so many interlocking rectangles I reflected that at Knossos with Evans's restorations one at any rate knew where one was. No, said the driver who took me to Mallia, he had not known Evans. But Blebbery—before the war he had driven Blebbery everywhere, east, west, along this very road. And using the Greek's phrase of esteem, 'a golden man', he exclaimed, 'a golden man'. And suddenly I knew the name. The Cretans had always found it impossible to pronounce the word Pendlebury.

From that moment my pursuit of the Evans legend grew complicated. The great ghost of the old scholar was everywhere in Crete: in the landscape, in the mountains, in the Herakleion museum amidst the spoils of excavation; at Knossos in the Palace of Minos which he had unearthed and reconstructed; especially at the Villa Ariadne. But often, as I pursued him in the memories of the Cretans, this other figure intervened; the young heroic figure of John Pendlebury. And not Pendlebury alone. The islanders wanted to talk about the British liaison officers who went in during the Occupation to help in organising resistance. They wanted to talk about a famous exploit, the capture by a party of Cretans and British officers of a German general. It was not always easy to identify the heroes, especially the foreign heroes, of such a tale. But little by little under the familiar Christian names by which the British were known in Crete in the war I discovered figures as distinguished as Patrick Leigh Fermor. I discovered my own friends: Tom Dunbabin, for instance. And I heard tales of the Cretans themselves, some still living, some killed in battle. Evans was not the only ghost whose presence could be felt at Knossos. For all these disparate characters, Cretans or British, were linked by place. They had been archaeologists, writers, farmers. But nearly all of them had been in some way connected with the Villa Ariadne. They had lived or worked at the Villa; their stories took flight from there or there came to rest. Their stories: not everything I heard about the war in my Cretan expeditions can be taken as simple fact, and what I repeat must sometimes be read as the accretion of myth. The record, like the tale of the Minotaur himself, is part-history, part-legend. The legend has grown round the people in the story. The Villa Ariadne gives the legend a basis of truth.

I

ARTHUR EVANS saw Knossos for the first time in the spring of 1894. That is to say he saw a rounded flowery hill known as Kephala, overlooking a stream and bearing on its surface, among the blossoms of anemone and iris, stone blocks with curious markings. Legend, endowed in Greece with a special tenacity, had preserved for scholars the identity of the site. Here Daedalus had designed for Minos, King of Crete, the labyrinth in which lived the Minotaur, half-man, half-bull. But to the Cretans Knossos was known by a humbler name. Sixteen years before Evans's visit an antiquarian from Herakleion, or Candia, as it was still generally called, had dug up some large ancient storage-jars on the spot, and the local people had come to refer to it as *sta pithária*—the place, as you might say, of the jars.

The remains visible on the surface—fragments of walls, gypsum blocks—had already attracted foreign archaeologists, and American, German, Italian and French enthusiasts had reconnoitred the hill. Some of them had thought of exploring. Schliemann himself, excavator of Troy and of the Shaft Graves at Mycenae, had proposed to dig, but the plan had fallen through. Possession of the land presented the greatest difficulty. As Evans soon discovered, the first requisite for carrying out an archaeological exploration was to be owner of the soil. But Crete up to the end of the nineteenth century was still under Turkish rule, and the Knossos site, he wrote, 'was unfortunately held by several co-proprietors, native Mohametans, to whose almost inexhaustible powers of obstruction I can pay the highest tribute.'

In Evans, however, the Mahometans had met their match.

He was a confident, slightly lordly figure; small but indomitably tough and capable of exceptional exertions; short-sighted but endowed with close vision of inestimable value to an archaeologist dealing with the minutiae of coins and seals. He came of a family of parsons and antiquarians who in the generation before him had joined forces with the world of industry. His father belonged to the company of Victorian polymaths. Denied an academic education, sent instead to work in the paper-mills of his uncle John Dickinson, John Evans learned mastery of the job; making a love match, he married the daughter of the firm; and finally came to run the business. But his ruling passion was elsewhere—in the fields of numismatics, geology and anthropology.

He amassed a vast collection of flint implements and prehistoric bronzes; his discoveries in palaeontology made him internationally famous. To his physical vitality the family circle itself was witness. He was three times married, the last time at the age of sixty-nine, and Arthur, his eldest son, was forty-two when of the third marriage a half-sister, Joan, was born. And in the grand Victorian manner the physical resources were matched by ceaseless intellectual and social activity. Treasurer of the Royal Society, High Sheriff of Hertfordshire, President of the Anthropological Institute, Chairman of Quarter Sessions—John Evans unmasked archaeological forgeries, fought against the excise duty on paper, resisted a vandal restoration of St Alban's Abbey, taught himself to make flint implements. He attended innumerable committees and congresses, he travelled incessantly, he carried on an enormous personal and business correspondence.

It was not surprising that at the age of twenty-four Arthur should have been condescendingly described (by the historian J. R. Green) as 'little Evans—son of John Evans the Great'.

Arthur Evans, then, grew up in an atmosphere of enthusiasm for learning. As a schoolboy he was already accompanying his father on archaeological expeditions. He inherited the habit of prodigious industry. For the first half of his life, however, his energies were dissipated. He became archaeologist, collector, administrator, journalist, above all traveller: in France, Germany, Sicily, Sweden, Finland, Lapland, the Crimea and the Balkans—in particular Bosnia and Herzegovina, later to be part of the Federal Republic of Yugoslavia but at the time of his visits first in Turkish hands and later under Austrian protection. His journeys and a certain romantic liberalism in his nature ranged him on the side of the Slavonic peoples. He was special correspondent in the Balkans for the *Manchester Guardian* and campaigned on behalf of the Bosnian insurgents. When in 1878 Turkish rule was succeeded by what he regarded as an oppressive Austrian administration—and by more insurrections—he continued to send fiery despatches to England, with the result that the Austrian authorities took him for a political conspirator, ordered his expulsion—and arrested him before he could leave. He spent seven weeks in a prison cell in Ragusa (now Dubrovnik), a city in which he had enthusiastically settled and which he had come to think of as his home. Fifty years were to go by before he revisited Dalmatia. To the official who in 1932 showed him round the prison he had once occupied 'I come back every fifty years', he said (adding, it is reported, in a soft obstinate voice, 'and I *will*').

In 1887 Evans had married the daughter of the historian Freeman, and with her after his expulsion from Ragusa he settled in Oxford. In 1884 he was appointed Keeper of the Ashmolean Museum, then a muddle of antiquities and curiosities housed in what is now known as the Old Ashmolean.

Ten years later—ten embattled years during which he had secured grants from the University; through loans, bequests, purchases and his own inextinguishable activity—had transformed the display as well as the collection itself; in short had created for Oxford an archaeological museum worthy of the name—the new Ashmolean he had fought for was being built. He was doing some building of his own too. While the Ashmolean battle raged he had conceived the idea of a house on Boar's Hill. With the financial help of his father he bought sixty acres of woodland, with a fine view, and began to plan. The house was to be a refuge from the frustrations of Oxford and a place of recuperation for his wife, who was ill, and as a start he built for her a kind of log cabin in the woods. In 1894 he was moving into the new Ashmolean, and Youlbury, as his Boar's Hill house was called, was finished. But it was too late. His wife was dead, and the big Victorian house in the setting of garden, lake and woodland had lost its initial purpose.

He was now forty-three; for most men those forty-three years might have seemed full enough. It was at this point that he set off on his first Cretan journey.

Of course he had been in Greece before, had visited Mycenae and Tiryns, met Schliemann, seen the great Mycenaean discoveries—and found them, understandably when you think of the direction his life was to take, much more stirring than the monuments of the much later classical period. Recently he had been thinking of the possibilities of Crete. He had come to believe that 'a prehistoric system of writing' was to be found somewhere in the island, but he had never gone to look. Now, with the Ashmolean fight half won and his domestic ties tragically broken, he came at last to Knossos.

He was not looking for the Palace of King Minos or the legendary maze through which Theseus sought the Minotaur. He came bent not on revealing and recreating a lost civilisation but on following 'a clue to the existence of a system of picture-writing in the Greek lands'. He saw a ring, a piece of an ancient vase, some engraved gems, traces of mysterious signs on stones, and these were the relics and the clues which changed the course of his life. Or, rather, gave his life its true direction.

Ranged on his side at this crucial moment was his powerful inheritance of obstinacy, energy, enthusiasm. And there was something else: money. He had never, all his life, truly known the lack of money. He had always possessed means of his own. There was an allowance from his father. There was a legacy from his grandfather. Always behind him there was the faithful backing of a well-to-do family. He needed to own the Kephala site. The obstructive Mahometans never stood a chance. Before he left Crete that spring he had arranged to buy a quarter share of the necessary land—a share which would later give him the right to buy the whole.

A year later he was back at Knossos. John Myres, a famous, romantic and adventurous figure from the ranks of ancient historians, was with him; they were eating their lunch in the open air on a slope overlooking the site when suddenly Evans announced: 'This is where I shall live when I come to dig Knossos.' The absolute certainty was characteristic, and here in fact it was that the Villa Ariadne was built.

But not yet. Five more years went by before Evans could begin excavation. Bosnia and Herzegovina were not the only places where Turkey was losing hold. Crete at the end of the nineteenth century was in revolt. There were massacres and counter-massacres. Greece landed an expeditionary force. Everybody expostulated, the Great Powers sent in naval detachments and the British took over Candia. In 1898 Evans was once again writing despatches for the *Manchester Guardian*—and taking part in relief work in the distressed areas of Crete. Meanwhile he went doggedly on trying to buy the rest of the Kephala site. Finally in 1899 the last of the Turkish forces left the island. Crete became autonomous (union with Greece came much later—in 1913). Prince George of Greece, appointed High Commissioner for the Powers, showed himself friendly to foreign archaeologists; and Evans wrote that 'after encountering obstacles and delays of every kind' he was able at the beginning of 1900 to purchase the whole of the Knossos area, 'this favourable result being due in large measure to the new political circumstances of the island'.

He was now a Cretan landowner and could apply for a permit to dig. But he had not yet come into his own fortune. He could not finance the whole operation, and together with David Hogarth, then Director of the British School of Archaeology at Athens, he organised a Cretan Exploration Fund.

The results were disappointing. 'Owing to the war in South Africa the contributions from this source fell far short of what was needed.' Nevertheless on March 23 he began digging. His assistant was Duncan Mackenzie, an archaeologist with experience of field work for the British School on the island of Melos. The workmen were both Moslem and Christian 'so that the work at Knossos might be an earnest of the future co-operation of the two creeds under the new régime in the island. Considering,' Evans comments drily 'that a few months earlier both parties had been shooting each other at sight, the experiment proved very successful.'

If allowances are made for the passage of time and the change in the value of money since 1900 the life briefly described in Evans's first report (published in the British School Annual) is recognisable to anyone who has watched archaeological excavation in Greece and particularly in Crete. The keenness of the workmen ('great intelligence in the more delicate parts of the work'); the dancing on a feast day; the hated south wind bringing clouds of dust—true that nowadays the archaeologists themselves and not the local women would probably wash the potsherd, that eight piastres (less than sevenpence in today's English money) would scarcely be a day's wages. But the general picture is familiar. What is not familiar is the immediate success.

When after the Cretan revolt of 1897 against Turkey, after the massacres and the intervention of the Great Powers, Evans had gone back to look at Knossos and the land, part of which he already owned, he had been thankful to find corn growing. The fighting had done no damage, nobody in that troubled year had disturbed the site. But then with the exception of the antiquarian from Candia and a former American Vice-Consul who also had reconnoitred nobody, as Evans presently discovered, had disturbed it, or at any rate much of it, for about three thousand years. He spent a week in preliminary excavation on the slopes of the hill of Kephala; when you dig you need somewhere to dump the earth, and you must be sure that you are not dumping it on ground which you will want to dig later. The trial explorations were more than enough to show that he was on the right track. After a few days he could have no doubt that the hill, the fields he had bought were the site, that the flowering soil was the thin covering of a huge complex of ancient buildings.

He had come to Crete—he said so repeatedly—to look for an early system of writing. Exactly a week after the first pickaxe had been driven into the soil there was his first piece of evidence, 'part of an elongated clay tablet . . . engraved with what appeared to be signs and numbers'. A few days later 'an entire hoard of these clay documents' was discovered. By the end of the season he had found over a thousand inscribed tablets, fragmentary or complete.

Not all used the same system of writing. A few had inscriptions in the hieroglyphic or 'pictographic' manner which he had found on engraved seals and which had drawn him to Crete in the first place; they recorded by signs, by stylised drawings ('the double axe, the bent leg, the eye . . . the branch or spray'). Ten times as many used a linear script. These turned out to be in not one but two kinds of writing, presently known as Linear A and Linear B. The latter, the more advanced, became a subject for savage controversy, and its deciphering would exercise scholars for the next half century.

But gratifying to Evans as this discovery was there were more spectacular finds.

Archaeology often brings to light relics—mysterious foundations, tumbled blocks, a charred sacrificial pit, the decaying stumps of dead houses—fascinating to the scholar but a stunning bore to the simple visitor. Knossos was different. It was not simply that the masonry of terraces and corridors persisted or that a passage was found to lead to a series of magazines with huge storage-jars standing over secret lead-lined storage-cists. It was that during their first season the explorers unearthed the remains of a civilisation fantastic in its aesthetic luxury. Still clinging to the walls or lying broken on the floor of portico or gallery there were frescoes brilliantly painted on plaster: groups, drawn in miniature, of court ladies with tiny waists, naked breasts, flounced skirts and hair in curls; the life-size figure of a young man—the Cup Bearer, as Evans called him—wearing an embroidered loin-cloth and silver ornaments, carrying 'a fluted marble vase with a silver base' and forming part of a long ritual procession. At one point the decorated walls were no more than a few inches beneath the surface of the soil. The excavators dug to find a room with paintings of griffins crested with peacock's feathers and crouched against a background of water plants and palm trees. On adjoining walls there was a painted landscape of hills, a river and flowering sedges; gypsum benches ran along the sides; between two benches stood a gypsum chair with a base and a high leaf-shaped back. 'The elaborate decoration, the stately aloofness, superior size and elevation of the gypsum seat', Evans decided, 'sufficiently declare it to be a throne-room.' A throne-room, then, a Palace with a throne-room. 'The seat itself', he wrote in his first report, 'is hollowed out to suit the form of the human body and, as it was probably also covered by a cushion, must have been a comfortable resting-place. In an adjoining room to the West a less carefully executed slab of a seat was found in which the hollowed space was larger, and', he added in delicate surmise, 'it seem probable that this was intended for a woman, while the seat of the throne seems better adapted for a man.' Refinement could scarcely go farther.

That year digging went on until the beginning of June, when malaria from the stream which runs at the foot of the Kephala hill made work too difficult. A nine weeks' season, nine weeks of success during which, as the annual report of the British School recorded, he had been 'fortunate enough to light upon the remains of a great prehistoric palace'.

'To light upon'—the phrase suggests a trust in the workings of Providence to which the energetic and self-reliant Evans would not have subscribed. Nor would he have entirely endorsed certain other comments made that year at the School's annual meeting. The chairman was Asquith, a few years later to be Prime Minister. Speaking not without irony of 'the days when Sir Charles Newton, with a firman in his pocket, a Company of Royal Engineers and Sappers at his back, and a British man-of-war lying at a handy distance in a convenient bay, was able to rifle at his will the half-hidden treasures of Cnidus and Halicarnassus', he remarked that since then 'a humbler and more apologetic mien' had been adopted by the British archaeologist. 'There is no longer pride in his pick or defiance in his spade'. Shortly after the meeting Evans was writing to his father about a second appeal for finance and the risks of placing everything in the hands of a Fund Committee.

The Palace of Knossos was my idea and my work, and it turns out to be such a find as one could not hope for in a lifetime or in many lifetimes . . . we may as well keep some of Knossos in the family! I am quite resolved not to have the thing entirely 'pooled' for many reasons, but largely because I must have sole control of what I am personally undertaking. With other people it may be different, but I know it is so with me; my way may not be the best but it is the only way I can work.

There was defiance in his spade all right, and nobody now would have called him 'little Evans'.

The fever which halted excavation in the summer of 1900 affected living arrangements too. In the first season Evans had shared with Hogarth, who was for a time engaged in excavating another part of Knossos, a Turkish house in the neighbourhood. '. . . We are busy giving it a drastic disinfecting and internal whitewashing, but it is a truly oriental abode with a kind of cascade fountain in the principal reception room and a small aqueduct running through the house.'

But the Knossos house was too near the stream to be healthy. For the 1901 season he took a house in Candia, and together with Duncan Mackenzie and the architect Theodore Fyfe, who had been called in from the British School to draw plans of the excavation, he rode out to the site every day on mule-back 'through a tunnel-like gate', as Joan Evans writes in her book *Time and Chance*, 'over the town moat, past the lepers congregated to beg outside'.

The Candia house was his headquarters for the next five years: five more years of epoch-making discoveries. Among the finds in that period were many which are familiar now to thousands of tourists: the inlaid gaming-board of ivory, gold, silver, rock-crystal and a pattern of daisy and nautilus; the 'Priest-King' bas-relief with crown of lilies and peacock's feathers; the acrobat carved in ivory; the bull-leaping fresco; the snake-goddess figure.

Sometimes the exploration, while it produced evidence of a rich lost civilisation, might have seemed to the layman to darken the mysteries. The 'ivory object in the shape of a knot with a fringed border'—a 'sacral knot', Evans called it; and those minatory 'horns of consecration' depicted on gems or shaped in stone (as you walk round the Palace you can see a great pair of them); the snake-goddess herself with her long aproned skirt and naked breasts and the serpents coiling round arms and hips and head—what did it all mean? All very well to say that the double axe—incised on stone, painted on pottery, fashioned in bronze to be offered as a votive, buried in tombs, erected as a thing to be worshipped—was a cult object, the sacred emblem of the Cretan Zeus ('labrys' was an ancient word for a double axe, and 'labyrinth' probably meant nothing more than 'the House of the Double Axe'). Scholars may explain and argue (Evans quotes W. H. D. Rouse as refusing to believe that the double axe could have been worshipped: 'The Greeks would be as likely to worship a pair of top boots'). But over the centuries the feeling persists of threat, secrecy, darkness.

Often, though, excavation gave validity to something which had existed only in the shadowy form of fable. In the legend Minos had exacted from Athens a yearly tribute of seven youths and seven maidens who were left to wander in the labyrinth, there to fall victim to the Minotaur. Gems showing a bull-man had already come from Knossos. Now not only were there seal impressions with the figure of a Minotaur; among the frescoes were scenes in which both young men and girls grappled with a charging bull; a girl seizes the horns of the animal, a young man somersaults over its back. 'It may well be', Evans commented,

that, long before the days when enslaved barbarians were 'butchered to make a Roman holiday', captives, perhaps of gentle birth, shared the same fate within sight of the 'House of Minos', and that the legends of Athenian prisoners devoured by the Minotaur preserve a real tradition of these cruel sports.

The terrible myth had broken through into history. Like Schliemann, who believed in the basic truth of the *Iliad* and found his evidence at Troy and Mycenae, Evans had a vision of a lost age and transformed the vision into reality. 'The Palace traditionally built for Minos by his great craftsman Daedalus has proved to be no baseless fabric of the imagination.'

As time went on excavation presented massive problems. Knossos turned out to be vast not only in area but in depth. The labyrinth was composed of storey upon storey, colonnade upon colonnade. A stairway had not one but several flights, and digging out the fourth of them was really 'miners' work'. Luckily two of the workmen had at one time been employed in the mines at Laurion and were equal to the job.

Next year, however, an upper wall was found to be heeling over and 'it became necessary to resort to heroic measures'. A section was cased in planks and no fewer than sixty men harnessed to ropes pulled it to an upright position in which it could be wedged and cemented. Monuments covered with soil for centuries and suddenly exposed to the weather may deteriorate; Evans had to roof in the Throne Room. What is more, he had to support the roof, and since a fresco had given him a model for the shape and colour of the original columns he decided to try to reproduce them.

It was the beginning of a long series of restorations. A Swiss artist, Gilliéron, was summoned to help in piecing together the fragments, often tenuous in the extreme, of the frescoes—and to supply missing arms, legs, faces and landscape backgrounds; critics began to suggest that restoration often became a work of the imagination. Architectural students from the British School at Athens were employed in solving structural problems. Walls were propped, pavements reconstructed, pillars replaced, upper storeys held in place; by the third season there was already 'a serious expenditure' on bricks, iron and timber. One winter there was alarming damage from rain. Part of the multiple stairway—the Grand Staircase, Evans called it—had collapsed. In the necessary rebuilding a hitherto undiscovered balustrade came to light. That led to the restoration, 'but in stone with a plaster facing in place of wood', of the original columns which had bordered the flight. Evans was entranced by his 'legitimate process of reconstitution'. 'To a height of over twenty feet', he wrote in one of his regal passages,

there rise before us the grand staircase and columnar hall of approach, practically unchanged since they were traversed, some three and a half millennia back, by Kings and Queens of Minos' stock, on their way from the scenes of their public and sacertotal functions in the West Wing of the Palace, to the more private quarters of the Royal household.

Naturally the size of the job—excavating, conserving, restoring—meant a growing army of labour. In the first season he employed a number of workmen fluctuating between fifty and one hundred and eighty. The following year he often needed two hundred. By 1902 that had gone up to two hundred and fifty, among them 'over a score of carpenters and masons'. The record offers an amusing contrast with the balance-sheet of most English archaeologists, lucky if they can scrape together the wages of a dozen pairs of hands; and there were times when Hogarth, who had been digging first at the cave on Mount Dicte which was the legendary birthplace of Zeus and later at Zakros in East Crete and who also drew on the Cretan Exploration Fund for his expenses, was inclined to remonstrate. But after all Evans, not to mention his father, a generous subscriber, had from the start contributed a good deal of his own money. He had bought the site. When in later years he spoke of the extent of his operations a note of unconcealed gratification crept into his voice. It was in his nature to live large, make the grand gesture.

Among the monuments of Knossos was a large paved rectangle with tiers of low steps on two sides: 'a primitive Theatre' which he judged might have been used for ceremonial dances. The German archaeologist Dörpfeld, former assistant to Schliemann, was accustomed during an annual island cruise to bring his party to Knossos. To this day the Cretans are splendid dancers; and one year the visitors were entertained in the 'Theatral Area' by a dance of the Cretan workmen and their womenfolk—'a dance, maybe, as ancient in its origins as the building in which it took place'.

As Evans watched the 'sinuous, meandering course' he reflected that the steps resembled the dance which, Plutarch says, Theseus instituted 'mimicking the mazy turns of the labyrinth'. For the sense of the dramatic was always with him. It was there in the picturesque names he gave, as the seasons came and went, to the quarters and the environs of the great Palace: the Court of the Distaffs, the Hall of the Colonnades, the Room of the Lotus Lamp, the Megaron of the Double Axes, the Magazine of the Knobbed Pithoi, the Hall of the Jewelled Fresco, the House of the Fetish Shrine, the Megaron of the Spotted Bull and—with a touch of perhaps unconscious indelicacy—the Room of the Lady's Seat.

Tirelessly his mind was busy putting the finds to work. The deep walled pits, now—might they not be prisons? 'The groans of these Minoan dungeons may well have found an echo in the tale of Theseus.' Surely the room with the grooved limestone slab and basin was once an olive-press. The stone benches, the low pillar with the hollow on top—the furniture, perhaps, of a schoolroom where clay for writing-tablets was kept moist; perhaps 'the art of writing was here imparted to the Palace youth'. And the stepped wall of terraces by the northern entrance—'it would be quite in keeping with Minoan taste . . . to suppose that these earth platforms rising step-wise beside the entrance way served as small garden-plots, planted perhaps with palms and flowering shrubs.'

It was natural that when he came to build his own house at Knossos he should give it a name from the mythical past.

By the end of 1905 he had been digging for six seasons. The accumulation of material was already enormous. Obviously he would be coming to Crete for many years. He needed to be at Knossos, on the spot. He had had enough of riding out to the site from Candia; patience was not one of his noticeable qualities. In 1906 he made up his mind. He would build; and he would build on the slopes overlooking the

Palace. 'This is where I shall live when I come to dig Knossos': now the words spoken to Myres eleven years earlier were justified. Evans planned the building himself 'with basement rooms', Joan Evans writes, 'for coolness, and a flat roof for air, and a steel and cement framework for strength'. Christian Doll, then architect at the British School, was brought from Athens to see to the work, and by October of that year the roof was on. The house was named after that daughter of Minos who gave Theseus the thread which enabled him, after he had killed the Minotaur, to find his way out of the maze—the Villa Ariadne.

The establishment of the Villa marked a stage in the Knossos story. The main work of excavation seemed to be finished; at any rate the outlines of the great Palace were clear. There were to be no more yearly progress reports from Evans himself, and respectful though one may feel towards the more subdued tones of the articles which between 1905 and 1908 Duncan Mackenzie contributed to the British School Annual one cannot help missing the high-flying style and the enthusiasm of the Old Master's prose.

Not that the discoveries had come to an end. There was always more to be done. But the explorers no longer lived in amazement. Their operations, with the Villa Ariadne as a working centre, took on an air of regularity. Mackenzie could live and study there. Gilliéron, reconstituting the frescoes, could settle there for months on end, and so could the succession of architects and draughtsmen who came to draw plans of the excavations and devise means of preserving and restoring the Palace. And Evans himself now had a permanent Cretan headquarters. For long periods it would be the centre of his life, and from it he would pour out a great stream of ideas, theories, plans and letters ranging from the exhilarated to the admonitory.

In 1908 news came from England that John Evans, now nearly eighty-five, was ill. 'There are over a hundred men at work, so you can guess that I have my hands pretty full,' Evans wrote to his stepmother. 'But my thoughts are very much with the Padre.' A week or two later John Evans was dead; to the last he had insisted that there should be no interruption in the operations in Crete. 'It is hard,' said the next letter from Knossos, 'to be away from you all at such a time, but I was glad to receive my father's message that I must do my work here.

Indeed there is no question of my getting away just yet, with so many responsibilities on my shoulders and so much that cannot be postponed.'

It is not only in the actor's life that the show must go on. Indeed the show could go on henceforth with a new assurance, for not only was there a paternal legacy. John Dickinson—the Dickinson of the paper mills whose daughter John Evans had married—had left a large estate first to his son and then to his son's sons. But the last of the grandsons died and Arthur Evans inherited. Fourteen years after his first visit to Crete he was a rich man in his own right. He could afford Knossos.

Between 1908 and 1914, then, the exploration of the enormous, enigmatic site and its surroundings continued. Perhaps a Cretan working in his vineyard would accidentally dig up vases and bronze fragments, and the hunt would be on again. A single tomb would be found, then a whole series. Explorers in Greece know that if you are looking for ancient graves it is no bad idea to take local advice. The vegetation gives clues. For instance fennel, which has long roots, is likely to grow in places where at some time or other, perhaps thousands of years earlier, the earth has been deeply disturbed; and Evans, recording the fact in his account of a successful excavation in 1910, gives full credit to his foreman, 'the most expert tomb-hunter of the Levant'.

This was the year of a particularly gratifying discovery. When one of a series of tombs was opened it was found to be of singular construction. Among the contents was a fragmentary pair of those famous bronze ritual double axes the worship of which had seemed to Evans's old opponent W. H. D. Rouse so hilarious a notion. The find in a grave was interesting enough, but the surprise came when the cist or burial chamber itself, long ago plundered and by now almost bare, turned out to be cut in the rock in the form of a double axe. The general architecture of the tomb, the disposition of such relics as remained, and various other pieces of evidence were enough to persuade Evans that the whole thing was not only a tomb but a funeral chapel. It might, he thought, have been used by the family for some kind of memorial service; its sacred symbols might have guaranteed divine protection: 'and,' he adds in one of his loftier flights, 'even in the shades, the direct guardianship of the Great Mother' might be thus 'assured to the warrior resting in his emblematic bed'. Anyway there was no difficulty in finding a name, and to the long list of romantic titles was added the Tomb of the Double Axes.

The discovery was described in a paper read by Evans at the end of 1913. Scarcely a year in his adult life passed without his writing some learned article or other (he usually managed to tweak a learned ear or two in the process). But papers and articles and reports were mere fragments of his work. Publication of the huge mass of the Knossos discoveries—an unknown civilisation to be recorded, a vast tract of prehistory to be charted—was the main job. There were always fresh questions to be answered. In 1913 he was back at the Villa, digging again in an attempt to answer them; by 1914 the materials for publication were, as he stoically put it, 'already in an advanced state'. Then came the 1914-1918 war.

Some distinguished archaeological figures were to play a part in it. Hogarth became the adviser of Lawrence of Arabia. Myres commanded small buccaneering ships in the Mediterranean (there is a story, apocryphal no doubt, that he once demanded identification of some sizeable British warship; back came the signal: 'Does your mother know you're out?'). And Evans, though at the outbreak of war he was already sixty-three, was far from inactive. He fought the War Cabinet's plan ('the breaking in of the jungle', he called it) to requisition the British Museum. He protested against the removal of enemy nationals from the roll of honorary Fellows of the Society of Antiquaries. One of numerous Presidential addresses to learned bodies gave him the chance to illustrate from ancient precedent the advantages of a through railway between western and south-eastern Europe—a project, Myres afterwards pointed out, 'which was in fact realised later by the Simplon Express'. When the war ended Evans hastened to attend the Peace Conference in the interests of the Southern Slavs.

But all this time he had been cut off from Crete. There were all sorts of adjustments to be made. New evidence had come out of the Knossos finds. Elsewhere Greek, American, Italian and French archaeologists were making discoveries which had to be taken into account. In 1920 he despatched Mackenzie on a confirmatory expedition in Crete. A year later—twenty-one years after the first campaign at Knossos—Volume One of *The Palace of Minos* appeared.

There were to be three more, the last in 1935, and a separate Index, the bulk of which Joan Evans compiled. The enormous discoveries demanded enormous exposition, and got it. And Minoan archaeology (it was Evans who first used the word Minoan) was always providing fresh material. The book changed as it grew; adapted itself to new knowledge; luxuriated. Of course he went on adding to his own discoveries. In 1922 he was back at the Villa Ariadne 'seriously implicated in digging'. There were finds 'below what seems to have been the Magazine of the Arsenal'. The discovery of 'another large staircase (or rather the evidence of it) in our West Wing' necessitated 'large works of reconstruction'. At Arkhanes, a big village south of Knossos, a circle of stone blocks under the projected living-room of a half-built house turned out to be a Minoan cistern. 'I have had what remains,' he wrote with typical glee in the audacity of the operation, 'excavated after pulling down the owner's front wall.'

His pleasure in the Cretan landscape was never blunted. The letters to his family during the 1920s sometimes mention the flowers. 'Here every bank is gay with dwarf iris, from blue to mauve, and many-coloured anemones'—he had a feeling for flowers; and the delight with which he had planned the setting of the Villa, that comes out too: 'The garden here has also been very pleasant with the growing palms and masses of roses and honeysuckle. The scarlet pomegranate flowers are just now in full bloom.' But something else was showing itself: an anxiety about financing the never-ending exploration of Knossos. The wages of the workmen had risen, and he was beginning to sell some of the antiquities collected by his father. 'It is sad', he wrote to Joan Evans in 1922, 'parting from some of the old things, but they have been already "researched" and I feel that my father would be quite content that they should serve as stepping-stones to other work.'

The same letter goes farther. 'I am trying to carry out a scheme for handing over the house and site here to the British School.'

Today it is extraordinary to think of a British subject owning not simply land and a house in Crete but the site of one of the most celebrated archaeological discoveries in the world; owning not only the ground on which the Palace of Minos stood, but the Palace itself. That phase of archaeological history ended long ago. But for a few more years Evans was to have absolute control. He dug, he conserved, he reconstructed (or in his word 'reconstituted'); he was the King Minos of his day. He finds evidence of 'a monumental stepped portico running up from the South'. Fragments of a fresco take four expert workmen a month to extract, and to piece the thing together he sends to Athens for young Gilliéron, son of the original restorer. There are 'extraordinary developments' at the deep pit which he calls 'the lair'—the Minotaur's lair. In his letters from the Villa references to the financial burden grow more frequent; the necessary 'restoration of the old structure . . . is rather ruinous on my side!' But he still has time and attention to spare for family affairs, and intertwined with accounts of excavation and discovery there is concern about the future employment of one young relative, there are exasperated comments on the matrimonial projects of another ('I had to write to him quite brutally').

And he still, at over seventy, is equal to the rigours of Cretan travel. 'I had to break off work here', he begins his account of an expedition in 1923, 'and took the opportunity of doing some exploring, camping out with tents in the very wild ranges of the South side of the island.' Mackenzie and the architect-draughtsman Piet de Jong were with him on this occasion, and the party settled for the night 'on the shore' he writes 'of Fair Haven where (as the sailors said it was safe) I pitched my tent a few yards from the sea opposite St Paul's island, the others camping more inland.'

St Paul's island—the Acts of the Apostles, reporting the Pauline voyages, has the relevant passages. '. . . We sailed', they begin 'under Crete . . . And, hardly passing it, came unto a place which is called The fair havens; nigh whereunto was the city of Lasea'. The master of St Paul's ship, however, finding the haven 'not commodious to winter in', presently sailed on 'close by Crete. But not long after there arose against it a tempestuous wind, called Euroclydon. And when the ship was caught, and could not bear up into the wind, we let her drive. And running under a certain island which is called Clauda, we had much work to come by the boat . . .' Evans had reason to recall the story. 'In the night', his letter goes on,

Euroclydon—it *was* the same wind—suddenly arose in his might, brought up the sea and nearly swept me and the tent away! Happily some sailors whose own boat was being swamped roused my men and the tent and myself were got off in the right direction—not before a large wave broke into the middle of it! It was quite weird. Next morning breakers rolled where my tent had been pitched!

'Got off in the right direction': Evans was night-blind. When he was dealing with coins and gems his microscopic sight 'enabled him', Myres says, 'to detect artists' signatures and other minute details of style'. But at the onset of darkness he was helpless. I remember once in Athens finding him ready even in the mild dusk of spring to take my arm as we walked across the British School garden. It was a readiness which had nothing to do with age; he was as spry as a sparrow. One can understand how gravely the disability complicated the Fair Haven mishap—which was to be among the most often-recounted of his adventures. After the lapse of nearly forty years Evans's servant Kosti was still eager to describe his own rôle in the event—a rôle presented as one of self-abnegating heroism. It is with satisfaction that one identifies the spot where Euroclydon struck. Kali Limenes, says the map: Good Harbours, or, in the New Testament phrase, Fair Havens.

Evans was not deterred. Two years later he was off to 'a place where the French are digging an early Palace'. The place was Mallia, about twenty-five miles from the Villa Ariadne. Today the bus takes you from Herakleion in an hour, but in 1925 it was an expedition involving some forethought, and Evans, again with Mackenzie as his companion, set out prepared to spend two nights in tents on the mountainside. He was interested but acid. At present, he wrote, the French 'are employing three men and two boys so it will take some time before they are through'.

His expeditions were not confined to Crete. On one occasion he went on 'a pilgrimage into the Morea in quest of a "magic ring" ... a great gold signet ring from a beehive tomb'. Though about this time the references to finance appear more often in his letters ('I have 45 men on the job, and wages are about double what they were, so you can see that I am absolutely reckless') anxiety is always brushed aside. Everything which holds up his work or impedes his curiosity is disregarded—the 'enervating South wind'; 'paths like torrent beds and once' (this was on the trip to Fair Haven) '12 hours at a stretch without passing a village'; temperatures of up to 105 degrees in the shade—'I resist, as the Italians say.' He went everywhere, said one of his workmen. Never, on his Minoan excursions, alone. Eye-witness accounts give the impression of a retinue—not only British companions, not only Piet de Jong and Mackenzie, but also Manolaki the current foreman, Kosti as cook and a boy as handyman. He would travel by car, when cars became available, as far as possible; then he would ride on mule-back. He never, according to Piet, slept in a village. Tents were always used; Evans had his own and, as the Fair Haven incident shows, his own ideas of where to pitch it.

Meanwhile visitors swarmed to Knossos and the Villa. There were parties of Swedes and Danes, Germans and Americans. Pierpont Morgan arrived in his yacht ('quite pleasant people'). In one month of 1926 Evans received three English parties, each of between a hundred and a hundred and fifty people; he entertained Dawson of *The Times*, H. A. L. Fisher and another scholastic character of whom he remarked, 'I never saw anyone expand so over his tea! . . . Mrs Edith Wharton the novelist', he added, 'is due, so you see this really is the hub.'

And there were local guests to be entertained. At Easter about thirty people would sit down to lunch in the Villa garden; caterers from Herakleion sent waiters; and domestic talent from Knossos —Kosti, and Maria in her black weeds, and Manoli Markoyannakis, at that time the houseboy, and probably Spiro Vasilakis, a reliable and respected member of the team of workmen—lent a hand. Recounting this long afterwards Manoli spoke with awe about the arrival of provisions from England, champagne, gin, whisky, jam, tinned meat—'Why,' he exclaimed, 'one year there were 29,000 drachmas to pay in customs dues on one single consignment of food and drink!' (At the time 29,000 drachmas represented in English money about ninety pounds). Perhaps the sum is not altogether surprising. Piet de Jong, who spent months living and working at the Villa, told me that the rest of the party might drink Cretan wine, but not Evans. He always drank French wine; occasionally, to celebrate a success or cheer himself up after a disappointment, he would broach a bottle of champagne which he shared with the others.

The choice of foreign wine is not to be taken as an instance of prejudice. Cretan wine does not suit everybody; I have known English visitors who developed a rash from drinking it. All the same by avoiding it Evans may have encouraged the Cretans to believe that he did not think much of them, and to this day some of them do believe that. They say that he spoke Greek badly, that Mackenzie was always at hand to act as his spokesman, or that Manolaki the foreman would pass on his orders. He did not want, they say, to speak Greek; he gave the impression of despising it. Probably he spoke as well as any of the travellers whom the local people will compliment warmly on command of the language. But then it was in his nature to hold aloof from the country society. 'They liked Pendlebury,' said one cosmopolitan Cretan, drawing a comparison, 'because he drank with them.' Certainly it is impossible to imagine Evans sitting down at a café table to drink rakí with the village elders. Nor were the lunch parties in the Villa garden given for the benefit of the citizens of Herakleion. Most of the guests, said Manoli, were foreigners, French or Italian archaeologists, with one or two Greeks—a Vice-Consul, perhaps—who had acted in some official capacity.

Once an impression is given reasons will be discovered to account for it. Evans, said one Cretan acquaintance of mine, began his excavations at the time when Crete had won autonomy. 'Under the Turks you were allowed to take out antiques—now suddenly you could take out only duplicates: this prejudiced him against the Greeks.' Somebody else had heard a tale of a misadventure with brigands in the Peloponnese which had affected the great man's feelings towards Greeks everywhere. Since Evans, after describing the obstacles put in his way earlier, wrote thankfully of 'the new political circumstances' which after the departure of the Turks had enabled him to buy the whole of the Knossos area it seems unlikely that he preferred the Ottoman rule. As for the story of the Peloponnesian brigands, so far as I know it is an invention. But other tales have more foundation.

There was, for instance, a moment in the 1920s when the Greek Government devised a simple form of devaluation. Any notes in circulation were cut in half (on another occasion a third was chopped off) and consequently became worth half their face value; customers watched wryly as shopkeepers brought out the scissors. An eye-witness (he was a boy at the time) has described the scene at Knossos.

Evans was sitting at one table and Mackenzie at another, ready to pay the workmen. Evans asked for a basin of water and a towel. He took a bundle of notes and tore it in half—then he washed his hands to show what he thought of Greek money. The men were angry and the cook—he was a Greek from Asia Minor—made a disturbance. Next day the foreman sacked him.

It is perfectly true that where taking antiques out of Greece was concerned Evans felt himself entitled to make his own laws. There was the case of the customs official at embarkation who asked him to open the parcel he was carrying. The story is famous; I have heard it from a dozen sources, on the last occasion from a Greek archaeologist.

I don't myself believe there were antiques in the parcel, but anyway Evans refused to open it. The official began to insist. Evans simply took the parcel and threw it into the sea . . .

It is a fine ripe example of high-handedness—but a high-handedness not, I should have thought, aimed especially at the Greeks; his autocratic manner, all the more splendid for being expressed in so conclusive a way, was recognised in England too. It could, I know, be alarming. War and Occupation never made poor Manoli forget an occasion when he was a house-boy and on the way back from the bank some money was lost (the folder had slipped down behind the seat of the car); when I talked to him nearly thirty years afterwards he was a middle-aged man with children growing up, but he still shrank into himself at the memory. Even sophisticated people were intimidated. I know a Greek archaeologist, later internationally distinguished, who has confessed that in his early days when he spoke only a little English he was unnerved by his encounters with Evans. But in general the Cretans, those of them with memories long enough to recall the grand days of exploration at Knossos, remained ready to see the joke. Old Kosti, describing his years as servant at the Villa, would launch without being asked into a story which for some reason had stuck in his mind. A bathroom prepared for the host was mistakenly occupied by a guest (it was John Forsdyke) who managed to drop the fresh tablet of soap; Evans, arriving for his bath and finding the piece on the floor, flew into a rage—and Kosti would mimic his master stamping, waving his arms and shouting. 'He used to strike me, he used to take me by the shirt and shake me'; then, with wondering admiration, 'a very strange man, a very strange man'. The physical violence is perhaps a myth, though one can imagine Evans threatening it. But nobody would question the authenticity of a remark often quoted by Kosti: 'Only God can change my mind.'

Certainly the older people of Knossos never ceased to mourn the Evans régime, autocratic though it was. The explorer may not have fraternised with the villagers, but he observed the local rules; the end of the year's dig would be duly celebrated by a *glendi*, a party for the workmen and their families. Do you have a *glendi* now? I asked—it was in the late fifties and the British School was excavating near the Palace. Heads were shaken, and in glum faces I could read regret over decline, the decay of a great age. The mimicry itself was never resentful. In moments of excited talk Evans used to scratch his head, running his hand furiously right to left through hair which never grew really thin. One of his former employees gave me a demonstration as amused as it was accurate.

Occasionally the stories had a touch of affection. When Evans was crossing the road from the Villa to the Palace the village children, little scampering boys, used to run to show him the coins they had picked up, a French centime, perhaps, or some tiny worn Italian piece. He would carry out a grave examination, reward the children— and leave them with their treasure. Next day the same boys would dart up, the same exercise would be performed; amiably he refrained from pointing out that the coins were the ones he had already seen. I remember once pressing Spiro Vasilakis for an honest opinion. What was Evans really like? 'He was good,' said Spiro, his humorous lanky face with its dark moustache smiling. 'Really?' I said. 'Tell me the truth.'

'Eh,' said Spiro, 'to me he was good.'

One must not think of Evans as a dry man. He had time for friendship. 'I had a very sad arrival here,' he writes from Knossos in 1925.

When in Athens I received a telegram to say that Mr Seager, a great friend of mine and an excellent explorer [Seager was responsible for excavations on the islands of

Mochlos and Pseira] had been taken suddenly ill on the way from Egypt and landed in an unconscious state at Candia. With Mr Blegen of the American School I was so anxious to do everything possible that I took steps to get a despatch boat given by the Greek Government—which they would have done—to take over the best doctor in Athens, but before anything could be done we received news of his death and arrived at Candia just in time for the funeral. . . . It was a very impressive public one in which the Government as well as the local authorities took part and we finally laid him in the little English cemetery on this side of Candia, beside British officers that he had known. He had just taken a little house near here and it is a great loss.

Cretans who remember the occasion have described the funeral procession with Evans getting out of the carriage to walk bare-headed behind the coffin; he felt the death, they said, deeply. The request to the Greek Government is characteristic not only of the man himself but of the decent international relations of the period. But his last tribute to Seager is all his own. 'He was the most English American I have ever known.'

In family relations Evans was warm, and despite the emphasis on the business of archaeology the long letters home find space for fun. The handwriting slanting and angular on the heavily black-edged paper which after the death of his wife he always used ('for protective colouring', says Joan Evans mischievously), the first page often boldly intersected, crossed by lines written at right angles (even the richest Victorians hated to waste a fresh piece of paper on a concluding sentence), they are observant, ironic, gay; to Joan, over forty years younger than himself, often likeably affectionate. There is a nice sensibility in his condolences on the death of her friend Miss Jourdain (one of the two authors of *An Adventure*, the account of ghostly apparitions in the gardens of Versailles). 'I am so glad that you were able to get some flowers at Youlbury—it is like having friends instead of hirelings. But I am so sorry for you.' Any asperity in his nature was softened when he wrote to his half-sister.

But the asperity was there. It showed itself in reaction to criticism and especially in the long quarrel with Wace, excavator after Schliemann at Mycenae, who held fundamentally different views about the sources of the great creative period of Minoan culture—a quarrel which was to trumpet on long after the death of both protagonists. It showed itself in comments on Mackenzie, who had been a tireless and faithful assistant since the first year of the Knossos discoveries but whose constitution a quarter of a century later was understandably beginning to falter under the strain of the long Cretan summers, the interminable detail of archaeological excavation and the terrifying energy of his employer.

Poor Mr Mackenzie is still very shaky from the 'flu that he had in January last. He drinks *warmed* bottled beer and reposes most of the time—going down to the site however now on his donkey. He told me that the nightingales (who now sing all night here and most of the day) had given him a 'set-back'! I really don't know what to do with all his hypochondria. I did stir him up once by saying that if he did not mend I could take no further responsibility for him and must send him to a nursing home! He walks with a slouch, stoop and stumble as if he was 95 at least. On the top of that he has a quite healthy appetite—but goes to bed immediately after dinner.

The date of the letter is the Greek Easter of 1926. Evans himself was not indeed ninety-five, but he was close on seventy-five. He still seemed immortal. That summer there was one of the earthquakes which periodically set Crete and parts of Greece trembling. With the historic mystery of the destruction of the Palace of Minos always before him he was naturally fascinated by the phenomenon. A few years earlier (it was in 1922) he had written to Joan:

Most curious has been the evidence of a great earthquake at the end of MMIII [Middle Minoan III, 1800-1550 BC in Evans's system of dating] which threw Palace blocks over smaller houses and crushed them with their fall . . . To celebrate this discovery we had a little earthquake here. The house rocked and rumbled and a traction engine seemed to lumber over the garden. No damage however was done, though the cook was nearly thrown over backwards.

The 1926 earthquake was a more serious affair, but he still preserved his scholarly detachment.

It was a very interesting experience, the earthquake as, curiously enough, I had been specially taken up lately with the effects of earthquakes on Minoan Knossos, which must have been as much a centre of them as medieval and modern Candia where on an average about two serious ones occur every century. As the last really good specimen occurred in 1856 I had strongly felt that one was overdue and even warned a lady here to expect one before the end of June! She and her husband had to rush out in their nightgowns into the streets of Candia—where a great deal of damage was done but it was a great piece of good fortune that it occurred at a comparatively early hour when most people were about—our two clocks stopped at 9.20 pm. I myself was lying undressed on my bed reading—and reflecting on my chances archaeologically, with cheerful effect . . . as my bed is in a basement corner of a very strongly built house—for the Villa Ariadne has walls a yard thick—I elected to stay where I was, tho' the rocking brought down things in the room and a full pail of water on the floor was half splashed out. It was so like a ship at sea and though the shock did not last more than a minute I began to feel squeamish by the end. Earth sickness is a new complaint!

Less phlegmatic (and not having retired early to the basement), the rest of the party in the house, Piet de Jong, Forsdyke and the historian H. R. Hall 'rushed out, passing the heavy stone table dancing on the terrace and dodging past the trees, that rocked as if they would fall, to the open . . . Things kept falling about, the whole house groaning and creaking and a deep roaring sound coming out of the depths.' When Evans finally emerged 'a great cloud of dust had risen, at first obscuring the full moon, and some lights from the village reflected on this gave the impression of a conflagration shrouded in smoke.' Near the garden gate children were rescued from the wreck of a small house. Some of the hill villages round Knossos were almost entirely destroyed. In Candia itself the damage was not only to houses but to the Museum which held the archaeological finds.

But the Villa Ariadne survived.

And something else. 'Hurrying down with the others . . . to the site of the Palace, I was glad to find that the reconstituted upper storeys had resisted the shocks.' That was lucky, for 1926 was the year in which Evans finally handed over in trust his Cretan estate, including the Palace site itself with its stairways and corridors, its colonnades and halls, its magazines, its terraces, its courts, its throne-room, all the vast works of restoration which had accrued in a quarter of a century. Possibly the Director and the Committee of the British School, which now became the guardian of Knossos, felt an occasional twinge of nerves. After all the next earthquake might not delay for half a century. It might happen in a year's time and bring down the whole structure of the Palace. But the transfer of responsibility was the obvious course.

The School was honoured and grateful. The gift was splendid. It included, outside the perimeter of the Palace, olive groves and vineyards; it included the Villa Ariadne itself, encircled by shady gardens. Generosity did not stop there: Evans gave also an 'invested endowment for maintenance and for the salary of a resident Curator'. It was natural and right that Mackenzie, for so long the worker in the field and, in spite of his 'hypochondria', Evans's right-hand man in exploration and research, should be appointed to the post.

Twenty years after its building, then, the Villa entered on a new life. Evans had often filled it with scholars and architects whose studies were predominantly concerned with Knossos. During his régime they had been his guests, his co-workers. Now the house became an outpost of the British School at Athens. Students would pay, just as they paid in the Athens School hostel, for bed and board, and would share a sitting-room and a dining-room. Evans's servants stayed on—Kosti as cook, Maria as cleaning woman; and Manolaki Akoumianakis, for some years permanent foreman of the Knossos dig, would come from his house in the village when he was needed. Excavation, after all, did not come to a dead stop. Forsdyke records that Manolaki, 'inspecting with the eye of an agriculturist the waste upper slopes which he had bought . . . noticed a hewn face of stone which he at once recognised as belonging to the diadromos of a chamber tomb.' Manolaki may not have been, like that earlier foreman, 'the most expert tomb-hunter of the Levant', but he was pretty smart at the game. Evans immediately excavated the grave, which proved to be part of a cemetery; he then turned over all the material to Forsdyke, who continued the exploration in the following year. It was 1927, and Humfry was having a first experience of field work. The cemetery where he was digging was of an early Greek period—from the protogeometric to the orientalising period in archaeological terms, tenth to seventh century BC. Evans, who had excavated one of the tombs years earlier, now not only handed over to the young archaeologist all the relevant photographs and drawings but made 'a generous contribution towards the cost of publishing some of the vases in colour'. It was not the last of his benefactions. At the lower end of the garden where it abutted on the road from Candia (by now it was generally called Herakleion) there was the small house which I have earlier called a lodge. I think it had once been a tavern; at any rate it had long been known as the Taverna. In 1928 he renovated the building 'so as to provide one single and one double bedroom, a sitting room, and workroom, kitchen etc., below, for the use, at any time, of members of the School independently studying the antiquities of the spot'. The School now had its own annex to the Villa, and Evans had added to his debtors the long list of students and visitors who were to stay in the cool, quiet, owl-haunted enclosure.

In spring and summer, then, the Villa was at the service of archaeological students. They worked in it, they used it as a base for research, they left to travel about Crete, in the 1920s no centre of comfort, and came back thankfully for clean clothes and baths and palatable meals. But the imperious shadow of its creator still lay over it, and in Athens or wherever in Greece British archaeologists congregated you could hear talk of his descents on Knossos. They were growing rarer. The bulk of his work as an explorer was done. Now he had to publish. In 1928, seven years after the first, the second volume of *The Palace of Minos* appeared—or rather a pair of volumes, for the huge instalment was in two parts. The third volume came in 1930—but it was still not the end of the book. It was not even all that Evans was writing. In those, as in all the other years, he produced an extraordinary list of studies, lectures and pamphlets—on numismatics, on the Glozel forgeries, on the Shaft Graves and beehive tombs of Mycenae, the centre of his running argument with Wace (he was never too busy for argument).

Meanwhile there were changes at the British School. In 1929 Humfry became director in Athens. In the same winter Mackenzie, his health failing, his nerves on the edge of a breakdown from which he was never to recover, retired and was succeeded as Curator of Knossos by John Pendlebury. Young men were moving into positions of command. At the Villa and especially at the Taverna, which had been reserved for the Curator to live in, John and his wife Hilda introduced an air which was a mixture of the domestic and the adventurous. Both archaeologists, they travelled enthusiastically and hardily in the island. But they were not only archaeologists, they were a family. Conversation in their company would turn from Minoan scholarship to topics—household furnishing, for instance—hitherto unfamiliar in the monastic setting of Evans's Knossos. They were in fact nesting, and in 1932, in a letter from

Youlbury to his stepmother, Evans remarked: 'I was just writing to Mr Pendlebury to congratulate him on a son and heir. A Knossos nursery will be a new feature!'

The next part of *The Palace of Minos* toiled on. 'I have about 6 sections of Vol. IV practically finished—not quite half I think,' he wrote in 1931. 'The total pages might well be about 400.' And there was life at Youlbury; work had to be done there too. The view from Boar's Hill over Oxford—it had been celebrated by Matthew Arnold in 'Thyrsis'—was in danger from speculative building. The Oxford Preservation Trust had made an attempt at saving it, but Evans felt more was needed. He flung himself into the cause; urged the acquisition of land; himself bought with the help of a mortgage a necessary field, and undertook ('with too light a heart', as he said later) to enlarge the view by constructing a mound on the heights—Jarn Mound, it would be called after the local name of the spot.

The job took him nearly three years: from January 1929 to November 1931. At the first attempt the structure collapsed; the clay suffered 'a general slump'. He tried again with different material, with a motor hoist, trucks running up inclined rails and the employment of twenty men a day. This time, success. The Mound, fifty feet high, was crowned by a dial with a plan of the surroundings; at the base 'for the benefit of future archaeologists', as he slyly put it, 'freshly minted coins of the realm' were buried. And now he began planting at the foot of the Mound a wild garden which should contain not only local plants and shrubs and trees, not only the flowers mentioned in 'Thyrsis' and 'The Scholar Gipsy', but representatives of the flora of all Britain. A booklet he wrote telling the story of Jarn Mound bears witness not only to the success of the experiment but to the range of his botanical knowledge. And to his love; there is romantic fervour in his catalogue of Spindle and Guelder Rose, Pasque Flower and Monkshood, Grass of Parnassus and Elecampane.

Often there were week-end parties. In 1931 he writes to his half-sister to acknowledge some iris seed she has sent him; he will sow it, he says, and adds: 'I am having the Paynes of the British School, Forsdyke and Miss Lamb [Winifred Lamb, then Keeper of the Classical Antiquities in the Fitzwilliam Museum at Cambridge] here for the week-end of October 17th—if you could join us it would be very nice.' That was the first time I met Joan Evans, but not the first time I was invited to Youlbury. In the years between his appointment to the School Directorship in 1929 and his death in 1936 Humfry and I spent a number of week-ends in the house, and its owner was at last becoming to me something other than the fabulous being—a Daedalus, a King Minos—whom the stories from Knossos had conjured up. Not that I altogether lost the sense of awe. Evans was always kind to me, and perhaps if I had ever talked to him alone I should have recovered my nerve. But at those Youlbury visits the company itself was enough to overpower me. There were times when I was prevented by my job—I was employed as a kind of Editor's dogsbody at the *Sunday Times*—from travelling down to Boar's Hill with Humfry on Saturday. Joining the party on Sunday, I would make a timid entry into a drawing-room which seemed to me full of revered names: the prehistorian Gordon Childe, H. R. Hall, author of a standard *Ancient History of the Near East*, Leonard Woolley, excavator of Ur of the Chaldees—all amiable characters, I am sure, but not men to indulge in small talk. And once I had the misfortune to arrive on the very morning when some enterprising but unin-structed interviewer for the *Sunday Times* had implied that Woolley was claiming the discovery of Noah's Ark. Both the famous archaeo-logist and his wife were among the visitors, and though the interview was nothing to do with me Mrs Woolley's implacable pursuit of the subject completed the destruction of my self-confidence.

Perhaps the house party sometimes included people as ill-qualified as I was for learned society. Perhaps the conversation at table was not exclusively academic and erudite. But my impression is of sitting nervously silent through talk about numismatics and the Ring of Nestor. Once I embarked desperately on some anecdote about an acquaintance who, I said, was 'the kind of person who had a very good cook'. It was politely but not enthusiastically received, and later that evening Humfry added to my discomfiture by remin-ding me privately that our host himself was the kind of person who had a very good cook. I took, I suppose, a kind of terrified pleasure in those week-ends. Indeed my fright coloured my memories. I was persuaded, for instance, that I had seen Evans flavouring his boiled egg with strawberry jam. Thirty years later Joan Evans convinced me that I had been inventing my own Youlbury mythology.

Yet some of the pictures which memory reflects are not imaginary: Evans at breakfast regally throwing over his shoulders the letters he had opened and read; Evans, a bit put out by H. R. Hall's insistence on catching an inconveniently early train, showing displeasure by making no arrangements for the visitor to have breakfast before leaving. And the timetable I have not imagined. In such a well-run household a gong would signal the moment for guests to go to their rooms to change for the evening. Evans did not like unpunctuality. Humfry was careful in conforming to the rules of good manners, and I was terrified by the thought that the errancies of hair or hooks (one did not in those days rely on zip-fasteners) would make me late for dinner. The thought of coming down late in the morning was even more appalling. I envied Mrs Woolley (at that date her husband had not yet been knighted) the social aplomb which sustained her in saying that she had a headache and would have breakfast in her room.

Evenings might give me another fright. Evans liked going to bed early, but courtesy would not let him retire before the women guests. At about ten o'clock, then, it fell to whoever was acting as hostess—Joan Evans, perhaps, or the senior among the wives—to make a move. But the distinguished characters who made up those scholarly house parties were apt to be unmarried, or if they had wives did not always bring them along. At any rate there was an occasion when I found myself the only woman there; I spent the hour after dinner half-paralysed with shyness and the thought that I should presently have to choose a moment to stand up, say I was going to bed, and take one of the candles which (though Youlbury of course had electric light) were arranged every night on a side-table, ready to see the visitors upstairs.

Once in the bedroom I could relax, read and wait for Humfry to join me. The wait would be fairly long. Our host would retire almost immediately, but the rest of the men would stay to talk and argue. Once, sitting up in bed with a thriller (there was always a supply of books in the bedrooms), I was startled to hear a sudden ringing of bells—not, as it seemed to me, a single bell, but bells everywhere in the house, deafening bells, an alarum. There were confused voices and running footsteps—not mine: perhaps in those frugal days I did not own a dressing-gown, perhaps I reflected that there were enough men in the house to deal with the emergency. Anyhow I stayed in bed and read on, and presently the alarum stopped. When Humfry came upstairs he told me that in the heat of argument and to demonstrate a point he had opened a glass-fronted case to take out one of a collection of Minoan gems; the case was wired, opening it set off the burglar alarm, and nobody except Evans knew how to stop the bell ringing. Probably, said Forsdyke, who enjoyed his host's lordly ways, it was set to ring from Carfax tower down in Oxford, too.

But I must not give the impression that the learned talk went on without a stop. On Sunday mornings guests would be taken for a walk through the grounds, past the lake where the Boy Scouts had permission to camp, up Jarn Mound for the view over Oxford and the soft languorous counties. In the afternoon there might be an excursion by car—in two cars, usually. Sitting beside the driver of the leading car, Evans enjoyed the impression of speed, or what in those quiet days passed for speed; there was a facetious rumour that from time to time he would hiss 'Faster, faster!' The second car, a hired vehicle which some of us felt lacked the agility of the first, panted in anxious pursuit along the country roads; married couples schemed to travel in one and the same car, preferring, they said privily, to die together. Meanwhile Evans, racing ahead, looked out on the hedgerows and the shrinking passers-by. 'There seem,' he once remarked with more than a touch of exasperation, 'to be a lot of *pedestrians* about today!'

But there were no mishaps. Indeed there were rewards. One of these excursions gave me my first look at Cirencester. I remember a visit to Wayland's Smithy and to Inkpen Beacon, where the remains of a gibbet still stood on the naked turf; on foot as well as on wheels Evans was in the lead, and we followed him breathlessly up the hillside. I think, but am not sure, that this was the day when on our return to Youlbury he began talking at tea about the encroachments of the armed services on the countryside; he was always the opponent of the despoilers.

'They've been using a stretch of downland for dropping bomes . . .'—the soft, elegant, rather high voice hesitated—'er, for dropping booms . . .'—at last, firmly and without embarrassment, 'for dropping bombs.' It was the only time I ever knew him to betray indecision about anything.

But though he now spent most of the year at Youlbury Knossos was never far from his mind. And getting to Crete had grown easier. He welcomed the possibility of travel by air (he was a wretched sailor), and in 1926 he described with delight 'a record flight to Paris—245 miles in an hour and 29 minutes, which works out at over 150 miles an hour'. Not that sea voyages could be entirely eliminated or that the journey to Crete was always simple. But his reaction to difficulties was as stoic as ever. In 1931, held up on his way by a freak April snowstorm, he took 'an opportunity for stirring them up like bees at Athens by sending to the *Estía*—the paper that Venizelos reads—a full account of the bad treatment . . . experienced both on landing at Piraeus and on attempting to depart from it, at the hands of the "Pirates of Piraeus" '. In those days when the island steamers still anchored out in the harbour and passengers were ferried by rowing-boat, most of us timidly endured the tyranny of the boatmen. But not Evans.

. . . A boatman had tried to prevent my entering the saloon, demanding four times the fare, 100 instead of 25 drachmas—though, as the weather was bad, I had tendered him 50. Next he pursued me into the small Saloon, where among the passengers seated—all of whom knew me—was the Greek Minister of War and other officials, who all looked away terrorised by this representative of the Piraeus *Camorra*! In my letter I took occasion to mention this . . . I understand that Venizelos took the matter up at once, so much so that I have just received a letter from the Captain of the Port at Piraeus expressing fulsome regrets and saying that the chief culprit had been made an example of, so I hope that something will really have been done.

Justice done (and the Minister of War presumably having taken to the hills) Evans continued his journey by air. But the seaplanes which in the 1930s made the trip to Crete used to touch down at Spinalonga off the east coast.

I had to cross about 7 miles of open sea to reach St Nicholas, the nearest port, in a motor-boat. This was too small for its job and, though the English Captain was very plucky, a gale blowing from just the wrong quarter made the sea so rough that we were beaten back three times in trying to make the headland that we had to pass, and returned ignominiously to the little hamlet of Elunda whence we had started.

The traveller was nearly eighty, but a mere gale was not going to stop him. 'I managed,' he goes on with the mixture of resource and Olympian self-confidence to which all who knew him would testify, 'to secure a larger motor-boat which took us through.'

That year he stayed into the heat of summer, and once more the Villa roused itself from routine.

We have had a burglary here, but I only lost about £10, representing some over from weekly payments placed in a drawer of my bureau. But the strange part was that it was accompanied by a letter in printed writing giving a false name and saying that if the police were put on the writer's track he would 'slaughter me like an ox'. . . . However, though the police have been trying to find out who the thief was ever since, I am still un-slaughtered! Our household have been examined twice over, and I have no reason to suspect anyone. I think the man must be partly out of his mind.

In archaeological affairs there was still greater drama. Convinced that the Palace was the home of Priest-Kings, Evans in the early years had hoped to find their royal burial-place. Legend said that the body of Minos, murdered when he pursued Daedalus to Sicily, had been brought back to Crete and buried in a vault with a temple over it; what Evans had looked for was a kind of double monument. But time passed without luck; he had almost forgotten. Now he had a fresh clue. In a vineyard south of the Palace a village boy had found a gold signet-ring. The site looked promising. Evans decided, as he puts it in *The Palace of Minos*, 'to organise a massed attack', and with John Pendlebury as director in the field and Piet de Jong at hand as draughtsman he dug. And there it was ('where I looked for it', he writes home)—horns of consecration, column-bases, double axe signs, the lot: an upper sanctuary, a pillar crypt and a sepulchre cut in the rock. Perhaps to call the strange complex the Tomb of Minos would have been going a bit far. He contented himself with naming it the Temple Tomb. Thirty-one years after his first epoch-making discoveries he had not lost his luck or his cunning.

This was his last exploration of any consequence, though a subsequent letter spoke of beginning 'a slight dig to investigate a stone passage that has come to light, near the Temple Tomb . . .' That was four years later, and in the same breath he said he would not attempt 'any considerable dig at present'. He had not visited Knossos in the intervening period. The seasons floated over the Villa and the garden, bringing scholars and travellers. In spring solemn eager students set out with notebooks for the Museum and the sites; in early summer the tourists, stunned by heat, antiquity and their own exertions, swarmed over the Palace; not until July—when in 1933 Humfry and Alan Blakeway carried out their first joint excavation—did the land fall silent. And yet the Villa, committed though it was to the general needs of the British School, still seemed a house in which, though the host was absent, one was a guest. It still bore itself as if it were Evans's house.

And so indeed, whenever the host appeared, it was; and in 1935 he made the grandest of his reappearances. On his way through Athens he was fêted. 'Six large entertainments in four days!' But he found time to gauge the political situation. Spring that year with an anti-Venizelist Government in power was darkened by a pro-Venizelist revolt and its aftermath: troops in the Athens streets, units of the Greek Navy, which was traditionally liberal, steaming rebelliously away to Crete and

. . . the state of affairs, consisting mainly of arrests and examinations of prisoners, being very unsatisfactory, especially as the opportunity has been seized to shut up many of the quite moderate people who had nothing whatever to do with the insurrection.

'However,' Evans adds, 'I was not shut up!' Far from it. The Cretans had long recognised the excavator and restorer of the Palace of Minos as their unending benefactor. Now they were to make a grand public achnowledgement. A bronze bust was to be set up within the Palace precincts and unveiled with suitable ceremony.

I am only just recovering from no end of a function regarding my brazen image, raised in the West Court of the Palace here. I was accompanied to it by the Metropolitan and found an immense concourse—all the Court and upper floor of the Palace packed with people, others on the trees and crowds outside . . . and I had to listen to seven addresses and to compose a discourse myself in the proper mixture of old and new Greek. I was made, among other things, an honorary citizen, with all kinds of privileges—exemption from all dues—and even 'right of asylum'!

The bust, he says, is 'on a—happily—fairly high pillar'. Next day another ceremony, but in Herakleion and culminating in 'a laurel crown'. The touch of deprecation does not altogether conceal pleasure. The junketings were exhausting. But observers detected a certain gratification; perhaps surprise as well. Years later I was talking to a Cretan collector of antiquities, Dr Yamalakis. Evans, he said,

was much more liked, or at any rate respected, than he himself supposed. When the bust was unveiled ten thousand people turned up. 'But I have no sandwiches for all these people,' he said to me, 'no drinks for them!' He was quite overcome . . .

Evans did in fact entertain what he called the dignitaries at the Villa after the function, and perhaps he was not actually contemplating as large an operation as the feeding of the five thousand. His concern is worth noting all the same.

He was now eighty-four, but the enquiring, exploring mind, perennially practical, still drove on. Back at Youlbury, he was indefatigable. That year was the silver jubilee of George V. Beacons were to be lit in celebration, and the job was entrusted to the Boy Scouts. Observing that one of the traditional sites was on his own land, he wrote in *The Times* a long article recounting the history of beacons in England and describing an experiment with a model. 'It consists of a straight oak trunk, cut for the purpose and allowing 20 feet above ground, which supports a capacious "fire cage", the handiwork of a local smith.' A fire of tow steeped in pitch and helped out by wood and coke burned, he says, for over two hours. Jarn Mound, the Wild Garden, the Beacon-Chain—increasingly he showed his feeling for the traditions and the landscape of his own countryside.

The following year there was a different kind of jubilee. The British School at Athens had reached its half-century, and an exhibition at Burlington House was organised. Evans made himself responsible for a room illustrating his work at Knossos. Among the exhibits was a reproduction of a fresco, much restored, which he had long maintained depicted a saffron-gatherer. Mercy Money-Coutts, who as a student had worked in Crete, helped with the arrangement. Some time in the 1950s I visited her in Canea where, married to a charming Cretan, Michael Seiradhakis, she was then living. I asked her about the problem of restoration. Yes, she believed the Knossos 'reconstitutions' were justified—except for the saffron-gatherer. It was really a blue monkey (an interpretation now generally accepted), and of that Evans himself, she said, was finally persuaded.

There were other matters on which time and the long bitter battles of research would prove the great scholar-adventurer mistaken. Nevertheless the structure of his work, huge, formidable, in some strange fashion poetic, outlasts criticism. An expert once grumbled to me that, since in the early days of excavation field archaeology lacked the precision acquired later, it was sometimes difficult to see what was actually found at Knossos. Reconstruction had often been deliberately carried out in the materials used in antiquity. Sometimes, he added, laughing ruefully, you can't tell the original from the restoration.

The ordinary visitor bears such complaints with equanimity. For with age the jagged walls, the stairways and corridors and roofs and pillars of the 'reconstituted' Palace have taken on a kind of grandeur; from the distance of the hillside opposite you recognise, crumbling but still splendid, the city which Knossos once was. Even my critical informant, admiring in spite of himself, admitted that if the explorer had not been able to indulge his passion for rebuilding the whole vast complex might by now have been fatally blurred. The gypsum which the Minoans employed in constructing the interior of the Palace dissolves slowly in water; rain would have gradually eroded it. 'The Grand Staircase has been worn down by exposure to the weather. But the cement which Evans had poured in the cracks is not affected. It still keeps its original level—you can see where it juts above the ancient slabs.'

The extraordinary machine of Evans's physical and intellectual make-up still, by the second half of the 1930s, had a few more years to run. But it was beginning to tire. In any case questions even more urgent than the conservation of Knossos were now exercising people's minds; a patch of threatened peace, and then a decade would go by before travellers would revisit Greece and archaeologists get back to their rightful jobs. Evans never saw Crete again. Perhaps in his magisterial nineteenth-century fashion he had cared for its past more than for its present; the feeling which survives him in the island may be one of gratitude rather than affection. But gratitude is there.

'After all,' a Cretan said to me a few years ago, 'after all he made Crete what it is now.'

II

i

'IT WAS the night after Mackenzie died.' Piet de Jong's voice with its flat tones and barely perceptible changes of pace always had a compelling narrative quality; as the eyes glinted under the whiskery eyebrows and the mouth under the enquiring nose drew in for a pause I felt a shiver of expectation.

I was in bed in one of the rooms downstairs at the Villa. And I heard footsteps, very slow, coming to the top of the stairs. And they hesitated. And slowly, very slowly, they came downstairs. And the door opened. And I looked up, and there was Mackenzie, standing there with a woman. And next thing I changed places, I was standing looking down at Mackenzie in bed. And once more I changed places, I was lying in bed, and there was Mackenzie again looking down at me. I woke up in a cold sweat.

Mackenzie died in Italy a year before Evans's last visit to Crete. Since the end of his Curatorship he had been suffering from severe mental disturbance. The trouble had begun earlier. Humfry, when as newly appointed Director of the School he visited Crete, was alarmed by what he saw of affairs at Knossos; and in *Time and Chance* Joan Evans says that her brother had found Mackenzie in his latter years with 'the gradual onset of his illness . . . exceedingly difficult to work with'. Nevertheless in the preface to the last volume of *The Palace of Minos* the author paid tribute to his dead lieutenant, to his loyalty and his understanding of the Cretans. Evans could be generous. He made amends for the asperity of his private comments on Mackenzie's 'hypochondria'.

One or two people, among them Piet and his wife Effie, would have said that he was making amends for something else. When Mackenzie moved out of Knossos three years had gone by since the Villa and the site had been handed over to the British School. Theoretically the job he left was a School appointment. All the same it is difficult to believe that Evans had no say in the matter. Certainly Piet and Effie had their own ideas on the subject. 'Sir Arthur came in one evening and found Mackenzie with his head on the table. Next day he sacked him.' Both the de Jongs were unshakeable in one thing: Mackenzie, they said, did not drink. 'He would sit for hours in a café with a small glass untouched in front of him.' Perhaps Evans did not share their belief, and to be honest there were other doubters among the fascinated observers of what was still the exotic, immured life of the Villa. But the de Jongs defended their dead friend: 'Yes, he had an unsteady sort of walk, but that was after he had a fall. He was riding his donkey and he fell, perhaps it was a stroke. After that he was never the same.' And Effie added a final word. Sir Arthur, she said (the de Jongs always referred to him as Sir Arthur), confessed to her later that he was sorry about the removal of Mackenzie. 'I think,' he told her, 'it broke his heart.' It is all long ago now, and the name of the first Curator of Knossos might, except to a handful of archaeologists, have disappeared under the dust which covers memories of so many romantic, adventurous, pioneering figures once connected with the Villa Ariadne, had it not been revived years later by one of the controversies which from time to time erupt in learned society. The controversy was over the Evans system of Minoan dating; dramatically enough those clay tablets with their linear scripts which in the very first days had seemed to the explorer to justify his whole enterprise were called to testify against him. And suddenly from the grave Mackenzie, the careful field archaeologist, the right-hand man, intermediary between Evans and the Cretan workmen, by virtue of his daily records of excavation became a key witness. It is an episode to examine which needs not reminiscence but a Minoan expert. Nevertheless I think I can say that the reputation which Mackenzie won in his prime has stoutly survived. Nobody has questioned it.

That fragment fits much later into the story, and anyhow I dare say the chapter is not finished yet. In 1930, however, when John Pendlebury succeeded Mackenzie, a new and a different era began.

After the interruption of the First War a young generation of archaeologists were beginning by the late 1920s to make themselves felt. They were sometimes distrustful of the work of their predecessors. In particular they questioned the conclusions of the great nineteenth- and early twentieth-century pioneers, whom they were inclined to regard as unscientific in sifting the evidence. Field archaeology had been an adventure, the unearthing of treasure, the confirmation of legend as historical fact. Schliemann had shown that Troy was a solid truth. Evans, following the clue of a myth, had recovered a splendid civilisation. Of course field archaeology would remain an adventure and of course the newcomers would build on the work of their elders. But the first major discoveries, having startled the scholars and the historians, had themselves settled down into history. Now a more deliberate and, it was suggested, a more scientific approach was the thing.

Naturally few archaeologists possessed the personal fortunes which had made possible Schliemann's work at Troy, Mycenae and Tiryns and Evans's work at Knossos. The post-Schliemann and post-Evans explorers operated with university grants, with funds raised by public subscription. A dig could no longer be a private venture. In Greece a British excavation would be undertaken under the auspices of the British School of Archaeology. Each national archaeological body in Athens—the German Institute, the French and the Italian and the British Schools—was rationed in the number of explorations conducted. For the Greeks, naturally enough, were jealous of their own history and their own honour. The whole system under which excavation was carried out was being tightened.

A new generation of archaeologists openly disapproving of what they regarded as the amateurish policies of the past and operating under considerable restriction on the freedom of the explorer —goodbye, one might have thought, to the good old traditions of obstinate individualism. Not a bit of it. Iconoclastic but devout in allegiance to the science they pursued, the new generation were to produce individualists of their own; outstanding among them, John Pendlebury.

John Devitt Stringfellow Pendlebury was a schoolboy when he first saw the Aegean. He was born in 1904, only son of H. S. Pendlebury, Consulting Surgeon to St George's Hospital in London.

In 1918 he went to Winchester College. His earliest interest in the ancient world was in Egypt; in fact he was once taken by his father to the British Museum to see the orientalist Wallis Budge, who advised, however, that the boy should read classics before making up his mind. By 1923 he had definitely decided to be an archaeologist; and his last Easter holidays from school were spent travelling in Greece with a Winchester master. At Mycenae the travellers encountered Alan Wace, at that time Director of the School at Athens; the distinguished scholar was impressed by the boy's 'anxiety to see things for himself, so as to be able to form a fresh, independent, first-hand idea of them'.

That autumn John Pendlebury went up to Pembroke College, Cambridge, as an exhibitioner. He was a classical scholar but not, according to a contemporary, a conventional one.

He did not work, like the ordinary run of undergraduates, in a litter of texts, lexicons, papers and notebooks, and he was always manifestly in training. My portrait of Pendlebury at nineteen is of a friendly athlete sitting on a hard chair with one book open, the book he was reading. It might be the *Iliad* or the latest volume of *The Palace of Minos*, or it might be Maurice Hewlett's *Forest Lovers*.

'A friendly athlete'—physical prowess was as important to him as scholarship. Fitness, stamina, endurance—it is a theme which runs through a lifelong correspondence with his father. Determination to excel in games and athletics marked him out as a boy. 'It was his close application to detail,' his housemaster wrote, 'that enabled him, for instance, to take catches on the boundary with the same certainty with which he cleared hurdles or the high jump bar.' And from the same observer: 'Watching him with others in all normal activities, nobody would have guessed that he had lost the sight of an eye.' He had lost it in infancy, and all his life he wore a glass eye. True, nobody would have guessed. Spirited games of tennis played at the British School on blazing spring afternoons, long ankle-breaking walks through a Greek countryside not yet tamed, mornings spent in museums, intent on the minutiae of the wreckage of the past— on all the occasions which I best remember nobody, watching him, would have guessed. A fantastic tenacity, a heroic resolve insisted that he should be not simply the equal but the superior of the normally equipped. The disability gave a kind of impetus to his life.

At Cambridge he was able happily to indulge his two passions. 'Never shall I forget,' Lord Burghley wrote two decades later, 'John's and my two most exciting races in the Freshmen's Sports and the Senior v. Freshmen's Match, before he concentrated on the High Jump. We each won one!' Presently John was running against Oxford in the relay race and the hurdles. Twice he won the High Jump for Cambridge. In his second victory he cleared six feet; it was half a century since anybody in the University Sports had done that. Parallel with success in sport there was success in work. When he left Pembroke he had achieved, after a Second in Part I of the Classical Tripos, a First in Part II with distinction in archaeology. Fine athlete, gifted scholar—the hero, you might say, of a romantic novel, a golden boy chosen by Fortune for her own.

The main lines of his career were already marked out. He would, as he had decided when he met Wace at Mycenae, be an archaeologist; he had begun to train for it. But what kind of archaeologist? There was his education in the classics and there was his inclination towards Egyptology. A first step was taken when he came down from Pembroke in 1927. Cambridge had a prize to offer and he won it; he was awarded the Cambridge University Studentship at the British School at Athens. But he did not relinquish Egyptology. Astutely he decided to combine two interests. He would travel in Greece. But the object of his studies would be not Greek antiquities but Egyptian artefacts found in Greece.

He arrived in Athens in November 1927. He was twenty-three years old. A photograph taken in the following year shows a young man in a grey pin-stripe suit and the stiff white collar proper to formal occasions; the brown hair crisp, very English-looking; the upper part of the face with its short, straight, blunt nose solid, resolute, but about the set of the mouth, about the slight forward thrust of the lower lip something mutinous. In 1927, however, stubbornness was overlaid by excitement. He was a little overcome, as well he might have been, by the company in the British School Students' Hostel, where a year earlier I had made my first acquaintance with archaeological society. I was newly married at the time. Humfry was still a post-graduate student; and for three months we dined at a table where nobody, to the best of my recollection, ever spoke of any subject outside the range of the antiquarian.

The phrase 'Students' Hostel' may mislead. The house was intended to afford board and lodging not only to young men and women just down from the University but to established scholars doing a stretch of work in Greece. John found himself mixing with some pretty formidable characters. 'I only wish,' he wrote to his father, 'everybody wouldn't be so obviously learned to the eyebrows. It makes me feel such an impostor being here at all. Most of them feel I think that a blue has put me beyond the pale!'

A Miss White made a comparatively favourable impression on him: 'The rest are definitely sub-human.' The schoolboy style of the letters marks the young graduate of the 1920s. It was before the days of drugs, political demonstrations and worrying about one's identity, and the products of the elder universities were often unquenchably cheerful. Perhaps John Pendlebury went on being youthful longer than most. A week or two later he was making a typical joke. He had gone with the favoured Miss White to explore the north side of the Acropolis, and there, like the Persian invaders twenty-four centuries earlier, had found a passage which led to a point high up under the walls.

Well, there was only one thing to do. I scaled the walls, put my head over the top and said to the astonished custodian 'Πέρσης εἶμαι'. [I am a Persian.] He was quite annoyed and only prevented from rushing at me by a yawning drain between us. I called him Themistocles, asked after Aristides and climbed down again.

He soon forgot the unnerving aspects of archaeological society. On an expedition to Phyle, an ancient fortress on the mountainous northern borders of Attica, he and Sylvia Benton, excavator of Ithaca and tough heroine of many tales and perhaps some myths in the annals of the School, vied with one another in accusations of fast walking; she said she had almost to run to keep up with him. He lost no time before getting out of Athens and into the country. Among his companions on a trip to Meteora and Tempe that winter was the Cambridge contemporary who was to describe him as 'a friendly athlete'—P. J. Dixon, later Sir Pierson Dixon, British Ambassador in Paris. In the later 1920s he too was a student at the

British School, and he it was who first prospected the site in Crete at Eleutherna which Humfry dug in the summer of 1929.

It was not long before Pierson Dixon abandoned archaeology for diplomacy. In the early 1940s he was at the Foreign Office and dealing with Aegean affairs. Sometimes I saw him there, for I was entangled in British propaganda to Greece and it was my lot each week to shuttle, bearing a few typewritten sheets grandiloquently described as a directive, between a Government department and the Office, as it was called. And again he came into the Cretan story, for it was a time when tragic news was coming out of the island, news in which Pendlebury was a major figure.

In 1927, however, John was writing home long, detailed, factual letters about his own personal affairs—the possibility of a studentship in Egyptology and the knowledge of language which might be required; or the ten miles of ancient road he had traced at Mycenae; or the interminable delay in getting a consignment of English cigarettes through control after control. 'I had the pleasure of telling them they were the worst postal service in the world and I believe I signed a paper to that effect.' He was taking lessons in modern Greek; or playing tennis; or going to a carol service at the English church on Christmas Eve but failing to find a seat on Christmas Day at any service anywhere ('It's rather depressed me'). His mother had died when he was a boy of seventeen, his father had remarried—a fact which John accepted with likeable tolerance and understanding; his letters are full of joking messages to 'Dickie', his stepmother, and his young stepbrother Robin. But there was no child of the second marriage, and the hopes of the elder Pendlebury were fastened on his son.

On the father's side the relationship showed a possessiveness which the boy, made financially independent by a legacy through his mother from his grandfather, the shipping magnate Sir Thomas Devitt, was perhaps fortunate to elude. But John was always dutiful, always grateful, always affectionate. He wrote every week. 'Dear Daddy', the letters begin. 'Love to all from John', they end. For twelve years every aspect of the months spent in Greece was described—work, controversies, expeditions, discoveries, encounters, jokes, tragedies. Not as a rule with eloquence. The thing was to get everything down, to convey precisely what had been achieved, walked, demonstrated; by example to assure his father of a constant industry, energy and resolution. Nevertheless from these undecorated accounts of jobs done, miles covered, sites found, the character of the writer emerges with clarity: ceaselessly active, concentrated on the work in hand, yet suddenly blazing with confidence, physical exuberance and English arrogance.

And even in the first months when the style has the flatness and shapelessness of youth, now and then there is a moment of observation, a flash of recognition of the magic inherent in a country which may have had 'the worst postal service in the world' but which would capture John Pendlebury and hold him and never let him go. He is at Mycenae; there is a village dance round a bonfire.

A man very ugly but a beautiful mover was leading the dance, he suddenly jumped into the crowd and pulled out a little boy whom he made to take his place. The child was just like a faun, leaping about and eluding him.

Meanwhile in Athens he keeps up his athletic skills. He plays hockey— 'outside left and managed to score all right'. He joins an athletic club, and of his first day on the track observes: 'Very fit and all the spring in the world, though I didn't try it. I think that I shall have a good chance of the Greek record, it is only 6 ft or just under I think.' And he is beginning the long expeditions which a few years later were to make his most important work possible.

Students at the British School in those years would be found not merely visiting the famous sites but exploring remote areas. While concentrating on the districts relevant to a particular subject of research they would make forays into unrelated fields and absorb something of the light and the landscape and the rustic society of Greece. In the 1920s and sometimes into the 1930s a good deal of discomfort might be experienced in the process. Roads were spine-wrenchers, buses when they operated bounced from rut to rut, and more often than not the most practicable method of getting from one place to another was to hire a muleteer with a pack animal for luggage and to walk. You were lucky if at the end of a killing trudge you found an inn with clean beds and food you could eat. Today comfortable buses cover the main routes and modern hotels welcome you at nightfall. But devoted travellers will still take to the goat-tracks.

It is a deeply satisfying way of 'learning the mountains', as the country people used to say. Indeed there is no substitute, and John Pendlebury belonged by temperament to the band of explorers who would never have needed one. By temperament and by generation. It was almost a matter of honour in his day for students to come back to the School with stories of trekking all day and bedding down with the mule. The times and the circumstances were made for him. Physique and training enabled him to finish journeys which would have exhausted even the toughest of normal walkers, and a natural pride in his athletic prowess (it was, Pierson Dixon wrote, 'his only vanity') egged him on. In his first months on the Greek mainland he is trying himself out. He walks from Kalyvia (a little station before Eleusis) to the convent at Daphni and along the coast to the Salamis ferry. He returns from a Peloponnesian trip with a brief reference to 'one walk that has not been done for 100 years or more, Poros to Hermione'.

Not all the excursions are directly related to his field of study, but there are always museums to visit, there is always the chance of material for the work he is planning, a catalogue of Egyptian objects found in Greece, together with as much information as possible about their provenance. His letters are made up of athletics, expeditions and Egyptology, and accounts of long walks jostle requests to his father to look up a reference in some archaeological book presumably not available in the School.

At the end of two months he was restless. He was at a standstill in his work; he needed to move farther afield. It was only natural that his choice of subject should now take him to that part of Greece which by its art was most closely linked with Egypt.

He arrived in Crete in February 1928. It was a cold wet introduction to the island. The little party of students crossed, as we all used to cross, by sea and at night; it was horribly rough (somehow it always was horribly rough). Nevertheless no sooner had they arrived than they set off for Knossos. 'Very confusing', John found the Palace, 'spoilt in some places by Evans's restorations. However a marvellous spot.' Next day—the Villa was not open and they were staying in a hotel in Herakleion—they went back; it poured with rain. They set off on a strenuous expedition by car and on foot to eastern Crete; the roads were so bad that they often had to get out and push. They were drenched to the skin at Sphaka; snow overtook them on a pass over Mount Dicte; at their first attempt to reach the islands of Mochlos and Pseira where Seager had dug it was too rough to cross and at the second the boat leaked in the storm and they were half-preparing to swim ('I got as far as undoing my puttees once,' John said). And a night in Sitia provoked him to write.

> Some talk of being bitten and some of being bit
> By wasp or bee or hornet, or by the humble nit,
> But of all the world's best biters you can commend to me
> The best of all is what we call the homely little flea.

Still, he was drawn to Crete, 'a wonderful country—much richer than Greece—the peasants finer men—more upstanding'. He was already enjoying the country talk. 'Their dialect is very nice. K before an ee sound goes to ch as in Italian, so does χ always.'

Once more in Athens (after, of course, 'a frightful crossing') he decided that he would have to go back in the spring. But he had not yet recognised the ties which would bind him to the island. 'Next year there is to be a dig at Knossos again, but I would sooner get really into Egypt.' Possibly his next visit made him think again. It was in May of the same year—1928. Evans was in residence and invited both John and Pierson Dixon to stay at the Villa; Mackenzie also was there, and Hilda White, who was staying at the Herakleion hotel, recorded her impressions of him. She said that Mackenzie had a very gentle manner. A snapshot taken about this time shows a tall figure with glasses and grizzled moustache and the crumpled wardrobe of a British archaeologist long expatriate—cardigan, dark baggy trousers, battered felt hat and mackintosh over arm. The expression is one of reserved irony, and Hilda recalls that, looking at some area of the excavations, 'I don't mention this to Sir Arthur,' he would say in his soft Scottish voice, 'but I have my own ideas about it.'

She found him always charming, always helpful. Perhaps, though, the end of his Curatorship was already casting its shadow; at any rate about now Evans was hinting ('secretly of course') that John might undertake a dig either on the south coast or at Knossos itself.

Certainly, the young archaeologist writes, there are chances. He even shows signs of softening on the controversial question of restoration. 'Evans seems to be rebuilding the palace completely in the most spendid style!' Nevertheless the letters give no indication that he is thinking especially about Crete. In between the two trips to the island he takes part for the first time in an excavation. It is conducted by Walter Heurtley, Assistant Director at the School; the search is for prehistoric remains in Macedonia; and the finds are of a type which classical archaeologists are apt to find dispiriting. But in spite of 'appalling rain and cold' John is stirred. Perhaps it is worth noting that with the ferocity typical of the newcomer he comments on a dig being carried out by a member of an older generation and another country:

He has destroyed a fine prehistoric site containing just what everyone wanted to know in the way of stratification. He is merely out for what will look well in a museum, employing over 100 men with no one to look after them. Twice a day he goes round asking the workmen—through an interpreter, of course—what they have found! and where! It is probably the worst dig in history.

And in almost the same breath he is asking his father to enter him for the High Jump in the Middlesex, Southern and AAA Championships and to secure a copy of the second volume of *The Palace of Minos*. Life is an exuberant confusion of travel, friendship, weather, museums, photography, plans to bring out the catalogue of Egyptian finds in the autumn, urgent messages about the transport to London of a dress suit, and what is the verdict on *The Vagabond King*?

Yet in spite of the excited range of interests the character is stable and the emotions are strong and constant. During his first winter and spring in Greece John Pendlebury had found a companion, like himself an archaeologist, gripped by the same enthusiasms and ready to undergo the same tests of endurance. Hilda White, in the early letters the subject of references which though engagingly off-hand betray a growing interest, was thirteen years older than John, and the disparity of age made it difficult at first for his family to accept her with the welcome she deserved. She was also a good many inches slighter, and the excursions which she shared with him taxed her hard. She was unconquerably game. From the start she was under the spell of his boyish absurdities, his intense but amiable vitality. As for him, he knew he was lucky, and to the initial protests of his father he wrote obstinately 'Hilda and I cannot live without one another.' One might not have expected from this confident, light-hearted young man with the airy English jokes of his class and his breeding an attachment beneath its casual façade truly devoted. When a year after their first meeting he married Hilda it was the beginning of a relationship happy on both sides.

ii

They went out to Greece together in the autumn of 1928, and characteristically spent their honeymoon on a strenuous expedition which in a week took them from Mycenae via Stymphaios, the plain of Pheneos and the falls of the Styx to the Gulf of Corinth at Xylokastro, now a popular camping site but in those days a quiet little place with pine woods fringing an empty beach. Most of the trip was done on foot with mules for the luggage and with the camp beds which, as John remarked, enable the traveller to sleep out on fine nights or to dispense with doubtful accommodation indoors. As guide they took a figure from Mycenae known, until his early death, to many Philhellene visitors—Spiro, one of the sons of the Belle Hélène family. It was a tough week.

Next morning we got up in the cold dark. We followed the path down to the Styx; crossed it by a bridge of trunks and branches; and climbed the steep side of the amphitheatre of mountains by the path leading to the plains of Xerokampos and Kalavryta. We did it quickly, for the cold was intense, and arrived panting at the top, 2,000 feet up; paused for a quick look back at Solos and across at Chelmos in the early sun. Xerokampos is a frozen waste of snow in winter and keenly cold in September. We were glad to put on coats and walk briskly in the biting wind.

Humfry and I had walked over much of that country. I know the precipices of Chelmos, I know Xerokampos; the names call up memories of long breathless climbs and the company of implacable mountains. Hilda Pendlebury's record—for this time it is Hilda who is writing—recaptures the excitement of those desperate journeys as well as their discomfort and exhaustion. It is amusing to compare the account (it was written after the passage of a good many years, but one recognises its accuracy) with a terse passage in one of John's letters.

We started at about 6.30 and had a terrific climb up a ridge below the huge Mt Chelmos. We then crossed a tableland about 5,600 feet above sea level and in about 4 hours reached Kalavryta.

John always knew and always recorded the times, the distances, the heights. But one must not be deceived. The letters were a hasty summary, a willing token of family devotion. The timetables which he regularly kept were the skeleton of writing to come when his feeling for the country and the people would be expressed with affection. 'Our last advice'—I quote from an article called 'Travelling Hints', and though it was written about 1930 (it was posthumously published) and conditions have changed since, not necessarily for the better, it still holds its value for the novice:

Our last advice is, learn a word or two of modern Greek, think of a nice-sounding name, look it up on the map and go there. Take to the hills and thank heaven for the fine tall gentlemen you meet. Eat and drink with them; ask what they think of the ruins and their history; and in a week you will learn more about Greece than twenty people who have motored everywhere for a month.

For the time being his interests, at any rate his archaeological interests, were divided. He had been busy on his catalogue of Egyptian finds. For a few weeks he went north to Salonika, where he and Hilda worked for Heurtley on the Macedonian finds. When he came back he found Athens agreeably cool and the School pleasant to stay in: 'We are almost sorry to be leaving for Egypt so soon.' For now he was to have a second experience of excavation, beginning at Armant, burial place of sacred bulls, on the Nile banks opposite Luxor, then moving on to Tell el-Amarna. City of Akhenaten, Amarna had been originally dug by Flinders Petrie nearly forty years earlier; later, German archaeologists found the celebrated head of Nefertiti there. At the time of the Pendleburys' first visit exploration was sponsored by the Egypt Exploration Society and conducted by Hans Frankfort with his wife Yettie— names, again, which call up memories, for the Frankforts had been fellow-students with Humfry at the Athens School, and when we were first married we spent a wedding cheque on travelling from

Greece to stay with them on their dig at Abydos, north of Luxor: a gift was never better employed.

In most of the years which followed John spent the winter months in Egypt and moved north again across the Mediterranean in spring. He always came back to Greece. He and Hilda were there in the spring of 1929, carrying out one of the Aegean tours, nine islands in thirteen days, which the trading and passenger steamers of the times made possible. Appointed Director of the British School that year, Humfry did not take up the job until the autumn, but in the spring he was in Greece and planning for his Cretan dig in June at Eleutherna. He invited the Pendleburys to go with him to look at the place. Evans with his retinue—Mackenzie and Gilliéron the fresco-restorer—was at the Villa Ariadne, but there was still room for the visitors, and John and Hilda joined Piet, who was working as draughtsman for operations at the Palace, in the Taverna.

For Hilda it was a first experience of the old régime with its touches of grandeur; Evans's chauffeur was down at the harbour to meet the ship. It was, she remarked, a good thing for one site at any rate to be reconstructed to give an idea of what a Minoan palace was really like; after all there were plenty of unrestored sites. Indeed Knossos was becoming positively habitable. 'I do think,' she added mischievously, 'Sir Arthur ought to live there in the end.'

Staying at the Taverna was a new experience too. The Villa had by now been handed over to the School, and during the months when it was open students would stay in it rather than put up at a hotel in Herakleion. But when Evans was in Crete it was still indefinably his house and run by his servants, though senior visitors and students might enjoy its hospitality and everybody went up for meals to the big house where Sir Arthur held court. An extremely generous court, as Humfry and the Pendleburys recognised on their expedition to Eleutherna. Provisions for the trip included a variety of tins from the Evans larder. Possibly these delicacies gave John the idea for some sybaritic suggestions in his 'Travelling Hints'.

Of provisions I personally recommend a few idiotic luxuries; caviare, asparagus tips, pâté de foie gras. These are the unessentials that make life worth living in a world of hard-boiled eggs and hacked meat.

Being an athlete never made him a puritan.

He still had no job, but archaeology had a few grants in its gift, and when the Cambridge studentship came to an end another benefit, the Macmillan Studentship, carried him on. It meant roughly eight months in the year in Greece, so in the winter of 1929 there could be no Egyptian interlude. But of course he was thinking about a job and corresponding with his father about it. The subject of a lectureship had come up, and with all the force and ingenuity of which a young and adventurous mind is capable he was putting up arguments against the idea. He could not get back to England early enough. He would not have time to compose a course. He was out of practice with suitable themes. He had been urged to apply for a permit for an excavation in Crete and a lectureship would mean abandoning that. At last out it came: '*I don't want* an academic life.' He had recognised practical archaeology as his real interest. Before he was twenty-five he was sure of what he wanted.

And fortune rewarded him. A few weeks later a wire came from Knossos. It was unsigned and headed 'strictly confidential', and it invited him, should Mackenzie retire in the autumn, to carry on 'at a slightly reduced salary and slightly shorter period of residence'. He paused for a moment, not to reflect on what cataclysm could have shaken society at the Villa but to wonder if the request came from Evans or from Humfry, the Director-Elect. Then with decent caution but presuming the former he wired to Evans 'Received wire unsigned answer affirmative.'

'It seems,' he commented when he wrote to his father, 'a pretty good show.' And so it was. His first book, the catalogue of Egyptian finds which he called *Aegyptiaca*, was nearly complete. His first job was in prospect. He had a Studentship to keep him going. There were hopes of digging—and in Crete. One more thing. The young archaeologists were taking over in Greece. When Humfry in the autumn of that year went out to Athens as Director he was twenty-eight, only three years older than the newly-appointed Curator of Knossos. It was lucky for them both. Whatever the difficulties in the administration of the Knossos estate Humfry had a contemporary to work with, and a contemporary who shared his approach to the business of field archaeology. For John the relationship was especially important. He knew that he had as Director someone who would not only support him in practical affairs but would understand his attitude to the pompous and the bureaucratic, someone who enjoyed the same encounters and the same vast excursions, someone, in short, who saw the same jokes. I will not say that Humfry and John Pendlebury were always united in their tastes and their reactions. But they were friends.

John was due to take over the Curatorship in the spring of 1930. There was plenty to do in the interval. The Pendleburys went to Sicily, saw the Greek sites, very properly liked best the huge tumble of stone which is Selinus and thought Taormina 'beautiful but filled with a portentous collection of English and Americans'. In south Italy they found the museum at Taranto half-shut (all archaeologists and their wives know the terror of the innumerable feast-days and other museum-closing occasions which can make some desperate journey pointless); and there also they had 'an annoying encounter with a plain clothes spy at the station' who, John said in his description of this enigmatic meeting, disliked the look of the visitors and strongly suspected them. At the School in Athens there were athletic activities—a hockey match against a British Navy team and a stupendous walk to Thebes over the mountain barrier which separates Attica from Boeotia, starting by moonlight in the middle of the night and arriving about six in the evening in time to catch the train back. There was even fencing—John bought masks and foils and was, he said, teaching Hilda and one or two of the students.

And for the first time he was learning about in-fighting in the academic world. An article he had written for a learned journal was attacked, and by such an established figure as H. R. Hall, then Keeper of Egyptian and Assyrian Antiquities at the British Museum. John was outraged. Was he expected, after piling up evidence, to refrain from drawing conclusions? Was it impermissible to scrutinise data (the subject concerned the golden shadows of Theseus and Agamemnon and the siege of Troy) which had long been assumed and to see if they would fit into history? He was suddenly and violently conscious of injustice—the injustice often felt by a young man making an early foray into fields appropriated and jealously guarded by his elders. 'My theory is not fantastic. Every remark made I . . . have quoted chapter and verse for.' And his next letter goes on, 'Everyone here is furious and says it is Hall who doesn't like new things.' In his angry defence there is the sense, familiar to those who have been observers of erudite society, that any minute world war will break out over the debated theory. 'I stand to it,' he cries. A fortnight goes by before he is ready to write to his father about much else.

There is, however, an interpolation. In the midst of the fray he breaks off. 'What happened,' he asks, 'in Pembroke's final of the athletics?'

But presently there were other matters to think about. In March he formally took over the Knossos curatorship, and he and Hilda moved to the Villa Ariadne. He now had responsibility outside his personal interests, and his life entered on a new stage.

iii

The novice in a job is the natural prey of attack, and John Pendlebury was soon entangled in another squabble, this time an Anglo-Greek one. British explorers have been generously treated in Greece. But an occasional outburst of nationalist irritation is understandable; in England a team of foreigners digging up Stonehenge might well get some sidelong looks. In the interval between the wars, too, a good many Greek archaeologists had their training in Germany, and there were instances of anti-British sentiment, possibly aggravated in Crete by Evans's moments of high-handedness. I remember one archaeologist in particular who was quick to resent what he interpreted as the arrogance of the British. 'Because we are a poor and oppressed nation,' he once wrote to Humfry, a Philhellene if ever there was one, 'you know you can trample on us.' John had recently had a first experience of academic warfare. Now came a first experience of official sniping.

While he was settling into the job at Knossos he heard of some early Greek vases in a house in Herakleion, and Humfry, who was in Crete at the time, joined him in going to look at them; a British School student who was doing research on the Protocorinthian period to which they belonged then proceeded to take photographs.

While she was thus innocently employed the police burst in. The vases were seized; the owners were arrested together with the chauffeur who had taken the British party from the Villa to the house; John received a furious letter from the Director of the Herakleion Museum, Professor Marinatos; and the local paper published an article accusing the British School not only of trying to buy the vases in question but of being involved in large-scale antique-dealing.

Anybody who has spent any time in provincial Greece will be familiar with the rumours, the scandals, the delighted perusal of appalling news. Probably the situation is not so different from that in any other Western country, but it manages to seem more dramatic; if a potentially hostile Power is concerned everyone will be ready to believe that it is parachuting radio transmitters into every vineyard. As a rule one can rely on the brevity of human memory; by next day everything will be forgotten. Antique-dealing, however, is rightly a grave matter in Greece. The finds of an archaeological excavation remain in the country. The law says also that all ancient objects found by an individual must be taken to the authorities. Small thefts from a dig are not unknown, and most travellers, pausing in some village or other, have been privily invited to value what is described, usually erroneously, as an antique. But the excavator has to be doubly careful, and a foreign School privileged to operate in Greece must have clean hands. The accusations in the Cretan newspaper could not be ignored. John flew into a rage. He immediately called on the local police to put it on record that the intention was merely to photograph, not to buy. Then he wrote to Humfry, who was back in Athens when the storm broke, and called for action. 'I am out for my pound of flesh and blood.'

The accused protested their innocence: the vases had been found years earlier and at once taken to the relevant archaeological official, who had pronounced them valueless and returned them to the finders. Humfry complained to the Ministry of Archaeology and the Ministry delivered appropriate censure. John demanded an apology and an apology was given. The incident is a pinprick; none of it matters now, nobody cares. Indeed most of the people concerned are dead. Only Professor Marinatos has survived the years and the war; today he is internationally famous. The story is an absurdity recalled because it illustrates the kind of trifle which could complicate the life of a young archaeologist. It illustrates also a hot temper in John Pendlebury. He would never ignore an offence.

Curator of Knossos: the title suggests a placid scholarly career concerned with little beyond keeping the lustral areas free from insect life and occasionally putting up a prayer for a respite from earthquakes. Far from it. A busy season was ahead. To begin with, the interregnum between the departure of the old and the arrival of the new Curator had combined with a rainy season to leave the Palace choked with weeds. In his latter years Mackenzie, perhaps beset, as Hilda sometimes suggested, by the loneliness of his job, had been increasingly losing grip. By now, John records, he was for the moment too ill to be moved from Athens by the relatives who had undertaken to look after him. The estate had to be reorganised. The land which Evans had handed over to the School included valuable tracts of vines and olives, and the new Curator had to attend to the disposal of superfluous material and the letting of agricultural property to local tenants. At the Palace not only was the Throne-Room in need of re-roofing, the whole site was in disarray.

Some of the people round have been allowing their animals to stray into the palace, where they break down walls and make a mess. I have given orders that any animal found there shall either be taken up to the Villa where I shall demand money for its return (if I do not eat it for dinner) or else turned away and tethered in a fine field of corn near the palace, so that the owner can have a bit of trouble with the farmer!

Meanwhile the visitors who had been a feature of the open season during Evans's majestic years continued to pour in. Venizelos makes a special visit. A party of Swiss arrive and depart leaving 'orange peel all over the palace'. Among the parties a couple of dozen Hellenic travellers on their cruise are given lunch at the Villa (the School and its Cretan subsidiary preserved the tradition of hospitality); Anthony Hope, Gilbert Murray, H. A. L. Fisher, Liddell Hart 'who wrote that book on Scipio', Ronald Knox—the list includes also Evans's stepmother who, as John remarked, was two years younger than her stepson.

Presently 'in great form' Evans himself arrived. It was an event which not only raised the level of activity but greatly contributed to

77

the general refurbishment of the place. Among the first decisions John had made at Knossos was to start a proper archaeological library at the Villa. 'Sir Arthur,' he writes, 'has just very generously given £50 for me to do what I like with for the library here.' Again, 'Sir Arthur has been extravagantly buying hard for the Taverna ... Cretan embroideries, rugs, a sofa, a desk and curtains to make it a self-contained place.' Meanwhile John had started work on the mass of pottery which from long years of excavation had been stored in boxes and ranged on shelves in the Palace itself where space was available. He planned to catalogue it.

A very long job and difficult considering that all I have to go on are the labels (written in pencil on worm-eaten wood in 1901 by a Greek foreman who can't spell and who called the places by quite different names!).

Evans's arrival brought other demands. There was digging to be done—in the 'Theatral Area' and outside the West Court. The results were considerable.

If you imagine a room 20 feet long, 15 feet broad and 15 feet high filled with pottery you can imagine how much came from one walled pit!

Piet, who worked intermittently at Knossos, had left for Perachora, where Humfry was making his first finds, and though Hilda always shared in the job there really was more to do than even John could manage.

I am having a fairly strenuous time 6 a.m.—6 p.m. solid on the dig trying to do three people's work. My own, de Jong's ... and Mackenzie's left over from many years.

It is not surprising that the inspiration of Evans's presence should have begun to pall. For the moment there was even a cooling in John's enthusiasm for Crete.

I really often feel that it would be better to go definitely over to Egypt, keeping say 3 months of the year free to keep up with what's happening in Greece. However I shall wait and see. Evans is obviously itching to get my time here extended. That I will not have. Three and a half months is enough for anyone, cut off from society, besides when one's work is definitely on Eg. Gr. connections it's a mug's game giving up one of them.

Evans's delight in finding a young man with the Pendlebury

qualities of knowledge, energy and efficiency is understandable. The Curator's private cry of relief at the end of the season is understandable too. 'We have got rid of Evans thank the Lord and can now concentrate on finishing up without his interference.' Really the two, Evans in his late seventies, John in his middle twenties, were matched in pertinacity. Neither would ever give in to a job.

A fortnight later the Pendleburys were on their way home ('Don't forget to get me some cricket if possible in late July'). In spite of his momentary disenchantment John had a special reason for persevering in Crete. In the midst of his three-men's job he had started on a guide to Knossos. 'Have decided to say "You" throughout. "One" is so lonely while "we" gives the impression that he is not alone and may move him to turn his head uneasily "as though a fearful fiend doth close behind him tread".' He must have felt his joke was too good to waste, for he used it again when he came to write his Guide.

One (if it is permissible to use the lonely pronoun) can see that he had changed during the three years since his first visit. He had not grown older. The activities and the enthusiasms and the satisfied vanity in bringing off a joke were the same; John never grew older. But the qualities of self-confidence and independence discernible at the start were developing. He had acquired authority. And he was going to need it.

After the 1929 season in Egypt Hans Frankfort had been invited to conduct an excavation in Iraq. This left the job at Amarna vacant, and John was asked to take over. He had worked as field assistant with Frankfort for only one season. He was still only twenty-six. Nevertheless he now held a responsible position in Egypt as well as at Knossos. The two jobs complemented one another, since his interest, as he had pointed out in exasperation with Evans's demands on him, was in the relation between Egypt and Greece. In the matter of time they were conveniently dovetailed. Winter was the season for digging in Egypt; by February the Pendleburys could be in Greece, ready to move to Crete and the Villa in March. In 1930, then, after the summer break in England which most Aegean archaeologists allowed themselves, John and Hilda took up work at Amarna.

It was a full-scale operation. The British party numbered six, the labour force of experienced workers and local boys and girls over one hundred. But his assistants could detect in John none of the apprehension which might have been expected in a Director comparatively green. He knew the site, he knew the people, he had made it his business to learn Arabic (he had already taken lessons in the summer of 1928); and Hilda, who modestly said only that she picked up what she could of the language from the servants, was there to run the household, to attend to the daily demands of workmen and their children for first-aid and elementary medical attention, and to join, as she always joined, in his work.

He did, an observer said, a prodigious amount; as well as directing and supervising the dig he handled all the photography and all the developing, a job generally undertaken by a specialist. One of the party at Amarna, Mary Chubb, later wrote an account of the season. In the picture she draws of John one sees a young man with a secret vision of himself as a T. E. Lawrence figure; and perhaps he had something of the complexity (though none of the self-torment) of Lawrence. On the first morning, she says, he appeared for work on the dig wearing 'a bright pink, open-necked shirt and navy shorts, with a many-coloured belt of twisted leather'. Those were the days of the sub-fusc. It was not done to wear bright pink shirts, even on an excavation, and Humfry and John Pendlebury were the only men I knew who broke the rule. Mary Chubb has an interesting observation to make. The bright-coloured shirts, she says, were a gesture.

When he doodled, as he frequently did when thinking out a dig problem, his doodles were nearly always of knights in armour, or crested helmets, or fine fifteenth-century gallants with wonderful lillypipe hats trailing to the ground.

She was not the first to see the romantic in him. 'In these formative years,' Pierson Dixon wrote, 'Pendlebury came to see the past through the spectacles of the romantic, or rather the chivalrous . . .' Mary Chubb recognised something more—the desire to introduce the romantic element into everyday life. That early photograph of the young man in the grey suit had indeed a touch of the mutinous in it. 'Behind his normal façade of conventional Public School and University man was someone pining for a slashed doublet instead of a neat grey pin-stripe.'

For the time being, though, the longing was nebulous; nothing much more, perhaps, than a fancy to cut a romantic figure. And even then Crete gave him the chance to do that. In the first summer of his Curatorship he wrote from the Villa Ariadne to his father: 'Have just got a Cretan costume—perfectly gorgeous, a great show.' Cretan Sunday best for a man consisted of a white shirt with turn-down collar worn under a waistcoat; enormously baggy dark breeches; a wide repeatedly-wound cummerbund; a black silk kerchief twisted round the head; high boots, preferably white; and a cloak of fine, blue, smooth French cloth, braided and lined. John's cloak was 'a soft darkish blue on the outside, embroidered in black braid with a hood folded back, and all lined with scarlet'. He indulged his romantic fancy by wearing it at Amarna as a form of evening dress.

The Amarna season was a success, and he was able to number among the finds 'A Mycenaean house. Gold and silver. The Princess's head' (a small sculptured head, possibly a portrait of one of Akhenaten's daughters). 'A splendid house belonging to an already known official with a magnificent painted lintel. Excellent small finds . . .'

He came back from Egypt with the offer of a job as well. One of the Englishmen who in the days of British influence held important positions at the Cairo Museum was leaving for America and John was unofficially invited to succeed him—'viz practically 2nd in command of the Museum beginning at £E.900 a year!'—an offer which he knew would not have been made if he had not been able to claim some published work (*Aegyptiaca* had appeared in 1930). From the early letters it is clear that his father had been persistent in urging him not to delay in both writing and publishing. 'I can't ever,' John now wrote, 'be grateful enough to you for spurring me on . . .' All the same he turned the offer down. 'I told them I was bound up in the Aegean for some time and refrained from saying that I wouldn't consider a stationary job for another 5 years at least.' Freedom to change, to travel, to explore was still essential.

iv

From Cairo the Pendleburys came back in February to Greece,

and for about a month they were based on Athens; in the intervals of work and travel John thought about the shape and scope of his guide to Knossos. It was in this spring that I first came to know him.

In Humfry's first year as Director of the School I had not been able to persuade myself to give up my journalist's job in London; I went out to Greece merely on holiday. Now it seemed foolish to hesitate any longer. I let the flat, packed my traps and took what was then a popular, reasonably fast and economical route to Greece—overland through Italy to Brindisi and by the Lloyd-Triestino line to Piraeus. By the end of January I was installed in the Director's house with servants over whom, since as yet I could not speak their language, I had no control, and with a teasing desire to escape from the formalities of Humfry's official position into the country.

The house was cold, and I fidgeted. In the mornings I took the tram (the bus was a later amenity) which plied between the Gennadeion Library opposite the School and the centre of the city; learned the way about; ran errands; mastered a few Greek phrases; and joined Humfry at the National Museum. His excavations at Perachora on the headland which, running westward from Loutraki and Mount Geraneia, separates the Corinthian from the Halcyonic Gulf would soon be entering on a second season. It was a remote, unfamiliar site, and of necessity the finds were brought to Athens for safe keeping; and morning after morning in one of the Museum storerooms he was engaged on the endless task of sorting the pottery, thousands of fragments of it.

Sometimes from the dusty confusion on the shelves he would pick out two pieces which joined; and gradually the delicate patterns of rosettes and palmettes, the miniature designs of painted griffins and lions with their mock ferocity would match, and a whole vase would take shape.

I knew nothing, I did nothing. In a kind of petrified respect mixed with slightly resentful jealousy I watched the operations of wives better equipped as archaeological partners—and readier, I am ashamed to think, to set their own personal interests aside. In particular I watched the Pendlebury partnership, for though Hilda was working on a Mycenaean study of her own she was always wrapped up in the job John was doing. Sometimes when I arrived at the Museum I would find the two of them in the store-room with Humfry, for John gave generously of his time to photograph the Perachora material. In the afternoon the Museum closed. We would go by taxi—Athens taxis were cheap—back to the School for lunch; after lunch we played tennis. Husbands and wives played together, urging one another on with anxious cries. Somehow the conventional phrases which John addressed to Hilda were invested with a curious mixture of the familiar and the courteous. We never exchanged partners; I was glad of that, for though he always preserved an unruffled good temper I felt I should have failed to live up to his ideas of feminine reliability.

Presently my desire to get out of Athens was satisfied. Together with the Pendleburys Humfry and I were to make an excursion along the north coast of the Gulf of Corinth. We would begin with Delphi; cross a shoulder of Gkiona, the high mountain which carries westward the chain of Helikon and Parnassos, and follow the Mornos valley down to Naupaktos; and go on to Missolonghi.

Humfry had made trips with John and Hilda before. He was accustomed to their long timetables, and anyhow he was himself an indefatigable explorer. In my longing for the adventure of the country trip I had forgotten the discomforts of spring travel and uncertain weather. Delphi indeed was a delight. We climbed to the Corycian Cave. We expressed proper dismay at the taming of the tall slit in the rocks where the sacred spring emerges; 'At Castalia,' John wrote to his father, 'they have made a very damnable cement path up the gorge so that the swine who go to the festival can go up to the fountain in bath chairs. They have quite ruined the place.' We none of us felt that the infirm or the indolent had any business in Greece; and certainly none of us imagined the motor-roads which later—and here I join with John—would violate the majesty of the mountains.

But the high pass over Gkiona was not for us. Over twenty years later I carried out part of the original plan—it was a kind of pilgrimage for me—and walked alone down the Mornos valley. At that first attempt we were defeated. The month was March and the weather broke. The route over Gkiona was impassable, and I was spared what later commonsense tells me would have been a pretty killing trip. We changed our plans. We renounced the Mornos valley and Naupaktos. Instead we took a car, drove north to Lamia and Thermopylae, and walked over Mount Oeta to Drachmani, which my companions assured me was the ancient Elateia but of which I remember only sleeping in a private house and a dirty bed.

We visited Chaeronea, where the marble lion which marks the grave of the Thebans killed in battle against Philip of Macedon was, as usual, rakishly crowned by a stork's nest. We saw Livadia and Orchomenos and Thebes; at the monastery of Hosios Loukas the almond-trees were veiled in pink blossom, and over supper an ecclesiastical dignitary roguishly recommended me to try, in the traditional Greek phrase, to make some children. Once, I recall, I was insecurely perched on not a mule but a small horse which slid sideways down a slope, leaving the pair of us mercifully unhurt but in an undignified tangle. Strangely, of the whole trip, ten days or so of it, I retain no more than such sporadic images, and even these are recovered only by reading John's record of our itinerary.

Perhaps my memory was temporarily frozen, for the weather was often cold and, as I have reason to remember, wet. I had no mackintosh. Idiotically I did not possess such a thing. I had set out in an overcoat—I suppose it was the only one I had—trimmed, absurd and even inhumane as it may sound, with monkey fur. One day there was a plan for an expedition to Gla, an ancient site on what was once an island in Lake Copais. The rain was pouring down, and the general feeling, in particular my own feeling, was that my clothes were unsuitable and that I had better not go.

Humfry felt he could not desert me, and for a couple of hours we sat in the local café, drinking village coffee and listening to the clatter of village backgammon. Hilda, I morosely reflected, would never have drifted into such a situation. Presently the Pendleburys returned with streaming mackintoshes and glowing faces. Gla, John wrote to his father, was an amazing prehistoric fortress rather bigger and more imposing than Tiryns. What was more, they had seen the Great Katavothra, one of the sinister outlets through which a lake will sometimes, foaming and gurgling, vanish into the earth, and which in this case helped to drain Lake Copais. I have seen other katavothrae, but I still regret the one near Gla.

But though I remember so little of those ten days I well remember my impressions of John Pendlebury: the figure—it was always ahead on any walk—fairly tall but compact, with an energy austerely disciplined. You would see him jump straight to the top of some little wall where anybody else would have stepped up. At our evening halts or during our picnic meals I observed his way of talking, clear, vivacious, quick without haste, the syllables precisely enunciated. One felt his glance fixed on one. Sometimes I found his manner daunting, but that, I fancy, was merely due to his looking at the world with one eye instead of two.

It was obvious that an excursion of the sort we had undertaken was a happy background to his private image of life. Each day took in some monument or some district associated with antiquity; that occupied the archaeologist and the historian in him and satisfied his desire, half-scholarly, half-romantic, for a relation with the past. The conditions of travel added a flavour of uncertainty. The discomforts of the trip were minimal, indeed non-existent in comparison with the exhaustion he would later inflict on himself in long walks in Crete. But everything joined to strengthen his idea of himself as an explorer, a figure in a continuing adventure.

v

A week or two later I saw John in another setting. The Pendleburys had moved to Knossos for their second season, and Humfry was paying an official visit to the site and the estate. I had never been to Crete before. Now for the first time I saw the Villa Ariadne, for so long a legend to me, and its appendage the Taverna. No students had arrived yet, and we had the Villa to ourselves. In the chilly March evenings fires were lit in the living-rooms; friendly but respectful figures swept the hall and served the meals. Gradually the Villa, from being in my imagination a mirage in a golden haze, a lodge to the Palace, perhaps, an annex to the Minotaur's lair, settled down as a sturdy stone house with an imposing balustraded flight of steps to the front door, standing amongst palms and olives and exotic shrubs on a slope with a drive down to the gate by the road.

In their first season the Pendleburys had been chiefly occupied with the Palace site and the reorganisation of the estate. This year in a breathing-space before the arrival of Evans they were struggling with the living quarters, getting 'the place in order and having the walls colour washed'. Domesticities mingled with the archaeological severities; for years Humfry and I used as a catch-phrase a question repeatedly overheard: Has the soap-dish come? Through everything John wore an air of contented authority. He was not only the explorer. He was the explorer with—I am sure he liked to feel—a solid family background.

The Guide to Knossos was taking shape in his mind.

A Preface. An Introduction. An architectural history—with a few plans, a ceramic and 'frescoic' history. The guide proper to the Palace. Four reconstruction sketches and the big plans on canvas at the end. Guide to outlying parts . . .

But a struggle was ahead. Evans wanted something far less ambitious. A few weeks later Macmillans, Evans's publishers, took a hand; the guide was to be described as based on *The Palace of Minos*. In exasperation John wrote to his father.

My name should be on the title page as author and I should receive a sum down for my contribution. This seems to me to be the very negation of what I intended, and in such a case I won't do it. First as I shall point out to him the actual guide part is entirely my own, secondly such a description on the title page would debar me from any personal opinions or disagreements, thirdly if that is what is intended any précis writer could boil down the P. of M.

Why nobody should be allowed to write about Knossos but Evans I don't know. Of course all future work must be to a certain extent based on him, but to maintain that a completely original guide should be dismissed as a sort of necessary work on the part of a devoted slave to be paid off seems to me to be folly. I should much rather have all the plans redrawn at my own expense and publish elsewhere.

There was no mollifying the young Curator.

I heard from Macmillan, who says that the partners don't see any profit in a guide. He wants to talk it over when we get back. Of course I'd like the CUP [Cambridge University Press] to do it but it would mean a lot of trouble about plans etc. The point I'm fighting for is that I shan't be too much associated with Evans and his reconstructions. I can't afford it!

Like many of his contemporaries he took a purist view of restoration, just as he took an austere anti-modernising view of Greek roads. It is amusing to find that while this battle of the generations was going on he was engaged as Curator of Knossos in supervising excavations for Evans. The year was 1931, and the founder of Minoan archaeology was almost at the end of his explorations. Four years later he would make a final visit to Crete, but there would be no more serious digging, and *The Palace of Minos* still had another volume to go. Nevertheless 1931 brought a triumph.

We have got what certainly looks like a royal tomb with side chapels and pillared halls. We are still a good six feet from the bottom and the top of a door leading farther into the hill has just appeared. It will be about the highest piece of ancient walling preserved and should be a magnificent monument.

The tomb in fact turned out to be the great complex of sanctuary and sepulchre which Evans named the Temple Tomb.

Once more John wrote about the Knossos guide and the argument with the publishers. Macmillans were represented by George Macmillan, at the time Chairman of the British School Committee, a dry old gentleman whose kindly efforts to adapt his hospitality to the needs of the School's young Director and the Director's wife caused us acute embarrassment. Once he took us in a family party to the theatre to see one of the jovial musicals, all canikin-clinking, of the time, *White Horse Inn*. 'I hear,' he said in patrician tones as we were conspicuously ushered into the front row of the stalls, 'that it is quite delightful.' I remember him chiefly for his habit of calling in the butler after dinner at his Yorkshire home, where he had been good enough to invite us for the week-end, and giving instructions before the guests about the suit of clothing to be laid out for wear next morning. His Victorian self-confidence could be intimidating, at least in my anxiety not to injure Humfry's relations with the Committee I found it so. But John was not to be rattled.

My point [he reiterated] is that if I do as Macmillan wants I shall really have to write it absolutely under Evans's direction which as I know well will mean one eulogy of reconstruction after another . . . I wouldn't have gone to Macmillan only there was the question of the plans.

Finally honour seems to have been satisfied, and in 1933 he writes from the Villa recording the arrival of *A Handbook to the Palace of Minos, Knossos*. The courtesies had been decently observed.

Evans had contributed a Foreword, and in his Preface John had said: 'Without restoration the Palace would be a meaningless heap of ruins, the more so because the gypsum stone, of which most of the paving slabs as well as the column-bases and door-jambs are made, melts like sugar under the action of rain, and would eventually disappear completely. The accuracy of the restorations has been ensured by careful study of the evidence during the course of excavation.' And this happy agreement was rewarded. The Knossos stock of copies was soon almost sold out; Macmillans had to be cabled for more; and when a batch of Hellenic Travellers visited the site they would, John said, have bought another fifty had there been any to buy. A last note will bear quoting. As usual a party of the Travellers were entertained to lunch at the Villa.

Among our guests . . . was Harold Macmillan, MP, a nephew and luckily I—by mistake—happened to mention in his hearing the stupidity of sending out here so few (copies). He said rather shamefacedly later that he would talk about it to the firm on his return!

In this academic struggle Macmillans bear the brunt of the attack of the new generation. Really, though, in the years of the Pendlebury curatorship it is the figure of Evans—little Arthur, as John took to calling him in a mixture of disrespect, admiration and liking—which looms over the whole scene: Evans who makes unscheduled additions in page proof to the *Handbook*; Evans whose restorations are ceaselessly argued over; Evans whose excavations keep everyone working beyond their time; Evans who rejects solicitude ('My dear Mrs Pendlebury', he says, taking Hilda's arm, 'don't worry, I *like* losing my temper!'); Evans who is obstinate, demanding, interfering—and generous. His table-talk is part of the background of life at the Villa.

Have you ever seen a geranium growing half-way up a fir tree without any roots in the earth? Evans's theory is that the gardener treed it when it was trying to escape!

His jokes are cherished. Nearly forty years later Hilda would describe dinner at the Villa—the warm, scented summer evenings, the rats scuttling blamelessly along the roof by the terrace, and Evans laughing delightedly at his own stories and stretching a hand over the top of his head to scratch the far side. There was even a certain gaiety of routine. On Saturday nights at this time, she said, they all drank champagne.

Keeping up with the indefatigable octogenarian (he was in his eightieth year when the Temple Tomb was discovered) was a job in itself. Nevertheless time was found to note the bizarre or the tragic event. The kitchen-boy had eloped with a girl from the village; a week after the wedding, John drily observed, the christening took place. Or there was the painful case of the English boy who went out for a walk at Delphi and disappeared. The accident, for accident it turned out to be, caused a good deal of stir in English newspapers, and a letter in *The Times* talked alarmingly of brigandage, murder and the perils of travel. 'A most extraordinary libel on Greece,' John called the letter, 'obviously written by one who has never been there or who if he has has never taken the trouble to know anything of the country.' (A fair amount of solitary travel since then has put me firmly on his side.) Like many Englishmen of his period he alternated between exasperation with the occasional delaying tactics of country Greeks and a total infatuation with Greece. But as time went on his affection for the Greek people grew.

The work of general reorganisation continued. By 1932 he had got those famous boxes of sherds from past years of excavation properly stored and plotted on the plan of the Palace. The boxes themselves, two thousand of them, had to be catalogued; afterwards he set out first with Hilda and later with two students, Edith Eccles and Mercy Money-Coutts, to catalogue the contents. Evans did not come out to Crete that year nor indeed in the succeeding years of John's curatorship: 'We are very peaceful here without little Arthur.'

The Pendleburys could settle down to a routine of work, excursions and domesticity. They made a tennis court in the Villa grounds. And there was an addition to the family. 'A Knossos nursery,' Evans had observed with amiable interest, 'will be a new feature.' David Pendlebury was brought out to Crete when he was still a baby, and with a son and heir about the place John could feel that his picture of himself as the adventurous head of a solid family was complete. He was a proud rather than a doting parent. Joan, the daughter who was born a couple of years after David, does not remember her father often playing with his children, to whom in a self-consciously offhand manner he always referred as 'the brats'. She recalls gestures of affection, and certainly the idea of fatherhood gratified him. It gave him the sense of an achieved manhood.

The new family responsibility did not interfere with filial feeling. There was a moment of anxiety for his father and stepmother.

By the way—this is rather difficult to put—I have unexpectedly left unused that £1,000 on deposit. I have also a comfortable balance in the bank here (£221) and am getting dr. 500 to the pound. If all this bother is, as it must be, hitting you and Dickie pretty hard mayn't I offer what I have to help keep up the family home? I won't say any more, because you know what I mean and what I can't say. But it really would give me enormous pleasure if I could be of any help. This between ourselves absolutely.

'I have unexpectedly left unused that £1,000 on deposit,'—the delicacy of feeling contradicts the casual exterior which he presented to the world.

In 1933 when he came back from his season in Egypt and, joined by Hilda and David ('he is certainly grown out of recognition and really is a fine young tough'), returned to Knossos he discovered that the foundations of the Taverna had given way. There were large cracks in the walls and the house was uninhabitable; the only satisfactory solution was to rebuild. In theory Evans had handed over to the School the entire estate, but in practice he was still very much in authority, and John wired to him as well as to the Director of the School. From Youlbury came the answer that rebuilding must begin. The opportunity was seized to make improvement, for example to reverse the normal structure of Greek village houses and put the staircase inside instead of outside. The usual local dramas enlivened the job and momentarily swung John back to a mood of English intolerance.

. . . Today I got fed up with the continual quarrels of the foreman and chief mason and told the workmen that the day after tomorrow I would sack the lot and get new ones. This I fully intend to do if they don't stop this eternal Hellenic bickering. Quite honest mistakes are reported to me as first class thefts.

But in a couple of days the trouble had been patched up, and by midsummer the little house was finished. It had cost three hundred and fifty pounds.

Nothing, however, interrupts the flow of work. There are students to be advised. There are visitors (including Prince Rupprecht of Bavaria, 'a very fine-looking old gentleman'). The letters home are full of references to proofs and articles and catalogues, to a lecture planned for an Amarna architectural exhibition and to the problem of funds for the Amarna dig, while from time to time the business of scholarship is interrupted by news of David's progress. And of course there are the expeditions—spending one night, for example, on a threshing-floor outside a village and another on the shore at Mallia and travelling 'through practically unknown country' to Elunda or Spinalonga. Spinalonga, where Evans's motor-boat adventure had begun, was a seaplane base for Imperial Airways. 'The Imperial Airways people,' Pendlebury remarks on this occasion, 'put us up on their yacht and did us proud.'

Up to the summer of 1932 the long exploratory walks had been undertaken partly for study but very largely for pleasure. Pleasure would always be an element. Now there was something else. He decided to write an archaeological guide to the whole island of Crete. It had begun as a bibliography of ancient sites. Rapidly it turned into a plan for 'a magnum opus, viz a real archaeological guide to Crete which will take some years'. Next, it 'looks like being about two volumes of the barest details, and these compiled only from our very limited library here.' A year later he had begun writing. 'It will really be my Index to sites made historical instead of topographical. I ought to be able to get quite a lot of new facts and some,' he adds belligerently, 'I hope unacceptable ones.' It would in fact be something which nobody else had the qualifications to undertake.

The extraordinarily precise and detailed notes he had always kept on any expedition were a beginning.

Friday 17th. Leave *Sphaka* 8.15. *Sitia* 1.45. (mule of Alexandros 175 dr.) *Hotel Athenai* 20 dr. a filthy bed. Good restaurant.
Saturday 18th. Leave *Sitia* 6.50 arriva *Palaikastro* 10.50. Leave 1.30. *Sitia* 5.40 (mule 150 dr.)
Sunday 19th. Leave *Sitia* 7.5 arr. *Sphaka* 12.5. Leave 1.55. *Pachyammos* 5.35. Alexandros mule again. 300 dr. (for wait etc).

This from his first visit to Crete in 1928. The mule, of course, was for the women in the party. Only twice in his life, according to the letters, once when he twisted his ankle—an incident which he reports with exasperation—did he break his 'record of never having ridden'. As time went on the notes grew fuller and the timetables more strenuous—and more and more taken up with the search for unrecognised ancient sites, the material for his archaeological guide. In 1934 Hilda was not with him. She was expecting her second baby and spending the last months of waiting in London in a flat which Humfry and I lived in but which was free while we were both in Greece. In her absence John describes one of his more backbreaking excursions, this time with as companions the Seton Lloyds (Professor Lloyd is an authority on Western Asiatic archaeology) and another friend; the plan was to follow the tracks of Evans in the 1890s. 'I am going to look over all the sites which he found before he ever began digging and to try and date them in the light of recent knowledge' The trip, a great if tiring success, as he comments in his tiny scholarly hand, began with a day in the mountains, whence the party descended to 'a clean hotel' in Sitia.

. . . The next day I got a boat to take us to various islands, round the NE corner of Crete and to Eremopolis (Itanos), where the mules had been sent. Unfortunately the boatman was a rogue. The motor broke, he couldn't mend it, didn't want to sail, couldn't row and it eventually came down to using horrible language and threats of violence to make them row us into a bay by the lighthouse on Cape Sidero on the extreme NE promontory of Crete. Here we luckily found the lighthouse keeper had a mule to carry Joan Lloyd and the lunch while I proceeded to get our animals to come and meet them. 10 miles in 1½ hrs over really rough country isn't bad going! I got to Eremopolis in time to look over the ruins and to go on, still ahead to Toplu Monastery to prepare for them. There we had true monastery hospitality and a chicken to take on with us. Next day Palaikastro where I searched the surrounding mountains in vain for unknown sites. Next day Zakro where we slept on the beach, next day I went alone to the SE corner of Crete and up a fantastic gorge back to Upper Zakro where we spent the night in a school. On the way I found a few sites and a wild shepherd boy who thought that all the world talked Greek and had been greatly put out by hearing animal noises (?German) coming from someone who couldn't do so last year. Thence over the hills to Zyro and down to the coast to Makrygialo by Palialimata. In this completely desolate place we slept in the telegraph office and for a joke asked if we could ring up London. To our horror the man said certainly! and began to do so. Luckily the director of the nearest exchange was having dinner and couldn't be got hold of.

Thence to Hierapetra and so to Pachyammos where I left them and returned partly by foot to Knossos. Last night I slept c. 14 hours . . .

The description is illustrated by a minuscule, spidery map; he often drew maps in his letters. But nothing save experience of a Greek journey of the sort can given any idea of the terrain, the distances, the exhaustion and the painful joy involved. Not even normal experience is enough. '10 miles in $1\frac{1}{2}$ hrs over really rough country'— it takes an athlete's physique to do that.

And John was combining exploration with an exacting job at Knossos. With the help of Mercy Money-Coutts and Edith Eccles the cataloguing of the Palace sherds was in its final stages. Meanwhile the property and the site needed attention. The Palace was being fenced with barbed wire to keep out animals as well as people. The cultivation of the vineyard, which this year was not being let out to a tenant, had to be supervised; the result was an unusually good crop and hopes of a profit of over ninety pounds, more than had been coming in for years. There were the customary crowds of visitors, including 'a perfect spate' of German tourists. 'Where,' John wrote with irritation, 'all these Germans get their money to go cruising round I don't know.'

The irritation was perhaps aggravated by the scarcity of British cruises which might well have boosted the sales of the Knossos Guide. What was more, when the English did appear there was trouble. That year when the Hellenic Travellers reached Herakleion the captain decided to anchor outside the harbour, and only about eighty people managed to get ashore. The passengers, inflamed by a mischievous rumour about reluctance to pay harbour dues and resentful of the number of free passages for lecturers, cut up rough, the more so since John, who seems to have made a practice of speaking his mind on these occasions, insisted that big ships could perfectly well enter the harbour.

Fortunately he had Canon Wigram on his side. Canon Wigram, annually the indomitable bear-leader of the party, it was who would arrive at the School in Athens with forty exhausted travellers panting for tea—or with equal sangfroid would telephone at the last minute to cancel the arrangement; the women passengers in particular were happily ruled by him, and he was indeed well-informed about the ancient sites included in the trip. At this juncture he wrote to Lunn, originator of the Hellenic cruises, to insist that Pendlebury was justified and 'evidently knew more about the coast than the captain'. Meanwhile the British Consul discovered that the port pilot had in fact advised entering the harbour, and the affair brought John a number of appreciative letters. There was even an invitation from the Duchess of Devonshire for the Pendleburys to stay at Chatsworth.

It is ironic that this period of achievement—the estate recovered from neglect, the Taverna rebuilt, the Palace put in order, the archaeological relics reorganised, the Knossos *Handbook* published and admired (Evans himself had expressed pleasure)—should have brought the Pendlebury curatorship to an end.

I have just had a letter from the Committee of the BSA saying that they are making more explicit the rules under which the Curator is appointed. The new clauses are that the Curator is to be responsible whether in residence or not for supervision and necessary action in emergencies and that therefore he is not expected to undertake direct responsibility for independent archaeological work out of reach of Knossos.

vi

Obviously for John the altered rules made the position untenable. He would have had to give up his season in Egypt. He would have been tied to administrative work. The freedom on which he had always insisted would have vanished. 'I feel very much that as a matter of courtesy they should have talked it over with me.' Nevertheless behaving, in spite of his hot temper and natural anger, with dignity, he enquired privately of the Chairman of the Committee (it was Sir John Myres) whether it would be easier for the School were he to resign at once or to stay on for his final term in office and advise his successor. Hilda away in London expecting a baby, his project for the archaeological Guide just beginning to look like a reality—at such short notice the loss of his job must have been an ugly shock. He took it philosophically enough.

Sooner or later I should have had to leave and this gives us a chance of leaving gracefully for a particular reason. I have now got Knossos into order and my only regret is that we shall be leaving the Taverna so soon after we have made it look so nice . . . Anyhow it will leave my hands free to do my own work and to travel about without always having to get back to pay the men on Saturday!

Five seasons in the post had brought out his essential toughness. He was less than thirty. But he was financially independent; there was ambition in his way of looking to the future; and when just before leaving Knossos to be with Hilda for the birth of the baby he wrote home he made it clear that he was not to be put upon by any Committee.

I am pointing out in my report at the end of the season . . . that things are happening agriculturally here from October to August and that there is no close season for antiquities to be found. If they hope to get someone who while nominally here for 3 months and paid for that period will either stay here for 10 months (and go barmy) or be permanently on tap in Athens they will be pretty lucky.
Actually I think they are trying to crack the whip—they don't realise a) that I have cracked too many whips myself to be impressed b) that it may serve with a lazy horse but that with a lively one that's doing its job they will be thrown!

Next time he saw the Villa he was no longer Curator. The Committee had appointed as successor a tall, pacific, unworldly Cambridge archaeologist and prehistorian, R. W. Hutchinson, whose domestic circumstances as well, perhaps, as his temperament were more amenable to the conditions of the job. By the spring of 1935 he was installed with his elderly mother at Knossos. Evans had not been in Crete since 1931, but he came out this year for the celebrations in his honour—the speeches, the festivities, the unveiling of the bronze bust in the Palace grounds; and John and Hilda arrived in time to see him 'crowned with bays'.

They felt in their new situation an embarrassment which was probably needless. They were in Crete to work, to travel; their position at Knossos, where they shared the Taverna with the Hutchinsons, was that of visiting students. But the Cretan servants could not immediately grasp the change of employers (the foreigner returning in Greece to the scene of a former happy relationship is always liable to be hailed as one of the understanding 'old ones'), and John and Hilda could not at first dissuade the staff from coming to them for orders. They refused, of course, to respond, and anyway it is unlikely that Hutchinson, affectionately known to his friends as the Squire, would have minded; as for Mrs Hutchinson, she had not yet learned any Greek. Probably the second Pendlebury anxiety was needless too. Evans was in the Villa Ariadne. The monarch might have abdicated but any spring he might want his throne back for a couple of months; and as a precaution John had 'told Hutchinson all the ways and traditions'. Nevertheless he could not quite overcome his fears of a regal explosion; and suddenly one has the impression, comic after the grumblings of a few years earlier, that the Evans-Pendlebury relationship had been idyllic.

Nothing, of course, happened. Sir Arthur expressed concern about Mrs Hutchinson's rheumatism, Sir Arthur duly left for Youlbury. Or perhaps something did happen. The grand, the royal days of the Villa came to an end. For John, at any rate, it seemed that there had been 'a sad break in the continuity of splendour'. And yet, if one looks back, it is hard to accept the idea of the falling curtain. It is still the trail of the great Evans which must be followed in that superhuman Pendlebury walk in 1934 through East Crete. John had once been expressing fervent though self-interested wishes for the durability of his employer, who had written that his fourth volume was going to take longer than he had thought and would be in two parts like the second: 'I only hope,' John commented 'he does finish it and that I'm not left with it expected by the learned world to finish it off.' Now the book is written and only its publication is awaited.

We got a wire just before he left to say that an important letter in connection with it was awaiting him, and he was wondering whether he had contravened the blasphemy libel and indecency clause in his contract!

And John, no longer responsible for the Knossos site, no longer in the employ of the insatiable discoverer, forgets his old disagreements and enjoys the joke. Next time he mentions Evans it is with recognition of kindness. 'I had a very charming letter . . . thanking me for Tell el-Amarna, which he found most readable, and for bits of information about sites.' In the long run few of us found the old giant resistible.

Perhaps in making 1935 the date of his last visit to Crete Evans chose the right moment to bid farewell. There was already disquiet in the air. He had spoken in one of his letters of the disturbances that year. The revolt petered out. But it left a bitter aftermath. There were arrests and trials; a number of officers, among them Sarafis, who was to be one of the left-wing leaders in the Civil War of the 1940s, were marched round the Athens barracks-ground and stripped of their insignia. In Crete, traditionally Venizelist, the feeling was violent. A trial was held at the naval base of Souda, and from a hotel in Canea, the nearby capital of the island, John reported the presence of 'rascally attorneys suborning witnesses for the court-martial'.

West Crete is full of the cry Τουφεκίζουνε τὰ κουπέλια (they are shooting the boys,) quite a sort of Irish They're hanging men and women for the wearing of the green . . . Many rumours here as to Royalist return backed by Venizelos of all people but not the old George of Greece but the Duke of Kent and ἡ Πριγκεπήσσα Μαρίνα [Princess Marina]. Their health has been drunk a lot in West Crete.

A Royalist return there indeed would be, though not by the Duke of Kent and not immediately. Greece settled down again in an uneasy fashion, and John returned to his normal preoccupations.

There were enormous walks, including a trip with the Squire (whom he greatly liked) up Mount Ida and on to Yerakari. Evans's foreman Manolaki Akoumianakis, who was still working for the School at Knossos, accompanied the party. Yerakari, a village in the Amari district west of Ida, was his birthplace, but he had not visited it for twenty-three years: now 'the round of visits was amazing'. John was still searching for ancient remains. 'Two more sites will make 100 in two years—not bad going for the hundred cities of Crete' (to which Homer had referred). Able to give his whole mind to the quest, by midsummer of 1935 he had found a total of sixty-one in that year alone. He was still the resolute athlete, given to skipping for a quarter of an hour in the early morning before breakfast ('I find it quickens up the muscles which walking is apt to increase but slow down . . .'). He was still the joker, full of repetitive family jests about drinking capacity, or delighted to relieve some social occasion by a juvenile secret game which involved inducing his companions to use some particular word ('My greatest triumph was getting him [the Squire] to say "bimetallist" and her [Mrs Hutchinson] "bivalve"').

But his travels were bringing him new interests. Cretans, as with the born explorer's pleasure he had noticed on his first visit, pronounced Greek differently from their compatriots. Their vocabulary too can differ, and he had the idea of collecting local words which 'thanks' as he put it 'to "education" ' were dying out. 'I believe I could go to the mainland of Greece—speak correct Greek and yet be quite unintelligible!' Soon he began noting down snatches of songs about Cretan villages. He was making friends everywhere. By now he had travelled on foot from one end of the island to the other. It was only natural that its people should feel affection and respect for the tireless young Englishman, his fair skin burned dark, his hair the colour of stubble, who turned up everywhere, slept anywhere, drank with them, talked with them, spoke their own kind of language. His letters are full of stories of welcome. And he began to be conscious of a special responsibility.

There are various things I'd like to say about Crete—speaking as one who I think I can say knows the island better than anyone in the world—and I have been asked to get my opinions as to various matters such as roads into English newspapers.

By the mid-thirties international discomforts were invading all our lives, even the most private of them. Back from Cairo one spring John foresaw trouble there. 'Fuad is ill—desperately. Farouk is 14 and a miserable lad. If God wills we—or the Sudan—will take over Egypt.' Even his incorrigibly boyish jokes would presently take on a political colour.

I sent round to the police station here today a bogus arrival form of Benito Mussolini—parentage unknown—religion Σατανολατρεία [devil-worship], profession white slaver. The commandant tells me that it took him in for a quarter of an hour and has fined me a dinner to pay for the cost of a wire to all the ports for information.

Nevertheless there was still a breathing-space. The spot in which he had established such forgivingly friendly relations with the local authorities was Tzermiadha in the central district of Crete called Lasithi. Here on the slopes of Mount Dicte is the rich, mysterious Lasithi plain, its flat expanse irrigated by thousands of windmills with sails flickering like a field of white blossom. At Psychro, south-west of the plain, is the Dictæan Cave down which tourists today are uncomfortably conducted; legendary birthplace of Zeus, it was excavated by Hogarth, who had just retired as Director of the Athens School at the beginning of this century when Evans was making his first discoveries at Knossos. In 1935 John, exploring the Lasithi area, had looked at a cave on the opposite, the northern rim of the plain. Evans had seen it years before, but though it contained early Minoan remains it had never been excavated. John decided to dig; and in 1936, with finance from various sources and a permit obtained through the British School, he and Hilda started work.

The cave had been in use before the sanctuary at Psychro; the deposit it contained stopped at the period when the Psychro deposit began. John was soon finding pottery and bone figurines of a local and hitherto unknown type. Some rewriting of his book, he realised, would be needed. Presently he knew that this was just the beginning.

We've got a programme for years here. It is so cut off a place that it has all sorts of queer survivals. Even nowadays they use more Arabic words than anywhere else and have Turkish gestures.

Next summer he was back, though without Hilda, who with her usual stoicism was undergoing a serious operation in London. The reports from the dig were cheerful: Neolithic burials, 'the first ever to be found in Crete'; a Middle Minoan building; quantities of pottery—in fact 'stuff of every period except classical and Roman'. And Marinatos, the Director of the Herakleion Museum with whom he had clashed at the beginning of his curatorship of Knossos, was now on the best of terms with the British explorers, and apparently prepared on his own authority to extend their permit to include not only Tzermiadha but the whole of Lasithi. Before the end of the season John had discovered 'a sub-Minoan Protogeometric Temple on a peak about 4500 [feet] up with all sorts of cult-figures—dove goddesses etc. which show the continuity of culture up here'. The site was called Karphi. On its rocky perch it disclosed what there was every reason to identify as one of the castles of the 'robber barons' thought to have taken over Crete when the great Minoan civilisation was disintegrating. And there were mysterious finds. Among the clay statuettes recovered (one was pieced together from 489 fragments) were figures crowned with discs and birds and equipped with feet separately moulded and appearing through openings in the front of their bell-skirts. 'The goddess,' John commented in *The Archaeology of Crete*, 'must have needed them to reach her lofty shrine.'

For two more years excavation went on. With knowledge and experience acerbity sometimes crept into his rejoinders. Once in the foundations of a house he came on a clay figure of a dolphin with, he remarked, on its back a man carrying a child. The presence of the child meant that the reference could not be to the legend of Arion, the musician-poet rescued from would-be murderers by one of the benevolent sea-creatures, and John was open to suggestions. Presumably the idea of a man carrying not a child but a musical instrument was put forward. At any rate a few weeks later he wrote: 'By the way tell E—that when I see a *cithara* with a navel and testicles I'll believe my find represents Arion.'

But in general the exploration of Karphi stirred no conflicts. The finds, especially the mountaineering cult figures, were notable enough, but the most satisfying results of the four seasons in the Tzermiadha district was the light shed on the prehistory of Crete, 'the real Dark Ages', as some have called them, when long after disaster overtook Knossos the arrival of a people familiar to students of Greek history, the Dorians, may have driven whole townships of the island's inhabitants to take refuge in the hills. Forty years after Evans's first revelation of a glittering Minoan culture John was filling in the gaps in the story.

The Lasithi interlude strengthened his ties with the Cretans. He made more and more friends. In 1938 when he and Hilda arrived at Tzermiadha they were greeted by 'five village elders—who had suitably liquored up for the occasion—with a gallon of wine and a set speech on the benefits we had conferred on the district'. At the end of the season there was a civic banquet in a garden in the plain, and the following afternoon they were accompanied by the Mayor and town council as far as the next village, where more refreshment was offered, while on their further journey towards Knossos they met two policemen who, refusing to let them eat their own food or drink their own wine, gave them yet another party. John was a proper recipient of the fierce proud hospitality of the island. As Patrick Leigh Fermor has recorded, he could drink even the Cretans under the table, could walk even the Cretans off their legs. And there was a kind of piety, as of a son for a father, in some of the relationships he formed. The famous Dictæan Cave at Psychro had, it is said, been discovered by a Lasithiot. In 1939 he died; John spent one of his free Sundays in visiting the grave of his old friend.

Savage political divisions have always been common in Greece, and at the end of the first season at Tzermiadha the Pendleburys, following a good old archaeological custom and holding a party in celebration, found that many of their acquaintances could not be expected to meet one another on a social occasion. But in the second half of the 1930s a new kind of unease was spreading. On a trip to Western Crete John and his party were taken by a policeman for spies. However on the impudent English suggestion that he should ring up the King or the British Consul to check, the man sensibly remarked that to telephone would cost twenty-five drachmas and it was cheaper in the long run to let the visitors take what photographs they wanted. Once later on, walking down alone from Lasithi to Knossos ('26 miles over filthy country in 6 hrs 25 m.') to get a document signed by the consul John was accosted by another local policeman.

You know we've just got a new law that all strangers coming through must show their credentials. But we know all about you and as long as that——little lawyer doesn't see you it's all right . . . He's got a feud on with the Inspector and will try to get him into trouble if he hears of your passage.

At that moment the lawyer himself appeared—and turned out to be an old acquaintance of John's.

How dare you stop famous friends of Crete—and mine. I hope the Kyrios will complain—and I'll back his complaint and you'll get sent off to the islands!

There were inconveniences not so easy to circumvent. Currency restrictions, for instance. In Greece, John remarked, posting 'an English cheque to an English bank to pay English cash for an English bill in England' was treated as sending money out of the country. To write to an English bank at all a special permit from the Bank of Greece was needed; otherwise the letter was automatically destroyed. His comments on financial affairs grew more and more acid. Exasperation over the difficulties of getting on with a simple job mounted.

Luckily he had his father in England to act as steward; and the extraordinary series of letters in which year after year, week after week he recounted the details of work and play, of digging and walking and joking and reading bore witness also to a relationship in which even money, among the English most private of subjects, held no secrets. To Hilda, no doubt—understandably she never quite forgot the elder Pendlebury's initial disapproval of her marriage—the unchanging interdependence of father and son must often have seemed less than a blessing. But if once or twice John betrayed a shade of impatience with the paternal demands, if he rebutted with a touch of asperity some complaint about a date unavoidably changed, about the 'tone' of a telegram, it really was only once or twice. For the rest the desire to please, to be worthy, was paramount. If the father found, as Hilda once told me he found, in the son his chief interest in life, the son at an age when most men have long since slackened the first parental ties responded with an exemplary duty and affection. There was an occasion when the older Pendlebury received some minor honour. 'It couldn't,' John writes, 'make me prouder of my father, but it makes me more pleased that he is honoured as he deserves . . . Your very proud son . . .'

Sometimes news of another sort reached the archaeologists in their far retreat during the Lasithi summers. In 1936 Humfry died of a relentless, a galloping infection of the blood. He was only thirty-five; none of us had thought that death could strike at our own generation. The Pendleburys knew him as a friend. They had made arduous expeditions with him, they had walked with him down to the headland in the Gulf of Corinth when the decision had been taken to make the Heraion of Perachora the next major School dig.

We shall miss him a lot. Our friendship throve on insult and abuse. I'm very glad to have known him, particularly on trips. 'My God, to think we're paid to do this!' on a very good day when we had found Perachora and were sitting on the hills above.

Always direct in his responses, John was deeply and truly grieved; again and again his letters return to the theme. But the news had another side to it. The sudden death of the Director threw the School into confusion. Peter Megaw, later Director of Antiquities in Cyprus, was Assistant Director at the time; resourceful, considerate and a kind friend to me, he took immediate charge. Alan Blakeway, who a year earlier had been digging in Crete with Humfry, presently secured leave from his Oxford Fellowship and came out as Acting Director. The Committee then began to look outside the list of obvious candidates.

Middle-aged men on retirement often have a romantic fancy to take up archaeology, but Gerard Mackworth-Young was different. He had been a distinguished Indian Civil Servant; he was also a good classical scholar; and he was determined. Engagingly modest, ready in the pursuit of his aims to accept an inconspicuous position, he had consulted Humfry on the steps to take. He was advised to master a craft which would make him valuable in any archaeological enterprise—in fact to specialise in photography. As a photographer, then, after enrolling as a student at the School, he came out to Athens; and when in the last years of his life Humfry was engaged on a catalogue of the archaic marble sculpture of the Acropolis Gerard joined the undertaking and produced the fine pictures for the book which resulted. In 1935 and 1936 he was gaining practical experience of another sort; together with James Brock he was excavating in the island of Siphnos.

The Committee had the answer to their problem. He was free; he had authority; and he was well-to-do, willing to take on a post paid at the rates available to a learned institution. When the next School session began he had been appointed Director, and he held the job until the Second War drove the British out of Greece.

In the months after Humfry's death when I was still within earshot of archaeological politics John was often spoken of as a candidate for the Directorship. I did not think he was the right man. The superficial flippancies, the persistence in undergraduate jokes seemed to me to unfit him for the formal, official encounters of Athens. Perhaps I was allowing an unacknowledged prejudice to affect my judgment. Certainly he was a far more complex nature than I was at the time capable of realising. Superficially tough, under attack he brooded. Arrogant in his views, in human relationships he could be forbearing and sensitive. His aesthetic tastes were undiscriminating. In his letters one finds references to books by Rose Macaulay and Robert Graves; a biography of Cromer stirs him; then he will describe some unremarkable popular novel as 'a first-rate book'; the best creative literature of the times seems to have passed him by.

And yet his own writing is not only direct and strong; it has on occasion a personal vividness. Half of him belonged to the society of scholars and artists. The other half lived in a world—empire-building, chauvinist—foreign to me. I saw the second half, and thought of him as an anti-intellectual. No doubt I was taking a conventional view, and now, reading the letters to his father with their severe undertones, I wonder if I was wrong anyway. It is true that they make no mention of a desire for the British School job. There is, however, a reference to the reappointment of Gerard in 1937; and here another name relevant to the story of the Villa Ariadne reappears: 'I expect the Committee are keeping him as a warming pan for Dunbabin whom the Oxford members are determined to have sooner or later.'

Tom Dunbabin—the quiet, handsome Tasmanian whom I had first seen, a powerful but temporarily bewildered figure, amidst the confusion of the Athens police headquarters—in the next decade would be contributing to a chapter in Cretan history. In the late 1930s he was a prospective Oxford contender for the British School post, and I dare say the rivalry between Oxford and Cambridge helped to colour the reference in Pendlebury's letter. Apparently John himself adopted an ambivalent attitude towards the Directorship. He blew, according to Hilda, hot and cold; he made no definite move to show he was in the running. His father insisted that he would have got the job if he had let people know he really wanted it. Anyhow he was passed over. He did not feel deeply about it, though he was disappointed or rather, perhaps, injured that he should not have been given the chance before someone such as Gerard Mackworth-Young who was not by first training an archaeologist.

But if he was merely disappointed about the British School his feelings about another rebuff were keen. From 1930 he had divided his energies between Crete and Egypt: spring and summer based on Knossos, then, after an interval in England, winter in Egypt. For seven seasons he directed the excavations at Amarna, and directed them with success. But no papyri were being found, and according to Hilda the Egypt Exploration Society hoped for papyri. Anyhow the Committee decided to move their operations. Hilda's view may well have been prejudiced, and the decision may not have been as sudden or as surprising as she represented. But whatever the circumstances, the first John heard was that Amarna was being abandoned and that a new director had been appointed to dig elsewhere.

In the first years after Humfry's death, though I travelled in Greece and cherished Greek friendships, I was inclined to lose touch with archaeological society, which in any case I had often found intimidating, and though I certainly should not have lumped them in with its austere ranks somehow I did not see the Pendleburys. I thus had no opportunity of judging for myself how John had been affected by his series of setbacks. But affected he certainly was. The curatorship of Knossos withdrawn from his reach; no hint of an offer of the Athens School—those two might have seemed injuries enough. But the loss without warning of the Egypt Exploration Society post really hurt him. To a naturally ambitious man—and he was ambitious—it might have seemed calamitous. Not to John. The self-confidence of the golden boy was not undermined. But he was embittered; Hilda saw that he was embittered. She had known only the bursts of anti-bureaucratic exasperation which interrupted, though never for long, his usual gaiety. For a time she was concerned about this new dark mood.

Possibly disappointment induced him to think willingly at last of a settled job. In 1935 before setting out from Knossos on a long expedition he had written

The fact is of course that I am more of a topographer than an archaeologist! I think my length of leg needs a mountain rather than a test pit to step over!

But in 1937 he was putting in for a post in Palestine, and though he was inclined, perhaps vaingloriously, to congratulate himself when he failed to get it ('I'd gathered it was a pure office job not adapted to longish legs still in their prime') the attempt shows a change in his attitude. Two years later still he applied for the Disney Chair of Archaeology at Cambridge. No luck again. But in defeat he was generous. About Dorothy Garrod, the successful candidate at Cambridge, he wrote: ' ... a very good appointment. A very nice person and a most sound excavator'. He had been temporarily embittered but not soured. After all he had enjoyed great success in a life still young. He had established a reputation based on both field work and published material in two areas of archaeology. He had produced a handbook and guide to Knossos which long years later, after all the intervening wrangles of the learned world, would still stand firm. And with the publication in 1939 of *An Introduction to the Archaeology of Crete*, evidence of a devoted scholarship in keeping with the endurance and tenacity of purpose it modestly displayed, he had joined the famous company of modern traveller-observers whose work in Greece began in the nineteenth century. He was the successor of Leake and Pashley and Spratt.

In the time which remained before the war he went on deepening his knowledge of the island. He 'managed to do the three peaks of Dicte in one day' (the optimists among us sometimes fancy themselves striding from one crest in the Greek mountains to another—until from some appalling height they see the nature of the terrain; only people like Pendlebury put the dream into practice). The same summer there was 'a trip up Ida and down south to Melambes to visit a cave. A pure pleasure trip, largely, but I've done all the possible routes up Ida but one and that impassable for mules' (it sounds like the one down which I crawled miserably sometime in the 1950s). 'Record time to the summit too and a resultant waist measurement, pulled in a bit, of 22½ inches.' The fantastic feats of speed multiplied. After a break from work on the Tzermiadha dig he walked back from Pachyammos,

this being quicker than the car! I left Pachyammos at 4.30 by a route which I thought would bring me here by about 2-3 p.m. To my surprise I arrived here at 12.30 having sat down for a good hour all told on the way. At 12 Hilda rang up the folk here to say that I'd be arriving about 3-4. The Postmaster said—in an aside—'bet you a million he's here within the hour!' Sure enough I was.

In 1938 Hilda shared some of his expeditions. In 1939 it was understandable that he should leave her with the children in England and go out alone. 'With the prospect of a good many pleasant seasons here,' he wrote from Tzermiadha, 'it would annoy one to have to begin trailing a pike in the Low Countries.' Time indeed was shrinking, and the Pendleburys would not again spend a summer together in Crete. The last months, however, brought some startling archaeological news. While in Athens John heard that large numbers of inscribed tablets had been found in the American excavation at Pylos overlooking the Bay of Navarino, where in the Greek War of Independence an Allied fleet under Codrington defeated the Turks. Was there a connection with the tablets which nearly forty years earlier Evans had found at Knossos? The explorer Carl Blegen invited John to look.

Blegen has got a Palace apparently of the Homeric period—really Nestor's!—and 185 clay tablets inscribed in a form of the Minoan script—though it seems to me probably not in the Minoan language, since the combinations of signs aren't the same as in our Knossian ones.

'Not in the Minoan language': another decade and more would go by before a young architect, making a fresh approach to decipherment, would revive one of the controversies which have always echoed round the name of Arthur Evans. There was no leisure now to linger over the significance of the Palace of Nestor. It was April already, Hitler was in Czechoslovakia, Mussolini was on the point of invading Albania. John had made what private provision he could.

In case of trouble [he wrote from the Villa to his father] I purposely leave all arrangements with you at home. Is there any way of extending a Power of Attorney indefinitely? If so let me know and I will have an affidavit signed before the Consul. I'm not panicking but I do want everything absolutely straight.

Greece, so often a battleground, is the most tense, the most rumour-ridden of countries in times of international crisis, and though by May when he was about to set off for Tzermiadha the atmosphere was less electric one can understand what he felt when he wrote:

The worst feature to my mind is that one is beginning to wish to God it would come soon and not hang over our heads.

Nevertheless the old enthusiasms ruled him. There were exhausting excursions ('better get in all one can in case of trouble'). There were recognised sites revisited and new sites discovered ('the book is well out of date already!'). And there was the dig. Some of the students from the Villa Ariadne went up to Lasithi to help him. The work went well. The workmen included a variety of picturesque characters: 'two gigantic purple masons straight out of Chaucer' and 'two Albanian wife-murderers who escaped when Zog opened the gaols'. The finale of the season was celebrated on John's name-day by the usual party.

It was the best we have had up to date. I really felt the village father!—pretty near 1000 people and dancing from 9–3! Total cost of making the whole village tight £7!

It was not, unluckily, quite the end. There was a spring on the heights. Before he left Tzermiadha that summer John built a fountain there; water would be piped down to the village, and in commemoration of the four years of excavation a marble plaque was designed and affixed. One morning he went up to the site to find the plaque chipped and the stone with which the damage had been done lying beside it. He reacted furiously: sent for the mayor, the schoolmaster, the police, refused to speak except on necessary business, declined all hospitality. He got no change out of anyone. Perhaps a village, however divided, if attacked will instinctively join forces against even the dearest outsider. Anyhow nothing was done; somehow in such circumstances nothing ever is done. There may have been a simple explanation for the arbitrary little act of violence. Probably a local family with a grudge against one of the masons were aggrieved that his name should, in accordance with custom, appear on one of the corner-stones; probably the wrong part of the fountain was chipped. John consoled himself with the thought that the story had spread throughout rural Crete. 'Tzermiadha is in for a bad time.'

But the incident was an affront to something more than his paternalistic relations with the villagers. His romantic feelings about the country were injured—those feelings which in all of us who care for the living Greece are a mixture of affection, enchantment and the gigantic spell of the past and which in John were strengthened by the inclination of his whole nature. The undergraduate at Cambridge sitting on a hard chair over *The Forest Lovers*, the young archaeologist at Amarna doodling, drawing figures from mediaeval chivalry—perhaps unconsciously he had formed a shining image of his rôle in life. All his adventures, his feats of stamina, his desire to extend himself in both work and athletics to the limits of endurance were an effort to fulfil the dream, an attempt to hasten its achievement. There was something, some goal of excellence he had to reach by himself. In spite of his jokes, his carousings, his friendships, in spite of the easy intimacy of his marriage, I see him as ultimately a solitary: the single horseman.

He left Greece in the July of 1939. He had a plan for a catalogue of ancient sites in the Cyclades, but though some of the preliminaries had been done that was for the future. For the present his job was complete—*An Introduction to the Archaeology of Crete* published and applauded; the excavation of Karphi rounded off; everything clear, everything tidy. When a few weeks later war broke out there was nothing to be interrupted except life itself.

vii

'I love being a soldier. I've forgotten all about being an archaeologist.' A common risk, danger, the sense of involvement in an adventure of universal importance—something in the atmosphere at the beginning of the Second War, something which a later generation has failed to understand, spoke instantly to the idealist in John Pendlebury. The disquiet in the air of the last year or two, the sourness which was invading casual human relationships, his own faintly lingering personal resentments, everything was wiped out. At last he knew exactly what he had to do.

Not that the soldier he became was an ordinary soldier; no 'trailing a pike in the Low Countries' for him. He had already in August been placed on the reserve of officers. When he came back from Greece he spent some time in Cambridge clearing up the last loose ends of work. That finished, he went with Hilda and the children to the Isle of Wight for a holiday; it was there that the family on the morning of Sunday September 3 heard the radio with Chamberlain's declaration of a state of war.

They took a car and drove straight back to Cambridge. There

was an interval when John served on a committee which interviewed candidates for commissions in the services. Then he was himself asked if he would prefer to join an infantry or a cavalry regiment. As one might expect he chose the cavalry, and towards the end of 1939 he was sent for training to the equitation school at Weedon. Perhaps, Hilda thought, hoping against hope, when he was posted abroad it would be to Palestine.

He was happy at Weedon, happy enough, perhaps, to forget not only about being an archaeologist but—since cavalry could hardly be deployed in Lasithi or the foothills of Ida—about the seeming break of his ties with Crete. For a few months he could live in the simple pleasure of learning the business of peaceful soldiery. That winter we all held our breath, incredulous in the lull. Occasionally he spent a contented week-end leave with Hilda. For the rest he was at Weedon until the fall of Norway and Denmark, defeat on the familiar battle-fields of the Low Countries and the invasion of France itself stirred the British out of a traditional reluctance to employ experts in expert fields. In May 1940 the War Office sent for him. 'Here,' somebody said, 'is this man who knows about Crete.'

Hilda once told me that some time that month John was flown over northern France. Beneath him he could see the jammed roads, the mortal debris of invasion, machine-gunning, bombing; he could see pitiful crowds of refugees driven as a screen in front of the advancing Nazis. A romantic view of history had always inclined him to admire the military peak-figures and the princes of the Renaissance, and when somebody pointed to their ruthless disregard of human suffering he would reply that this was 'necessary policy'. Now he was confronted with the reality of 'necessary policy', and he could not endure it. 'After this experience,' Hilda wrote, 'I saw him, his face set like a rock as he told me he could hardly wait to take his personal vengeance...' Vengeance is not, I think, the word for the part he was to play in the war; it is too confining a word for his high-spirited patriotism. But the part was soon to be assigned, and his companions were soon to be chosen.

In my time in Athens I often heard of a student of the School who was an especially resolute traveller among the discomforts and the ferocious sheep-dogs of Epirus and Albania. Nicholas Hammond was to be known later as an authority on the history and archaeology of the district. At this juncture of the war, like John Pendlebury he was summoned to London, and there in 'a dingy, dark and depressing basement room in the War Office' the two men, friends from their days at the School (both had taken part in that famous all-night all-day walk to Thebes), met again. Both had volunteered for 'special service'. Hammond says that his initial discouragement on a first encounter with official flummery and general vagueness was dispelled by the practical grasp which John immediately displayed.

In his mind's eye he was planning the organisation of Crete for resistance with a clarity of purpose and a care of detail which were fully fledged . . . he talked to me of swordsticks, daggers, pistols, maps; of Cretan klephts from Lasithi and Sphakia; of hide-outs in the mountains and of coves and caves on the south coast; of the power of personal contacts formed by years of travel, of the geography of Crete, its mules and caïques, and of the vulnerable points in its roads.

One can see how confident, in the terrible uncertainties of that summer, John with his quick enthusiasms, his persistently youthful taste for adventure, above all with his dedication to the job in hand must have appeared to his companions. The news was disastrous: France cracking, the British in retreat to Dunkirk. Here was a man who was absolutely sure of himself, who looked forward with something like joy to his own field of battle. There was to be the minimum of preparation—a few days in London 'learning the tricks of the trade', a few embryonic and according to one participant faintly ridiculous experiences with explosives. Meanwhile the troop trains were arriving loaded with survivors from Dunkirk, and we all wondered how long it would be before Italy entered the war.

Hilda knew, of course, that he was being sent to Crete. The wives of that heroic band of buccaneering adventurers always knew—and always kept silent. When John learned the date of his departure—he was at the War Office for no more than a fortnight— he sent for her. She left the children with her mother, went back to Cambridge, packed some things he needed and came up to London. His luggage included a swordstick. He had, Hilda said, an idea— fantastic, absurd, who, since the outcome was to be at once glorious and obscure, can say?—that it would be the ideal weapon against parachute troops. Then one night at the beginning of June husband and wife dined together at the Oxford and Cambridge Club. After dinner they were joined by two men who were strangers to her. Time was urgent, 'So,' as with her own special brand of laconic courage she put it, 'quite soon John came out with me and we actually said goodbye on the pavement outside the Club.' Next day he left on his last journey to Greece.

Nicholas Hammond was in the party which set off that morning for the Middle East. They were, he said, 'sent off from London by a staff officer in full-dress Guards' uniform, a spectacle which even in those days struck us as incongruous'. They made a roundabout journey by air via Corsica, Bizerta, Malta and Corfu; John, asking questions about roads and harbours in Albania, was busy preparing himself for the possibility of fighting on the Epirot frontier. But Greece was not yet involved. The Albanian campaign was still to come, and when the party, undercover but suspiciously military, arrived at Athens the authorities looked understandably askance. John was allowed to land. Nicholas Hammond, the Albanian expert, was among those sent on to Egypt. It was nearly a year before the two men met again. For the interval one has to rely on a few scattered letters from John to Hilda, on the piecemeal accounts of eyewitnesses, on one's own knowledge of his character and his relationship with the Cretans, and on the myths which have accumulated round his name.

He was not able to write often. There were four letters home, three to Hilda, one a round-robin which he invited her to share with his friends. The first mentions the Villa Ariadne; it is written from Knossos. He must have gone almost immediately from Athens to Crete, and for some time he lived at the Villa. Here a bizarre fact emerges; I had quite forgotten it. The date is June. Europe is ablaze, Britain awaits the Luftwaffe—but archaeology must go on, or at any rate appear to go on, and the Squire is still in residence, together with his elderly mother, as Curator of Knossos. He did not wish to leave the Villa and the Palace without supervision. At the same time he was concerned to prepare for the storm, and with two representatives of Cable and Wireless in Herakleion he worked part-time on compiling a list of Cretans who were reliably pro-Ally and Cretans suspected—these, one feels, must have been few—of being pro-Nazi.

John himself had to wear his civilian hat. His captain's uniform, as his amused friends knew well enough, was kept ready in a box. He was working for Military Intelligence. But ostensibly he was Consular representative, Our Man in Herakleion. 'Elliadhi,' he writes in that first letter (the name is that of the affable practical joker who once entertained Humfry and Alan Blakeway and myself to an embarrassing lunch)—'Elliadhi is being very nice and helpful in instructing me how to be a Vice-Consul.' The disguise cannot for a second have deceived the watching Germans. John, the Squire reported, said of himself that he was the most bogus Vice-Consul in the world. Certainly though Greece may have still been officially neutral there was not much neutrality in Crete, as he found when he began to travel about the island.

I had a short but very nice trip in the West—going up to Omalos and spending a night at Anoyia and going up to Nidha [the plain high on Mount Ida]—though not to the top.
Anglophily is rampant!

The job of Vice-Consul was a disguise accorded only the faintest observance. It is clear that from the start he was busy recruiting and organising guerillas against the possibility of attack; I have heard stories of his expeditions through the island in 1940 and the beginning of 1941, expeditions from which he returned blindly exhausted, to drop and sleep where he lay. It is clear also that the desperate situation of the times—the first letter is dated June 20, and France had already fallen—merely stirred defiant impulses in him.

I hope things aren't too depressing at home. Here we sadly lack news but at all events the one thing we know is that we shall never give in. First Θὰ πάρωμεν τ'ἅρματα νά φύγωμεν στά Μαδάρα [we will take our arms and flee to the White Mountains]. If England was overrun we'd fight from the colonies I know.

The letter was taken by the Squire to be posted in Athens. Communications were difficult, and for much of the time the Pendleburys relied on telegrams. Three months later John himself was on a thirty-six-hour visit to Athens, and from there despatched a fond, gossiping letter, the kind of letter which with its scraps of trivial news and its undertones of anxiety must have been typical of a thousand letters from soldiers serving abroad to their families during the Luftwaffe attacks on England. He had met old acquaintances in the street in Athens. In Crete there had been a heat wave. He had bought a puppy from his muleteer Kronis (for many years the Pendleburys' faithful servant); it was black with white legs and was to be given the Cretan name for a dog with stockings, Kaltsoni. For a moment the old mischief peeps out. The date is September 16 and Greece is not yet at war.

There is an old Italian skipper here with two ships who is getting very annoyed at people—I'm afraid at my instigation at first—going up to him and asking how it is that with Italy mistress of the seas, he doesn't go away!

There is a touching note of nostalgia. Beneath the gaiety, the adventurousness, the nonchalance in his nature an enduring affection had taken root. The boy had felt it, the man knew it.

I hope you got the wire on the anniversary of our wedding day (twelve years man and boy bless you!). I went down to Vianos that day and had a stroll on to Amira.

Then the anxiety. By now he had moved out of the Villa and was established with Kronis as servant in the offices of the British Vice-Consulate in Herakleion. Hilda with the children was in what he hoped was safety in North Wales. But who in those days could be sure? He felt, as many soldiers in the nervous quiet before the storm must have felt, restless; even, though he of all men had no reason to feel it, left out of things. The longing for danger, action, heroism teased him.

I hope everything has been peaceful in your part of Wales. It's dreadful sitting here not knowing. I suppose I am doing some good. It makes me very jealous to hear of what people are having the honour to do in England and Africa.

A month later Metaxas rejected the Italian ultimatum. Greece was at war, and in the bitter winter Greek troops were fighting in the snowy Pindus mountains.

For John the need for pretence was over. Temperamentally he must have delighted in the excitement of his undercover activities. But he delighted in display too. Now he could take his captain's uniform out of its box and wear it; the transformation satisfied a certain vanity in him, a pleasure in sartorial show. Or perhaps vanity is too sharp a word. An observer on the spot adds a comment. C. J. Hamson—brother of the late Denys Hamson, who played a gallant part in mainland Resistance, notably the destruction of the Gorgopotamos Bridge—had come to Crete as an SOE officer (later he was to be Professor of Comparative Law at Cambridge); the sartorial display, he writes, 'had a quality of disarming innocence—a klephtic panache, a Byronic posture: pour encourager les autres, et pour s'encourager un peu soi-même. One could do with all the encouragement one got.'

Pendlebury had fresh scope now for encouraging. With the entry of Greece into the war he could confer openly with people from his own country, working in his own kind of field—members of SOE among them. But the situation had disadvantages too. Since he was in uniform his ideas for guerilla action were subject to British military authority; for with the changed conditions the British had sent a Military Mission to Crete, and his job was that of Liaison Officer between them and the Greek military authorities. He was convinced that if attacked the island could be successfully defended. He knew the terrain. He knew the people. In the months since his arrival he had been working out a plan. He reckoned that for success—so I am told by Professor Hamson—he needed ten thousand rifles, and in November 1940 he asked for them.

For the British this was a black moment in the war. London was under nightly air-raids; the country was grimly on the defensive. Arms were needed for Abyssinia. Egypt would be fought for, but an attack on Crete seemed a long way off. Some observers say that had his plan been adopted the island might have been saved. But John, so Hamson believes, lacked the final conviction needed to impose his will upon his superiors. 'With his authority, his knowledge, he could have insisted. He could have refused to carry on in Crete. If he had insisted he would, I think, have won. He very nearly did win; he very nearly was a great man. He was a greater, certainly, than any I met on the island.'

He did not get his rifles. Whether those desperate treks in the last months before the attack, those home-comings half-dead with exhaustion marked a struggle against frustration one cannot know. All one can say is that his few surviving letters of the period are all confidence.

'Greece behaving grandly very proud of Crete' says a telegram; there was a Cretan division fighting in Epirus. But the island itself waited. That Christmas the authorities—'they'—allowed John and his kind to send a free letter home by air mail—'but one only and written only on one side'. He sent his message to Hilda but addressed it 'To all it may concern'; it was a general despatch to his friends. I have seen the letter. It is written on the thinnest, the most transparent of paper, yellowing now, frayed, tattered, almost extinct. But the writer is gaily alive in it, up to his old jokes.

What a show the Greeks are putting up. Did you see that Mussolini has complained that a) the sword and bayonet are barbarous weapons which only Greeks would use and b) that they have been sending savages from Crete! But I'm sure nothing to the savages that can be sent.

With the war coming closer he no longer feels out of things. He is active in a new way now, not only tramping the mountains to organise guerilla bands but receiving numerous visits from compatriots; everyone, he says, who comes to Crete has heard of his presence and been instructed to get in touch with him. There has even been an Old Wykehamist dinner. Of the Cretans—his Cretans, already indulging a taste for the brigand aspect which characterised the andartes, the guerilla fighters, during the Occupation of Greece— he writes with amused affectionate delight. 'All old friends here are going well, either twirling their moustaches (the vine disease got into mine and I had to have it out) or relating catastrophes.' He is even playing—it is significant in view of what was to happen—a brigandish game of his own. 'On his more nefarious expeditions,' a friend reports, 'he used to take out his glass eye and wear a black eye-patch. He would leave the eye on the table by his bed—if you found it there you knew he was away on some excursion or other.'

Frustrated or not he must have been enjoying himself. Romance was waiting round the corner. When the time came he would fight beside his island friends with the twirling moustaches; Crete would be his battlefield. And now one sees the man—different from the efficient administrator, the scholar and traveller of the letters to his father, different again from the husband gratefully remembering his wedding aniversary of the letters to Hilda—whom Patrick Leigh Fermor met when Crete was truly threatened at last and John visited the HQ cave outside Herakleion.

His florid handsome face, his single sparkling eye . . . his slung guerilla's rifle and bandolier and his famous swordstick brought a stimulating flash of romance and fun into that khaki gloom.

A few more months went by before the crisis, and as his round-robin letter shows he wasted no time.

I have been carried shoulder-high round five towns and villages and have been blessed by two bishops and made a number of inflammatory speeches from balconies.

Meanwhile the anti-bureaucratic irreverence which had marked all his adult life burst out. His position in Crete was still anomalous. The regular services, as Nicholas Hammond was to point out, had not yet fully recognised the groups of experts to which both he and John belonged. The man on the spot had 'to win the personal confidence of the local naval and military officers, who at first regarded his nose as false and his schemes as harebrained'. On this level John won the confidence all right. His unique knowledge of the island, his command of language and dialect, the absolute loyalty of his Cretan friends—he was irreplaceable. His relations with higher authorities were acrimonious.

I am making a grand collection of 'tickings off' usually beginning 'In future you should not repeat not . . .' Every Government cypher or code has obviously been made up on the assumption that the recipient of any original either has been, is, or will be doing something wrong. My best rebuke was for using the word 'bastard' in a wire to the Minister. In reply I pointed out that as it was in the code book the word was obviously meant to be used, and that the Minister was old enough to know the facts of life and that it was the only word that fitted the individual referred to.

But the self-felicitating disrespect serves to cover a passionate concern about the war.

This is hardly a Christmas letter but do know that I am thinking of you and hoping that you will have as happy a one as you can. Goodness knows where I shall be. However since we shall win—mainly owing to you people and the Greeks—it doesn't matter.

Still, life went on in comparative quiet. Sometimes he fretted over the difficulties of communicating with his family; letters from Hilda in Wales came in batches after long delays and in the wrong order. But the trickle of telegrams with their comments and their scraps of gossip continued. Hilda must have heard some fragmentary wireless despatch: 'Not me on radio though present', he cables back. He is regularly in touch with Knossos, for he relays a message not only from his servant Kronis but from the staff at the Villa: 'Kosti Manoli Maria all send love to you and children.'

Meanwhile the Squire and his mother pursue their calm career. There are occasional visitors to the Palace, the Villa and the Taverna must be attended to, and the Committee of the School, so far as one can make out, never reflect that with war blazing in the Mediterranean Crete is a risky refuge for an elderly lady suffering, as Mrs Hutchinson suffered, from severe rheumatoid arthritis.

Not that either the Squire or his mother would for a moment have considered leaving unless obliged. Years afterwards I asked him what they had proposed to do if the war reached Crete. 'Oh', he said airily, 'my mother would have gone up to the mountains.' In the meantime he went on being Curator of Knossos. The references in John's letters, however, show that he also travelled about the island. Was he, I asked once, engaged on some kind of official job? Not exactly, said the Squire. But there was his work with the Cable and Wireless representatives in Herakleion. And on John's behalf he was doing a certain amount of reconnoitring as well.

By 1941 the telegrams were growing scarcer, but early in March there was a reassuring message: 'Can again cable all well delay unavoidable.' A few days later a letter came. 'My own darling', it began; after thirteen years of marriage all his letters to Hilda began with an evidence of devotion which from his outward manner one might not have divined. It had the usual ending: 'With all my love from your loving husband.' He was, he said, still getting letters from home written in September and October; obviously he longed for news. Had the publication of Karphi, his dig at the Lasithi fortress-site, come out yet? Were his staff allowances and pay as Captain, to which since his despatch to the Middle East he had been entitled, being properly credited to his bank account? How were

Evans ('little Arthur'), Myres, Mercy Money-Coutts 'and all the vogue of yesteryear'? He had given up trying to keep a diary because for the present so much had 'to stay unwritten'. He had nearly but not quite got over his fears of caïques 'but not of rowing boats'—a feeling which will be shared by many people with experience of the Aegean or the Cretan Sea. His letters, he admitted, had been irregular, but so had his life. Occasionally, though, he managed 'to get a peaceful day up at the Villa and have a bath'.

Questions, messages, fragments of news—the last paragraph had a warning note. 'At present we seem as safe as you, though by the time this gets to you we may not be so!' The date was March 7. There was still nearly a month to go before Germany joined Italy in the attack on Greece and sent in tanks from the north. But John recognised the approach of trouble. He had, it seems, from the start intended, whatever happened, to stay in Crete and lead the Resistance; 'He never,' Nicholas Hammond wrote, 'talked as if any other course was possible.' As Hammond has remarked, this was very much a personal decision.

... On the Greek mainland, where plans for forming nuclei for guerilla warfare were too late to be effective, it was not intended that English personnel should remain behind; nor, so far as I know, was this either contemplated or done in Jugoslavia. John's plan was therefore original and daring, and given his personal qualities as a leader in a limited area with a more or less homogeneous population the plan was full of promise. It required more resolution in an Englishman to stay behind voluntarily and be submerged by the German tide than to return later as many did when the ebb was likely to set in. But for John the choice did not exist; he felt himself a Cretan and in Crete he would stay until victory was won.

At last there was to be no watching from the sidelines. Ahead of him John saw the romantic adventure which had lived in his imagination—dangerous, bloody, but to be entered upon in the company of people who trusted him: a noble adventure, a debt of honour to his friends, perhaps to himself. After March 7, 1941, no more letters came; perhaps there was no time for letters. But there was one more cable. It was dated March 17. Did he feel that the adventure was to be both his crown and his finale? Hilda believed that he knew he was going to be killed. Certainly the last words of his last cable, the last words she ever had from him, were valedictory. 'Love' he wrote 'and adieu.'

From that moment the stream of letters, telegrams, reports, the jokes, the anecdotes, the accounts of everyday life, the records of exploration, the timetables, the traveller's tales in the minuscule handwriting with the tiny spidery illustrative maps, everything stops, and a life so precisely documented suddenly becomes a matter of other people's memories.

viii

On April 6, three weeks after John's last telegram, Germany moved into Jugoslavia and Greece. By April 22 the Greek armies in Epirus and Macedonia had been forced to surrender, and a day later, with the British and Commonwealth troops in retreat and headed for evacuation, the Greek Government announced that it had moved to Crete.

Suddenly Knossos was in the thick of things. The Greek King arrived at the Villa Ariadne, where he slept in one of the stone-floored basement bedrooms which Evans had built against the heat of Cretan summers. His agreeable friend Mrs Brittain-Jones and his sister the Princess Katherine had lodged themselves at Neapolis in Eastern Crete, but almost immediately joined him; his servants found rooms in the village. The Squire, calm as ever, took the opportunity of showing the party round the Palace; Otto, the royal dachshund, celebrated the occasion by nosing out on the site a family of hedgehogs. But soon, with German troops already in Athens, the women were hurried to Egypt and the King moved on to Canea; and from there, accompanied by the British Minister, the Greek Prime Minister and a group of New Zealanders, he undertook the tough and indeed risky trek across the White Mountains to the south coast and eventual exile.

By now the pressure of events was getting too much for even the Hutchinsons, and on April 30 they left the Palace, the Villa and the Taverna for the duration. They were to be taken off by destroyer. That night they went down to the harbour at Herakleion. Mrs Hutchinson did not feel inclined for unfamiliar company, and while her son dined at the Officers' Club John Pendlebury stayed to talk with her. When the time came to say goodbye he made another valedictory gesture. He had £10 in English money; he gave it to the Squire, who later in the war used it to send parcels to prisoners in Germany. That was the last of their exchanges. The rendezvous was with a destroyer about a quarter of a mile away. In the April night a launch took the English pair out; Hutchinson recalled with amusement that when they reached the ship he was the only person who had any sort of light to signal with. Somehow the arthritic but indomitable Mrs. Hutchinson was got up the usual rope-ladder. The party were aboard; beleaguered Crete faded in the distance; and the journey began to Alexandria, to Port Said, at last to Cairo, where the Squire settled down to work for the rest of the war.

The story is now taken up by Nicholas Hammond, who was in the group which left England in the June of 1940 but who was refused permission to land in Greece and went on to Egypt and later to Palestine and Cyprus. After the war he contributed to a memoir privately printed for Hilda and John's father; and it is mainly on this memoir that I rely for the interval, or at least much of the interval, between John's March cable and the Battle of Crete.

After the voyage to the Middle East Hammond had heard reports from Naval Intelligence officers in Alexandria of Pendlebury's efficiency and resource. At last—it was in March 1941—he was himself allowed into Greece. He was stirringly and heroically involved in the retreat to the southward-looking ports; reached the Cretan naval harbour of Souda Bay; joined the company of HMS *Dolphin*, an armed caïque captained by Mike Cumberlege, another of the adventurous heroes of the war in the Mediterranean; and on arriving at Herakleion went up from the harbour to see John. It was the first time they had met since June 1940. John, he writes,

had a much clearer sense of impending crisis than we whose nerves had relaxed after experiencing the evacuation from Greece . . . The loss of the entire Cretan division in Epirus, as a result of the Greek armistice, was particularly galling and he spoke of it with the same warmth as the Cretan people, who had approved the assassination near Canea of the divisional commander for escaping without his men. If only the older generation of Cretans could be armed, they would give a good account of themselves; but the arms were not available, and even his own men, who were organised for guerilla warfare in the event of Crete being overrun, were far from adequately armed.

Nevertheless John, in spite of the frustrations which beset him, looked to the future with the mixture of resolution and robust gaiety which Patrick Leigh Fermor saw on the occasion of that visit to the headquarters cave. He had already made a reconnaissance raid on Kasos, the nearest of the Dodecanese islands. Now with Cumberlege and the *Dolphin* crew he planned an operational raid to bring back Italian prisoners and perhaps learn what preparations were in hand for an invasion of Crete.

There were matters to be cleared up first. The *Dolphin* party had the job of finding beaches suitable for landing troops and supplies on the south coast of Crete; and Cumberlege for his part was already looking for concealed inlets handy for bringing in small groups should the island be completely overrun. John drove with the explorers from Herakleion to the top of the hill where, midway across Crete, you look towards Gortyna, Phaistos, Hagia Triada and the Mesara plain; discussed his own scheme for mining this strategic road; suggested sites to be considered; and left the party with an introduction to one of his own men—'Pendlebury's thugs', as more conventional belligerents called them.

Once more in Herakleion, Cumberlege agreed with John on final arrangements for the Kasos raid. The two men had greatly taken to one another.

Both were men of vigorous speech and independent ideas, with great force of character and abundant humour; and both possessed that clear-headed audacity which undertakes the apparently more dangerous course after a detached study of the advantages and disadvantages. They possessed too a simplicity of motive in facing or inviting danger, something much more spontaneous and automatic than the ordinary man's sense of duty, a rare quality which I only met once again during the war.

The two parties, sea-fighters and land-fighters, were forming a harmonious interdependent group. John had become 'an honorary member' of the *Dolphin* crew, and they in their turn were welcome at his headquarters, where Kronis in Cretan dress stood guard. A letter from a friendly observer gives an idea of the happy, unmilitary disorder of the office 'with its two Lear watercolours and a somewhat rickety wardrobe filled with guns of all sorts, piles of paper money bundled in with every sort of other papers etc.'. The situation had the air of easy classless camaraderie which for the foreigner is the charm of rural and provincial Greece. The traffic policeman himself used to come down from his platform under an umbrella in the middle of the town to share a drink with the Englishmen. And when John gave a pre-raid dinner he insisted that the party should include a member of *Dolphin's* crew, Saunders, who had served seventeen years on the lower deck and who as a regular seaman 'was somewhat abashed but greatly delighted at dining in an officers' mess'.

By the night of the dinner party German bombing raids had spread from the naval port at Souda Bay to Herakleion airfield and harbour. The attackers, usually thirty of them, came over at dawn and at dusk 'and had shot down the three gallant Gladiators which went up to engage them whatever the odds'; as they flew low machine-gunning, *Dolphin* would reply from her quayside moorings. That evening John borrowed one of the caïque's machine-guns; whether he used it one does not know. Presently the friends dined together; the menu included 'fresh fish collected by the fishermen when bombs had concussed them'.

Excitement, the approach of the crisis for which all his life had been a preparation, and—for this is not a factor to be dismissed—the stimulus of simple Greek food and wine taken in good company: John was happy that night; it is good to think that he was happy. Before the party broke up the final details of the Kasos venture were settled. A new assignment—perhaps lucky, perhaps unlucky, who can say?—had necessitated postponing the raid. Cumberlege and his crew were ordered to Hierapetra on the south coast of East Crete. Today Hierapetra is a pleasant little seaside resort with a wide calm bay, tree-shaded cafés and a leafy corner with a ruined house where, people will tell you, Napoleon spent a night incognito. But in May 1941 the place was under bombing attack, and the *Dolphin* party were to see if it would be possible to salvage the cargo of guns and ammunition of a ship which had been sunk in the harbour. After that, Kasos. The date was fixed. It was to be the night of May 20.

The *Dolphin* party, then, set off—Mike Cumberlege and his cousin Cle, formerly a Major in the Royal Artillery but now in charge of the little ship's guns; Nick Hammond himself; Saunders; a young South African private of the Black Watch named Jumbo Steele; and Kyriakos, a sponge-diver from Kalymnos who had escaped from the débâcle in Epirus and had been given permission by the Greek commander of Herakleion to join the expedition. They would return on the 19th to collect John and his guerillas.

Once again there was delay. The party had to wait for a message from Souda, and Hammond telephoned to John to say their meeting might have to be two days later. Still, *Dolphin* was soon on her way back. It meant a voyage up the east coast of Crete and round the extreme north-east tip which looks out towards Kasos. Cumberlege decided on one more reconnaissance trip. Since they were already so near they would cross to Kasos and back and check the timing. It was the night of May 20, the night originally fixed for the raid. They would sail an hour before dark.

And that evening the engine would not start.

While daylight held Jumbo Steele struggled with the motor: in vain. The waiting crew watched four seaplanes flying low down the strait which separates Crete from Kasos, but tucked in under the rocks as they were—*Dolphin* had moored by an offshore island—they were not themselves detected. Night fell. Presently they could hear gunfire in the Kasos strait; the darkness was noisy. But when at dawn next day, the engine having repented, they rounded the north-east point and reached the little port of Sitia all was calm. Nevertheless Mike Cumberlege had decided that 'due to the extraordinary amount of air activity' in the strait the raid would once more have to be postponed.

At Sitia, then, they landed to telephone to John. Inexplicably they could not get through to Herakleion. They sailed on westward. It was annoying to be fired on from the shore; but perhaps the Cretans had not been told about *Dolphin*. To be machine-gunned as the caïque came to Herakleion, however—that was different. Alerted, Cumberlege brought *Dolphin* in at the far end of the mole, and his cousin and Hammond went ashore 'with a Mauser apiece'. And now in the soft May dusk they could see the swastika flying over the power station, they could see the bodies of British dead, they could hear the sound of battle from where Greek soldiers and civilians— the main body of the British and Commonwealth forces were holding Herakleion airfield—were fighting desperately in the streets.

At that last happy party with his friends John had suggested that after the raid Nick Hammond should stay on in Crete and, if it came to fighting, fight in the Resistance with him. Too late. In the gathering darkness *Dolphin* 'put out to sea pursued by angry bullets'.

And now John vanishes—vanishes into history, into legend, into the heroic memories of Crete.

ix

It was early on May 20 that the German attack on Crete began. By the morning of May 21, when had the Cumberlege-Pendlebury raid kept to its original programme *Dolphin* might have been returning across the Kasos channel, thousands of parachutists had been dropped in the area of Canea, Souda and the Maleme airfield; at Herakleion; and at Rethymnon. Everywhere they met a hot reception. At Herakleion not only did the British and the Greeks fight a successful defence (a battalion of the Black Watch gave a particularly good account of themselves) but, as one historian reports, the invaders found themselves quickly disillusioned about the assurances of their Commander, General Student, that 'the Cretans would prove friendly' (*The Struggle for Crete* by I. McD.G. Stewart). Greek villages are rarely short of a fowling piece or two, and the islanders, though hardly equipped for so professional a battle, fought with what weapons they possessed and what they could take. They fought, a Cretan told me, with knives, with sticks if they had nothing better; they snatched arms from the dead and went on fighting.

By the afternoon of the 21st, however, when Nick and Cle Cumberlege had walked along the mole at Herakleion and seen the bodies of the dead, John, who according to one source had been fighting 'rifle in hand', seems to have decided that now was the time for him to join his guerillas in the Ida district. Of the next few hours no British witnesses, so far as is known, survive. Indeed the confusion which surrounded the Battle of Crete was such that for months after the fall of the island, after the struggling, tragic attempts at evacuation, after the individual escapes of British and New Zealand and Australian soldiers, it was impossible to discover what had happened to John Pendlebury. But the faithful Cretans kept the record, and it is from their stories—though these, perhaps, are sometimes coloured by fantasy and the lurid light of war—that the tale can be pieced together.

On the afternoon of May 21, then—Tom Dunbabin, like Nick a contributor to the Pendlebury memoir, would outline the story —John 'left his office, seized a rifle and made for the Canea Gate with a few Cretan followers'. At the Gate, which leads westward out of Herakleion, he parted from Captain Satanas, one of his local leaders, but arranged to rejoin him later at Krousonas, a guerilla centre on the slopes of Mount Ida. Then he went on by car, alone except for his driver. Less than a mile farther out of Herakleion he saw a fresh wave of parachutists dropping. Clearly he had no idea of turning back. He left the car and climbed the hill to the right.

A Greek company had been stationed above the road. That afternoon Stukas had attacked; after them, it was about half-past four, came the parachutists. Since they were outnumbered and ammunition was anyway running out—once again the inadequate equipment of the Cretans must be emphasised—the Greeks were ordered to withdraw to fresh positions. One of them, however— his name was Polybios Markatatos—did not retreat. Presumably he still had ammunition for his machine-gun; anyhow he says he went on fighting. 'Suddenly'—let us hear the statement he made after the war:

Suddenly I saw on the higher ground above me an officer whom I did not know by sight, and for a moment I was alarmed. Seeing that I was afraid he reassured me, telling me to have courage and keep cool; at the same time, standing upright, he fired at the parachutists with his revolver. Presently four parachutists appeared at close quarters and there was a hand-to-hand struggle in which the unknown officer killed three with his revolver and I the fourth. Immediately afterwards he told me to direct covering fire toward the road so that we could advance westward. He went first and kneeling at the corner of a cottage a little ahead he continued to fire at the Germans who appeared. In this position he was wounded in his right breast, and seeing this I ran to help him, but when I asked him what had happened he replied: 'It is nothing, but give me some water.' This I could not do because I myself had no water and it was impossible to find any because of the Germans all around. I asked him again what we should do, and he said: 'Stick to your post, courage, and victory is ours.' It was impossible to move the wounded man and we were in a desperate position, so I went on firing at the Germans until my ammunition was exhausted, when we were both taken prisoner.

'Stick to your post, courage, and victory is ours'—through the stilted official phrases into which the story has been translated the mad brave truth glitters. Polybios Markatatos was taken to a prison camp at Tsalikaki Metochi about three miles farther to the west. In the camp, he says, he was told that the unknown officer was the English captain John Pendlebury.

The English captain was not herded together with the Greek prisoners at Tsalikaki Metochi. The place where he lay wounded— it is called Kaminia—is today a straggle of buildings, a dusty suburb. Even then it was scarcely outside Herakleion; there were houses and farms bordering the road. In one of them the women of a family, living away from the town for, as it was supposed, safety, found themselves in the thick of the Stuka raids and the parachute-drops. The group included a mother and her daughters; two names, Aristea Drosoulakis and Theonymphe Manousakis, have survived from the obscure horrors of that day. They had all been told not to go out of doors; they sat waiting. Suddenly—I have this part of the story from Theonymphe—there was a knock on the door. Outside stood a group of Germans, armed. Somehow they made it clear that they wanted a blanket; then they pointed at her. Terrified, she went out with them. She could not imagine what the blanket was for; she thought she was going to be killed. At last she understood. A wounded man was being brought in; covered with blood he was carried into the house and laid on the bed. Then the Germans went off, leaving him in the care of the frightened women.

Frightened but brave. The account which Theonymphe gave me in an emotional encounter over twenty years after the event is more dramatic than the statement which together with her sister Aristea Drosoulakis she swore in 1947 and which like all sworn statements is drained in translation of its passion. Nevertheless the two stories confirm and complement one another. Theonymphe when I saw her told me that the wounded man repeated his name—'John.

John'—and that at last they recognised his surname, 'Blebbery', the nearest most Cretans can get to Pendlebury. The statement, which adds certain details—that the Germans searched the house before bringing him in and that two Greek villagers who had been taken prisoner helped to carry him—is naturally, since it was made so much nearer the experience, more precise. The women realised that they had an English officer in the house. He had, they saw, been hit in the right breast and the wound pierced through to his left shoulder-blade. When the Germans had gone, Aristea—for though both women signed the statement she is the one who tells the story—went to the bed and asked his name and if he knew Captain Hamson and Captain Mitford, in whose confidential service her husband was employed.

When he heard the names of the two captains he was astonished and asked me who I was. I replied that I was the wife of George Drosoulakis and that I would gladly give him what help I could. He then told me that he was the English Captain John Pendlebury, which frightened me because from earlier conversations with my husband I knew about his activities. I asked him what had happened to my husband and he said that he was well and was taking a message to the village of Krousonas to the English Captain Hamson; then he asked for a doctor and for some water.

It was hardly to be expected that in the circumstances a doctor could be fetched, though Aristea says that she and her sister tried hard to find one. At about eight o'clock that evening, however, three Germans appeared; one of them was a doctor who treated the wounded man kindly and bandaged him. When this second party of Germans had gone Aristea and Theonymphe asked anxiously what had been said. John reassured them. The Germans themselves had brought him into the house; he had made this clear, he had insisted that the women must not be harmed; and now they had better do as the Germans had advised and show lights in the house so that it should not be fired on.

About 10.30 in the evening another German doctor came and gave the wounded man an injection and promised that though the wound did indeed go right through his body it was not very dangerous and that in the morning he would be taken to hospital for better treatment. And the behaviour of this German doctor, like that of the first, was excellent.

All that night Aristea and Theonymphe together with the two

captured Greek villagers, who had now been released, sat up with the Englishman and looked after him as best they could. 'He soothed us,' says Aristea, 'and thanked us again and again for what we were doing for him, and encouraged us, telling us to be calm and victory would be ours.' Next morning he told them to send away the mother and remaining members of their family, and from this moment the other witnesses disappear from the story. Aristea and Theonymphe still stayed on to look after him.

But now there was a new danger. That morning a further wave of parachutists was dropped, and the two women saw a small field-gun being set up outside the house. At this John gathered his strength. He ordered them to leave him. He even wrote a note which they were to hand to the first English car they happened to meet; he guaranteed that they would be looked after. It was now May 22. Maleme airfield was still in Allied hands, the naval harbour of Souda Bay was still holding out, the British and the Greeks, the New Zealanders and the Australians were still fighting confidently, and at Herakleion the invaders were in fact being hard pressed. Nevertheless Crete would be lost. Naturally neither John nor the women trying to save him had any notion of the true state of affairs; but they too were holding out.

And from the tangle of legend which would cling to his name, what I believe to be the final truth emerges.

'We refused,' Aristea's statement goes on, 'to abandon him, and waited for the Germans to take him to hospital.' Meanwhile they tried to find the German doctor who was to take charge. And then the laconic, the resigned cadences of the story of pain remembered. 'But while we were trying we were seized by the Germans, who took us by force to the camp at Tsalikaki.'

The darkness is closing in on John Pendlebury, lying wounded and alone in the empty house at Kaminia. But the tale is not quite ended. At all events there is one more witness. Aristea and Theonymphe were taken to Tsalikaki in company with about ten other women. Among them was one Calliope Karatatsanos; and as they were being marched to the camp she told them what she had seen when near the house that morning. Six years later she too would make a sworn statement before the police, a statement which no official interpreter has re-shaped. It is written in a sprawling and by now faded hand, ungrammatical, unpunctuated, Greek in that it does not translate the English words but writes them as they must have been heard, in Greek letters. I will not blur the naked lines of truth by dressing them. Here, then, is the last eye-witness's story.

I declare that I know about the execution of the officer Pendlebury by the Germans at Kaminia that on Wednesday at eight o'clock in the morning when they put him outside the door of a house when they asked him where are the English forces he answered No No No they gave the order Attention and shot him in the chest and the head and he fell.

The obstinate romantic had won for himself the death he would have wished.

III

i

'Worshipful mistress' the letter to Hilda begins. I have seen it in translation only; the original probably has one of the conventionally respectful forms of address, but perhaps the English phrase sets fairly enough the tone of what follows:

I tell you again that I am your brother because I regard you as a sister for we had sworn with your husband an oath of brotherhood and brothers we were. You should be proud that your husband was killed in Crete. Your husband lives, and will live, and his name will live for ever in the world and history will write much of him. I who know all his great deeds will make it my task to publish them when the time comes . . . I cannot write to you details, because when I remember him and his deeds my brain won't work and I forget everything . . . I have lost my children and I do not know if they are alive or not. I am here alone with my wife. Kiss your children from me . . . Whatever else you seek from me it is yours, and my life too, and all that is left to me is yours.

The writer is one of John's devoted followers. He had fought in the Battle of Crete. According to Mike Cumberlege, he claimed to have killed Hitler's cousin, a Major Hitler; in support of this proud boast he would display a revolver and cap badge. Like many Cretans he had been a hunted man. After the Allied withdrawal there was a price on his head; however, he was brought safely out of the island by Cumberlege, and the letter—flamboyant, self-felicitating, composed perhaps by one of the professional letter-writers sometimes called in by the Cretans—was sent from Cairo. It was dated September 1942. John was killed in May 1941. But though by the autumn Hilda knew he was dead a year went by before his death was officially announced.

The account I have given of his last days was elicited through searching enquiry by the Squire and by Hilda herself when in 1947 they interviewed the witnesses. It is accepted by responsible British officers who were in Crete during and after the war; it has been checked and re-checked. But fact often has gaps in it. Fact may be an outline round which twine details contradictory, extravagant, difficulty to verify—and yet imperious in their demand to be counted. Fact on its own tells only part of the story. It gives you the young archaeologist killed in war, it fails to give you the scholar-traveller driven all his life by some obscure passion to prove himself, to walk farther and drink deeper than the Cretans themselves, to show the world a man. The stories, fanciful or not, which have gathered help to show, reflected in other people's eyes, the image of John Pendlebury.

A fragment of fact to begin with. When the *Dolphin* crew put out to sea under fire from Herakleion harbour they were not at the end of their adventure. Back in Souda Bay, the engine gave out altogether. They transferred to another caïque, and with the evacuation of Crete at an end were on their way to North Africa when they were attacked by a Messerschmitt; Cumberlege was wounded and both his cousin and Saunders were killed. The survivors knew nothing about the fate of Pendlebury; nobody outside Crete could know. They refused to give him up for lost. After all he had from the beginning said that he would stay and fight in the island. Probably he was somewhere in the mountains. There was still a chance of getting help and supplies to him. And they tried. Later on, Cumberlege went back to look for him; others did the same. In vain; but there is something touching about the obstinate faith of John's friends.

There seemed to be reason for hope. An officer who escaped from Crete reported that John had been offered a place in a caïque which was taking a party out, but he had refused, saying that he must stay with his guerillas. There were persistent tales of an Englishman who had been seen at Hagia Galini, a village on the south coast near Tymbaki; what was more it was an officer who had lost an eye.

German propaganda strengthened the belief that John was leading a Resistance group. From Alexandria Cumberlege reported two enemy broadcasts: 'The bandit Pendlebury,' they said, 'will be caught and he can expect short shrift when he is found.' Nearly three weeks after the fall of Crete a newspaper spoke of small forces of British, New Zealand and Australian troops who had evaded capture and were carrying on guerilla warfare under the command of a British officer 'well known to the islanders. He moves freely about organising raids on German posts, depots and aerodromes, and spurring the islanders to continue their resistance.' A friend of Hilda's in the Foreign Office declared that she had every reason for believing the story. 'It will,' she wrote, 'be the greatest saga of the war, when it can be told.' With every Cretan who escaped to join the British in Egypt the rumours, cruelly raising hopes, multiplied and fantasticated.

By the autumn of 1941 the stories were taking another form. There had been a British officer in the mountains, but he had long since been taken prisoner; anyway it was not John. Friends were reluctant to give up hope, and fresh arrivals from Crete were stringently questioned. The shadow of the truth fell gradually. 'Missing, believed killed'—there were those who still refused to believe. But by the time John's death had come to be accepted as fact a new sort of rumour had spread. The mode of death it was which now became a painful uncertainty. Brilliant weavers of myth, the Cretans, not all of them unwilling to claim a share in possible glory, were apt to cloud still further the darkness of the final days.

Again a fragment of fact. The car in which John had driven out of Herakleion was found by Allied officers. It was abandoned and the door had been wrenched off. But there were no signs of a struggle. His cap was on the front seat, but not his tin hat. Again the confused reports. He had stopped at the Canea Gate, one story said, to speak to a group of his guerillas who had come to draw arms; he told them to make for a rendezvous in the hills, then drove on alone—to be intercepted by the next parachute drop. His Cretan followers, said another account, had begged him not to attempt to break through the parachutists who were even then landing in force west of Herakleion, but he insisted and went ahead, accompanied by one Greek machine-gunner and by a Greek civilian whom he had come across on the road. And from what a friend described as 'a hundred conflicting stories' a third version emerges. Realising that the *Dolphin* raid on Kasos was now out of the question, John had collected a group of his followers to fight under the orders of Brigadier Chappel, who for a short time before the evacuation of the mainland had been in control of all Cretan defences but was now in command at Herakleion; he then 'volunteered to clean up a farmhouse where some parachutists were hidden'. And now the weapon which in the enthusiastic days of planning John had thought appropriate reappeared. In this story it is with the famous swordstick in his hand that he leads the attack.

A battle is not to be read as if it were a balance-sheet, and if an extra two or three figures slip into some corner of the fight one need not begin to talk about inaccuracy. The tally of those who were with John or who saw him fall on that May afternoon is obscured by the smoke of war. Polybios Markatatos we know about, and one or two others had their own stories to tell. Some who might have heard the tale first-hand did not survive the war. One of John's agents—it was a man whom Mike Cumberlege, hoping for news, sailed to the south coast to find—was killed in what one must call domestic circumstances. Even during a war the normal exchanges of life continue, and he was murdered 'in a fit of rage' by another Cretan.

Nevertheless stories of John's death began to come out of Crete, and in October 1941 a friend at the War Office wrote to Hilda: 'I am afraid the original report . . . is authentic.' There were still no details. But early in the following year Lieutenant-Commander Pool, who had been in charge of the Imperial Airways yacht at Spinalonga in the 1930s and who had often befriended and entertained the Pendleburys during their expeditions in East Crete, sent Hilda an apparently definite account.

I have made the most searching enquiries about his death, and for a long time I believed that there was still hope. He was wounded outside the Canea Gate at Herakleion, and managed to reach the house of one of his men at Stavromenos [the crossroads on the way to Krousonas] where he was looked after by the man's wife until he died. He is buried in a little vineyard on the left of the road leading into Stavromenos, and his grave was marked by a small cross. This information was given to me by a mutual friend of ours, who saw the grave . . .

It sounded convincing enough. But then every month brought confused reports. Not long after Pool's letter to Hilda, Cumberlege wrote to John's father with a sinister tale. It came from the author of the high-flying phrases quoted at the beginning of this chapter. Messengers, it said, sent to enquire about John had come back with a terrible report. A fresh wave of parachutists had broken into the house where the Englishman was lying unable to move; he was unarmed, he was helpless; they shot him where he lay.

Cautiously Cumberlege hinted at an imaginative quality in local reporting. Some of the Cretans, he wrote, were given to 'highly coloured accounts of their experiences'. Looking back now, one recognises in the story passed on to Mr Pendlebury details which later writers would take as probably accurate: that the newly arrived parachutists searched the house where John lay alone, took his identity disc, perhaps noted his glass eye; that they left him and went away, to return an hour later on a deathly errand. But of the death itself, as Cumberlege emphasised, no eyewitness had yet appeared. He himself, one suspects, was not convinced. Nevertheless for some time this was the generally accepted version; and Hilda had to live with it. Another fragment had been added to the Pendlebury legend; and not until after the war, when Aristea and Theonymphe could repeat their story and Calliope could at last come forward and tell in public what she had seen, was the truth established.

ii

In the disorder of that summer, after all, it was hardly to be expected that there would be any immediate certainty. Crete at the end of May 1941 was the scene of a Dunkirk which, for all its heroism, nobody could interpret as anything but a disaster the more appalling since so many of those involved could not believe in their own defeat.

Italy's attack on Greece in October 1940 had enabled the Greek Government to call for help from the British. Air support at first, later on troops from Britain, New Zealand and Australia—such forces as were available in those stringent times were despatched from Egypt to the Greek mainland. A small contingent arrived in Crete, the defence of which the Greeks, anxious to send Greek reinforcements to Albania, asked the British to take the main responsibility. Defence was difficult enough in all conscience. There was one major road; it ran along the north coast and connected the three ports, Herakleion, Rethymnon and Canea. There was one airfield—at Herakleion. In the months before April 1941, when Germany attacked Greece, airfields at Maleme, west of Canea, and at Rethymnon were being constructed. Whether in Crete there was enough sense of urgency that spring one cannot say. Certainly the proper means were lacking, and one can see why John Pendlebury never got the ten thousand rifles he had asked for. When at the end of April the last of the British and Commonwealth troops evacuated from the Greek mainland reached Crete some pretty strenuous improvisation was called for.

For the British, the Greeks, the New Zealanders and the Australians the tragedy was that improvisation, no matter how rapid and brilliant, and no matter how courageously it was supported, was not enough. Ten days after the beginning of the airborne attack the Allied troops, most of whom had already experienced defeat on the mainland, were once again retreating before the victorious Germans. They had no air cover. At best there had been fewer than forty British planes available; finally only six were left, and since so tiny a force could be of little help these were withdrawn on the day before the airborne assault began. The Navy, though it suffered heavy losses, protected the retreating troops from a seaborne invasion. And the Navy was there to carry them to Egypt, some from Herakleion, most from the little harbour of Sphakia on the south coast. But not all of them. There were the dead and the wounded and those with no choice but to surrender; there were those who, with the enemy closing in, had to be left behind.

Later on military historians would find a major source for the Battle of Crete in the recollections of hundreds of individual soldiers. To the story of the fighting and the aftermath the contribution of single human beings was a record of courage indeed, but also of frustration and hideous confusion—frustration because in spite of failures in preparation and deficiencies in equipment the battle was so close-run; confusion because it left such a trail of mortal havoc.

Here and there in that human detritus one recognises the features of a friend: Joanna Stavridi, for instance, earliest heroine of the disaster. She was the daughter of Sir John Stavridi, a British banker of Greek origin. In 1939 she was a tall, dark, deep-voiced girl in her early thirties who had not yet found her path in life. She lived in London with her parents, hoped to be an artist, studied at an art school. When war broke out she volunteered as a nurse, and two months later she was on her way to Athens, where she trained at the Red Cross Hospital. Suddenly she understood what she had to do; she could not think why she had not been doing it all her life. Throughout the Albanian campaign she nursed in Arta. When the Allies evacuated the mainland she left with Embassy staff and a party of other British civilians in a yacht which was bombed and sunk. The survivors reached a deserted island off Kimolos in the Cyclades, then Kimolos itself, where with cool resource Joanna looked after those of her companions who had been injured. From Kimolos a caïque took the party south-east to the craggy volcanic island of Thera; from there the final crossing was made to Crete.

Boatloads of troops were arriving from the mainland without arms or equipment. Still, there was a breathing-space, almost three weeks before the next assault. The defenders collected themselves. Joanna reported to the British Consul; she was assigned to the Seventh General Hospital between Canea and Maleme. Her Greek brother-in-law was with her at the interview. With horror he learned that there would be no other women nurses, only orderlies; the evidence was clear that desperate perils were ahead. But there was nothing he could do. Joanna went off to her job.

An ironic touch. The orderlies had their own mess, but on arrival she was told that King's Regulations forbade her as a nurse to have meals with the rest of the hospital staff. She could have a drink at the bar with them but she could not eat with them; instead a tray with food was brought to her bedroom. Events, however, soon put an end to such formalities. The hospital, she says, was absurdly placed between the sea and the main Maleme road, precisely in the track of any hostile bombers, and sure enough when the airborne attack came the wounded had to be moved to the caves on the beach, three caves for the patients, one for the doctors and orderlies off duty. Soon there were five hundred stretcher cases, British, New Zealand, Australian, Cypriot—and German; the casualty rate among the parachutists was appalling. And the staff, flattening themselves against the cliff as in their lethal situation they moved from cave to cave, worked twenty-four hours on and twenty-four hours off.

Perhaps a week later—time was hardly calculable, and she can no longer remember the dates—the hospital received orders to move inland with all the walking wounded to a place called Neochorio. In this crisis Joanna was given a special task. She was put in charge of two patients, two doctors who were sick but not stretcher cases. Transport would be provided; she was to take the hospital gear, the instruments, and she was to get her charges and the material and herself to Neochorio. But it was too late. The final retreat of the British and Commonwealth troops had started, and the hospital was never moved to its new quarters. It was expected that Joanna would be taken instead to Sphakia, where the defenders from the Canea and Maleme area were headed.

Years afterwards she met the New Zealand colonel who was to have seen to it that she embarked for Egypt. 'What happened to you? We waited,' he said, 'as long as we could.'

But she was out of luck. In the frantic mêlée the promised transport failed. The little group were left behind, and Joanna, taking her two patients and the hospital gear, with fantastic courage went back to her post in the caves. The only wounded left were stretcher cases; she went on nursing. Two days later she had her first close view of the Germans in action as they came, fighting, through the caves. Fighting whom? I asked her once. She did not know. Lying face down on a stretcher and waiting, as the wounded and the hospital staff lay and waited, she could see nothing but German boots.

When the battle was over the invaders found five doctors who had volunteered to stay. They found a dozen or so orderlies. And they found Joanna. She was not merely the only nurse. She was the only woman left in the whole area. Presently news began to seep out of Crete. Every English paper carried the story of the dedicated young nurse in the Cretan caves. But when they found her the Germans could not make out who she was or what she was doing in the middle of a battle. During the worst of the action she had been wearing battledress, but on the approach of the enemy she had hastily changed into her Greek nurse's uniform. Do you belong, they asked, to a religious order? When they learned the facts they behaved correctly. Where, they enquired, do you want to go? To Athens, she said. When do you want to go? And her answer, too, is heroic. 'I will go,' she said, 'on the last plane with the doctors when my men have been taken off.'

At last she was flown to Athens, and there she was deposited in the heart of the German-occupied city, in Constitution Square. She was carrying a suitcase and a British warm. She had no money and nowhere to go.

The rest—the kindness of the American Embassy; nursing for two more years; then, when nursing came to an end, keeping alive under the Occupation by teaching English (and risking death by helping to hide two British officers who had escaped) is another story. The fate which left her behind in the evacuation of Crete was a fate she shared, though only temporarily, with thousands of the troops who in that minor Dunkirk crossed mountains to embark for Egypt—and failed to be taken on board. History, drawing on their memories, has recorded many of their names. But again it is from a name one knows, from the voice of a friend, that one receives the sharpest impression.

Myles Hildyard went to Crete from Palestine in February 1941; he was an officer in the Sherwood Rangers. He was stationed at Kheleris in an old prison overlooking Souda Bay. With a friend, Michael Parish, he shared a motor-bike, and on a trip to Herakleion they met John Pendlebury. A man of aesthetic interests both refined and far-reaching, 'I have always,' Myles says, 'been curious about archaeology.' Indeed at Eton, where the boys were allowed to choose an 'extra study' for one hour a week, he chose Minoan civilisation— never thinking that he would one day go to Crete. Now John Pendlebury showed him round Knossos. The acquaintance stopped there, and of the encounter he remembers nothing much more than a cheerful confident figure, John in the mood which characterised his last days. Presently Knossos would see fighting. But by then John, most likely, was dead; and Myles was at Souda with guns which, he says, were never used; like some of the fortress guns at Singapore, they would fire only seawards.

When the order for evacuation came Myles and his group were in the long line which struggled painfully, only rarely getting a lift, over the pass through the White Mountains to Sphakia. It was a forty-mile march in the almost waterless heat of a Cretan May. With bombing and machine-gunning all day, movement was possible only under cover of darkness. After three nights and four days the exhausted company came stumbling down the last stony track towards the sea. 'We formed up,' Myles wrote in his diary—he was to have plenty of time to keep a diary—

about 11 p.m. and with some difficulty and jostling got into our position. But unfortunately about then the rearguard began to arrive and pass through us. We moved slowly down towards the beach, down a steep and stony path, in bursts as a load was taken on board in front, and long halts. It was very slow and the fatal hour when all ships left for the night came closer and closer. We were getting quite near the water when there was a complete stoppage. At last officers were summoned to the front; we were told that the boats had gone and would not return, and that we would be surrendered in the morning.

His account goes on to describe something else which historians would record. By the morning the defenders had surrendered; nevertheless German planes bombed and machine-gunned the beach and the village. Myles went to look for his men. He found that they had climbed back to a valley above Sphakia.

There when it got light they proceeded to cook the little food they had, and they were sitting around doing this, thinking themselves prisoners and perfectly safe, when the German planes came over and machine-gunned them. One of our men was killed outright. The wounded were in a little church, and among them was our sergeant-major Fountain with twelve bullets in him. We heard later that he died. Three Germans who ran out shouting and waving to the planes to clear off were also killed.

That afternoon the surrendered troops began the march under guard, 'a mile-long column of men, and planes overhead photographing us'; shoes in tatters, feet raw, they trudged back up the ravine, back up the pitiless road over the White Mountains. On the third night—Myles with a cut wrist and a bullet-hole in his leg—they were back at Galatas in a prison camp.

Four days later he and Michael Parish escaped.

As a form of disguise they were carrying buckets and spades. Both were wearing their hospital coats. Myles had blue pyjama trousers, Michael Parish wore a blue pyjama-leg on his head. They had no plan except to profit by the disorder in which victory had left the invaders; they simply climbed through the camp wire and, all innocence, wandered past the guards. In the first village, Myles nonchalantly records, they met two German soldiers.

'What are you doing here?' they said in German. 'Do have a grape,' we said in English, handing each a bunch of unripe grapes about the size of green peas and devouring them ourselves. 'How hungry we are. Notice our spades, we are a work party; our clothes too, so striking. And we are so pleased to see you, anyone can see that.' 'Where do you come from?' they said. 'Where are you going?' They point, we point, all in the same direction, back to the camp, of course, where else? They walk on up the village, stop, look back at us. We sit, eating the uneatable grapes. They walk on and we leg it.

It was June 7. For two months the fugitives were fed and clothed and sheltered by Cretans who risked their own lives to save them, two months of hiding and waiting, of savage marches and cold nights sleeping in the hills, now and then punctuated by days of resting in the high villages or on the Omalos plain in the White Mountains where life assumed a kind of pastoral peace. Later during the Occupation an escape route was organised, and years afterwards in a village on the slopes of Mount Ida I talked with a schoolmaster who, he said, had helped in smuggling 1,800 soldiers out of Crete. In the June and July of 1941 nothing was organised, everything was improvised, haphazard. Nevertheless in the middle of August Myles Hildyard and Michael Parish with a party of about forty escapers, British, New Zealanders and Greeks, set off in a twenty-foot caïque from the Cape Spatha peninsula west of the bay of Canea. Rowing and sailing, they reached Cythera and Cape Malea, where the majority of the Greeks landed, leaving the rest of the party to a fortnight's risky voyage via Monemvasia, Milos, Kimolos and Paros to the Turkish coast and Ephesus. And in Turkey Miles's adventure dovetailed with the adventure of Joanna Stavridi.

When the yacht in which she sailed from Greece was sunk off Kimolos a steel box of papers went down with it. The survivors told a friendly fisherman that if the papers were found they should be somehow conveyed to the British military authorities. The fisherman recovered the box; resisted a Greek policeman who advised him to destroy it; told German interrogators that he had in fact thrown it into the sea; and on the arrival of Myles's party entrusted them with his find. Since the papers turned out to be secret communications between the British command and the Greek King concerning the evacuation of Greece their discovery in the caïque when it reached Turkey understandably caused local officials some excitement. Myles Hildyard and Michael Parish refused to yield up their steel box. Accompanied everywhere by a Turkish policeman, they made a special journey to Ankara, where they handed it over to the British Military Attaché. They were not prevented from travelling on to Egypt; pleasant to think that both came out of the long adventure with the Military Cross.

iii

From chaos, then, single figures emerge. There are those who survive, and there are those who mourn, among them the two sisters who spent with John Pendlebury the last night of his life.

Aristea Drosoulakis and Theonymphe Manousakis, together with the other women who had been rounded up, were held in what they described as a 'fortress' for a week or more. Aristea says eight days, Theonymphe says twelve; tragedy in a peasant country is extensible. When Herakleion was safely under German control they were set free.

The tale of their return is there in the statement about the wounded Pendlebury which the two women swore in 1947. Even about that formal account, typed and witnessed and stamped, there hangs the smell of death. But the typewritten story is without colour, without feeling. 'You can't,' Theonymphe said to me, 'imagine what it was like if you weren't there.' When I saw her two decades had gone by since the battle and its aftermath, and it was with difficulty that I had tracked her down in a dusty suburb of Athens. Aristea's daughter, then living in Athens, gave me her address. A policeman, when I asked for help, stopped a bus for me at green lights. A passenger—I remember he was carrying a huge water-melon—walked with me from the terminus to the road. A woman in the street led me to the house. I say the street, but it was unmade and unnamed; shanty would be a word more precise than house; and there, sharing with neighbours a minuscule yard, living with her son in a room clean, swept and furnished with truckle beds and a single chair, was Theonymphe.

After twenty years the horror was still alive for her. In their prison camp, she said, the women wept despairingly. 'Where is my husband?' they cried; some of them scratched their names on the wall. At last the 'fortress' was opened and they straggled back to their homes. 'There was no light,' said Theonymphe. 'There was no water. There was no food. Nobody had any money. Everybody was in rags. You could hear nothing but women crying. Human corpses lay on the ground among the bodies of dead mules.' Perhaps she was luckier than some. Her husband survived, at any rate for a time. After the battle he was in a concentration camp in Crete; he was released. It was later, and of a heart attack, that he died.

The story Aristea had to tell was darker.

Unlike her sister she had not left the neighbourhood of Herakleion. She lived, I was told, near the Canea Gate—that Gate linked by so many stories with the last days of John Pendlebury. I had gone a little way westward down the road out of the town. 'You can see the house where he was taken,' Hilda had said, 'you will know it by the pine-trees.' And there indeed were the pines, there on the left of the road was the cottage, empty now, forlorn. On the right, another cottage: broken roof, dusty walls; here, I thought, John may have taken cover before he was wounded. Corn was growing on the hillside behind. It was a day of sun with a little cloud, hot; he might have seen the parachutists dropping from just such a sky. Children sitting on a doorstep cried 'Goodbye!' as I passed (it was their only English word). But when I spoke to them they fell silent; and when I went back through the Gate nobody recognised the address I asked for. The name, though, that was familiar. 'Ah, Aristea! Of course— she has gone out, she will be back. That's where she lives, in that house over there.'

A quiet woman with greying hair, resigned in black, cherishing in her tiny house her extraordinary memories, she took me at first for

Hilda, whom she had seen perhaps only once; an Englishwoman enquiring after Pendlebury must surely be his widow. Simply a friend, I said; 'Mrs Pendlebury told me about you.' It was enough. There was no need to question her; unasked she told me the appalling tale.

When she and the other women were released she had learned from Calliope of the death of John Pendlebury; she still had no news of her own husband. With her sister she hurried homewards, searching. When they came to the house they found John's body outside; it was lying in a ditch. Thirty paces away Aristea saw another body. It was her husband. Between the official and the spoken story the distances vary; they shrink, they swell. But I can still see Aristea's heartbroken gestures: 'My husband's body here ... the body of Blebbery there.'

George Drosoulakis had indeed been in the service of the British. 'He was,' Professor Hamson says, 'Pendlebury's man—indeed they all were.' It seems that he had not managed to get through to Krousonas to deliver the message of which John had spoken. Professor Hamson says he is 'morally sure' that he did not receive a message in writing from Pendlebury: 'It would have been invaluable.' The documents poor Drosoulakis was carrying when he was intercepted by German troops betrayed him. Some time earlier he had been suspicious about the movements of a submarine; John had written to him about the affair (a fiasco, apparently) and he had the letter on him. When the two sisters found his body this and another letter were tucked just inside his jacket. Aristea with the terrible eloquence of Greek hands showed me how the papers peeped out.

'They lay,' she said, 'over his heart.'

The letters, when I saw her, were still extant. 'They are all I have,' she said. 'Would you like to see them?' She unlocked a cupboard and brought out a packet wrapped in paper—John's letter about the submarine; fragments of an identity card with her husband's photograph and her own; a torn-up letter promising the dead man 'a better job'—all stained with blood from the heart over which they had been lying, the brown stains of blood twenty-one years old. 'I watered them' she said—yes, she really used the sad formal phrase—'I watered them with my tears.' And once again in tears, 'A better job!' she cried. 'All he got was death.'

There were other relics. The official testimonials which after the war were given 'in the name of the Governments of the peoples of the United Nations' in recognition of 'services to the struggle for freedom'—she had two, one for her dead husband, one for herself; the name stamped at the end was Alexander. 'You must be proud,' I said. But now the story took on the sombre shape of Greek tragedy. The Cretans were not allowed to move their dead. Aristea and Theonymphe, then, covered the bodies of Pendlebury and George Drosoulakis as best they could; later, one gathers, the two women buried them where they lay or near by. History, however, had not yet done with John Pendlebury. German Intelligence had for months known about his work with the guerillas. But the invaders needed to be sure that he had not escaped; the broadcasts reported by Cumberlege suggest that nobody was sure. Presently the web of myth and fact, hearsay and official testimony was still further complicated by the later accumulation of witnesses and by the element of personal drama with which those inheritors of saga the Cretans would decorate the tale.

Aristea in the statement made jointly with Theonymphe introduces two new characters, her husband's brother and sister who, she says, under threat were forced to tell the Germans where Pendlebury was buried. Reluctantly they led a party accompanied by Dr Kassapis, a Greek doctor who was in charge of a Herakleion hospital. Some Cretans were inclined at the time to censure Dr Kassapis for collaboration, but later they changed their minds; they say he was an honourable man, and certainly it is difficult to see what would have been achieved if he had refused. The body was exhumed, it was identified by its glass eye and buried again at the same spot. Even in this unadorned form the episode—the invaders' need to be assured that a dangerous opponent had been scotched, the identification by that famous glass eye—has the ring of some dreadful legend. Telling the story herself, Aristea gave it a savage excitement. The force of the sacred number three must not be overlooked.

'Three times they dug up the body to make sure. "Yes," I said, "it is the English captain, it is Blebbery." "Are you sure?" they said.

"If you are not speaking the truth you will be shot." Three times I was put in the line to be shot . . . It was lucky for me that the glass eye was there as proof.'

But there is another witness, this time a man not mentioned in the official reports. 'Michael Vlakhakis,' somebody said, 'Michael fought with Blebbery. You'll find him at Knossos, he may be able to tell you something.'

Long absence from Greece, from Crete, perhaps from a well-remembered village wipes names from one's memory. But there were still Cretans who had not forgotten the days when Humfry and Alan Blakeway and James Brock dug at Knossos, and Michael was among the first to recognise me when I went back. Thin as a ploughshare, the body twisted by wounds and illness, the skull like a bent axe-head, he had limped to greet me out of the kiosk where by the bus-stop and the café he sold cigarettes. Now we sat over a drink in the shade. Yes, he had been fighting in a field outside Herakleion, he had been near John. He heard the Englishman call 'I am wounded, can you help me?' But he could do nothing. The firing was intense, almost immediately he himself was wounded; later he was taken to hospital.

Some days afterwards the Germans came to question him. Was it, they wanted to know, really Pendlebury who had been killed?

'Then they took me from hospital in a car to the place where Blebbery was buried—he was buried, you know, on the spot— and dug up the body. It was wearing, if you will excuse me, only a shirt. "Yes," I said, "that is Blebbery." He had been buried for some time, and you will understand . . . but I knew; "Yes," I said, "I am sure." Then they took the glass eye and they cut a piece from the shirt, from the collar, and they buried him again.'

To all the contradictions and obscurities another obscurity is added. Why the piece from the shirt? Michael could not explain. Perhaps, he said, the Germans wanted to know what kind of shirt the Englishman was wearing. Perhaps the women who nursed him had changed his blood-stained military shirt for a Greek civilian shirt, and the exhumation party were looking not only for identification but for an excuse for his murder. A German doctor who saw Michael Vlakhakis in hospital later on was disturbed. 'If

Pendlebury was shot like that,' he said, 'it was a crime.' Not only a doctor; a parachutist too 'often said that if Pendlebury was killed in cold blood and not in the fighting it was a great mistake'. But the story of the shirt remains enigmatic. When after the war Hilda went out to Crete to learn for herself the truth about her husband's death she saw Polybios Markatatos who had fought with John, she saw Aristea and Theonymphe who had nursed him, she saw Calliope who had witnessed his execution; no doubt in her search she saw many others. Michael Vlakhakis says he told her about the piece of the shirt. But he did not tell her about the decomposing body and the removal of the glass eye. 'It would have been,' he said to me, and not for the first time I recognised in him an inherent delicacy of feeling, 'it would have been painful for her.'

The body of George Drosoulakis was presently removed from the place where his widow and her sister had buried it and reinterred in a Greek cemetery. 'At the same time,' Aristea says in her formal statement, 'I sought a permit to remove the unforgettable Captain but it was not granted.' Exactly where after the exhumation Pendlebury was first buried it is difficult to discover. A letter from Mike Cumberlege, who speaks of 'a small vineyard', at any rate corroborates the report from Pool, who added: '. . . It will comfort and please you to know that the Cretans place fresh flowers on his grave every day.'

But there was still no permanence. According to Tom Dunbabin's contribution to the Memoir the site 'became too well known and was a source of inspiration to the men of the hill-villages who came in and out of the Canea Gate'; the body was accordingly moved again. Possibly it was at this time that John was, as Dunbabin records, buried in the British part of the Herakleion cemetery; for Aristea says that when after living for two years in a village she returned to the town she found the grave she had dug empty. In May 1945 a visitor to Crete who went in search was immediately led by attendants to a grave 'side by side with five others whose names are not known. They described the grave as that of the man with the glass eye, gave his name in a corrupt Cretan form as Pendlebury and quite obviously knew all about him from his past fame amongst them.'

The visitor then had a cross with name and details set up in the cemetery. Not until after the war, however, did the body of John Pendlebury come to a final resting-place in the British military cemetery at Canea.

At the time of Hilda's visit to Crete in 1947 there had been much talk of commissioning a bust of Pendlebury. An executive committee had been appointed with the Metropolitan of Crete as observer; information was to be collected and an estimate drawn up; and the bust when finished would stand in the gardens of the Herakleion Museum. Meanwhile an imposing wooden cross marked the hillside at Kaminia where the Englishman's sudden appearance in battle had so much startled Polybios Markatatos. Captain John Pendlebury, said the inscription: 'He fell fighting the 21/5/41.' To squeeze 'fighting' into the upright bar of the cross the Greek word had with touching casualness been split and hyphenated. A memorial service was held there early that March. Prayers for the repose of the soul of John Pendlebury were chanted by the Metropolitan and his assistant; the Mayor of Herakleion placed a wreath; and the company included the Prefect, the Chief of Herakleion Police, several generals, an assortment of archaeological representatives, members of the Resistance movement and a party of John's Cretan brothers-in-arms. Aristea and Theonymphe were there too, and behind Hilda in the photograph one can see among the eminent and the learned the figure of Kronis Vardakis, 'the faithful muleteer', as she wrote on the back, 'of so many journeys'. Still more people, the Squire said drily, would have turned up if it had not been announced that the service would be in church; only at the last minute was it transferred to Kaminia.

When long afterwards I went to look the cross had gone. The outskirts of Herakleion were changing: houses being built, factories beginning to sprawl over the slopes. On a later visit the deserted cottage, the crumbling walls once stained by battle, they too had vanished. Forgetfulness was washing over the landscape; no bust of John was to be seen in the Museum gardens or anywhere else. But his name was remembered.

The year was 1959. In Rethymnon I had called on a former member of the Resistance, Theocharis Saridhakis. Two days later—

two days of travelling by purgatorial bus and by donkey—I reached a remote village; I had letters to a Cretan who was to give me lodgings and act as guide next morning. He was away; he had gone, though in the opposite direction, to Rethymnon; but he would be back. At last he arrived and I gave him my letters. To my alarm he had a letter for me. I tore it open. It was from Saridhakis. 'The day you left,' it said, 'I wrote this song for the hero John Pendlebury; perhaps I will publish it on the anniversary of the Battle of Crete as a memorial to him.'

The poem, in rhyming four-line stanzas, celebrated John's work for Cretan archaeology and his fight for Cretan liberty. You earned, it said, the laurel wreath, your friends are happy in the belief that you sleep with the smile of triumph on your lips. But those wolves, it went on, grunting sought you out even in the tomb. 'They plunder your sacred corpse and though you are dead THEY SHOOT YOU AGAIN.'

The Pendlebury legend was still alive.

IV

i

'Here am i, still alive,' Evans is reported to have said, 'and that young man with all his promise is gone.' It was the summer of 1941, and the tales of John Pendlebury's death already seemed only too well founded.

For the second time Evans had been cut off by war from Crete, from Knossos and the Villa which many of us still could not help thinking of as his personal estate. Now the break was final, He had just undergone an operation, the second in three years. Not that he had stopped working. A Roman road crossing his property had been discovered, and when friends called they found him sitting—Myres describes the occasion—in his library at Youlbury.

On his knees was a well-used Ordnance map, showing his Roman road, and in reply to a question he showed the fair-copy of his account of it, and said brightly, 'It is finished, it will go to *Oxoniensia*.' It was his last contribution to learning.

The visitors had come to congratulate him on his birthday; he was ninety years old. Three days later he was dead. Joan Evans has recorded that once when he was asked about his beliefs he answered, 'I believe in human happiness.' It was as good an epitaph as any for his life of confident endeavour.

But human happiness, particularly at Knossos, found the going hard during the next few years.

Under the Hutchinson régime the Villa Ariadne had preserved during the first eighteen months of the war a vague scholarly calm. Neither the tasks of counter-espionage hinted at in the Squire's reminiscences nor the occasion of an expedition to deliver arms to some loyal village or other ever quite broke that quiet surface. Even the visit of the Royal fugitives from Athens, dachshund and all, was accepted, at any rate by the Hutchinsons, with composure; and according to the Report of the British School the King and the Princess 'expressed their appreciation of the beauty and comfort' of the house. How did Kosti and the rest of the Villa staff take it all? I asked the Squire once. Oh, he said in his usual equable tones, they seemed to manage all right.

After the night of April 30 and the reluctant departure by destroyer of the two Hutchinsons the place was left without a Curator. But Manolaki as overseer and Kosti as house manager 'gallantly' says the Report 'remained at their posts, and undertook to hand over the keys to HBM Consul, M. Elliadhi, when the Villa ceased to be occupied by the British or Greek authorities'. It was occupied all right. When the airborne invasion began the house was used as a British military hospital; soon it was taking in German wounded also. Once it was shelled by a German mortar, but the damage was not grave. Presently, when Crete was wholly German-controlled and it became clear that there was to be no handing the keys over to the British Consul just yet, Kosti went back to his village in the hills; that at any rate is where he spent most of the Occupation and where I found him long afterwards.

Manolaki's story takes a different course.

A little before the turn of the century Manolis Akoumianakis had come from Yerakari in the Amari district among the western foothills of Mount Ida. He was a boy when he left his village; according to one of his sisters he was no more than fifteen. Yerakari is known for its cherry-crop—in particular morello cherries, which Greeks preserve and use to make a cool summer drink called *visinádha*; Manolàki, as he was called, came to Herakleion with cherries to sell. He did not go back to Yerakari. As Pendlebury found on taking him on an expedition to Amari, he rarely went back.

It was about the time when Arthur Evans had at last succeeded in buying land at Knossos for excavation. Presently the boy went to have a look at the dig. He was interested, he asked for a job, and together with the Maria who later became one of Evans's servants at the Villa he was set to washing and cleaning the sherds which the excavation was producing. He soon showed that he was quick at distinguishing the different shapes and types of the fragmentary vases in his hands; and Evans, recognising the gifts of the young workman, put him in charge of the group of sherd-cleaners.

Clearly Knossos was the place for Manolaki; there he would settle, marry and bring up a family of seven children, sons and daughters. He had the instinct for archaeology sometimes found among shrewd and perceptive Greek country people. As one might expect the record is threaded with myth. One night, the story goes, he woke, got out of bed and went to look for a spade. Startled, his wife asked what he was doing. 'I have had a dream,' he said. 'I must go up the hill and dig.' Dreams of buried treasure are part of Greek folk-lore (and not only Greek). I cannot even say how much was previously known about the tiny Byzantine sanctuary called Hagia Paraskevi. But he did in fact carry out an excavation there. He was, you might say, an archaeologist in his own right.

Working for Evans, he was in time promoted to foreman. I have been told that when the moment came to build the Villa Ariadne he was sent to Athens to buy palms and shrubs for the garden. As the years went by his employer came to rely on him (in an exasperated mood a Cretan, remembering perhaps some high-handed British action, once said to me: 'I think he was Evans's only friend in Crete'). When the excavation of Knossos was halted by the First War—I have the information from Micky, his eldest son, whom I had seen as a child carrying messages on the Fortetsa dig—it was Manolaki who diligently cared for the Palace and the Villa. And Micky says that as a boy he read letters to his father in which Evans gave instructions for the maintenance of the property. But war, which destroys so much, did not spare these small records, and they were lost when in the 1940s Knossos and the Villa were German-occupied.

By the time I first visited Crete Manolaki was a respected and well-known local figure. Indeed long before I ever went there I had heard praise of him from Humfry, who had not forgotten that in 1927 as a novice in excavation he had owed much to his foreman. Manolaki possessed the experience in field archaeology which Humfry lacked. He gave the newcomer some tips which, though science may by now have outdistanced them, were certainly useful then: how to judge from the soil and the vegetation the possibilities of an unexplored site. And Humfry drew for me a portrait which I fondly set against the background of my golden Knossos and the legendary Villa which I had imagined. I saw a tutelary figure climbing hillsides white and powdering in the sun. He was always a little ahead; now and then he stopped to prod a dry patch of earth or tug at some obstinately rooted plant. I had never seen a man's Cretan costume, but I had been told about the cut of the breeches, and in my picture the voluminous pleats over the buttocks wagged steadily as the figure climbed. When he turned to his companion his face, bearded like the face of some bronze Zeus, was immensely benevolent.

When I met him in life I thought I had not been so far out. We exchanged greetings on that short first visit to Crete; of the occasion I recall a shrewd smiling face, a slightly grizzled moustache and an attitude of tolerant respect. Later, in the summers when Humfry and Alan and, in the second season, James Brock were digging I could watch him more closely.

He was in his fifties; to me he looked ageless. The face, wrinkled and walnut-coloured from sun and wind, with its vertically-lined cheeks and the deep furrows of the forehead, was set in a mould of ironic amusement; he was, I felt, an observer. And at a time when regional Greek costume, especially in the more sophisticated villages, was beginning to lose ground to the drab suits of Western Europe, he stuck to Cretan dress—the huge bunchy breeches, the waistcoat with the decorative fringe of bobbles, the cummerbund and the high boots; in summer when I knew him best he always wore a wide-brimmed straw hat. Whether he ever thought of putting on conventional urban clothes I cannot say. Evans, I have been told, liked him to wear Cretan costume; it suited, I dare say, the feudal picture which the discoverer had of his domain. Anyhow Manolaki never changed his style. For formal occasions he would simply appear in the splendid braided, red-lined cloak which is Cretan festive dress. His children would adopt the ways of Western Europe; but not he.

Evans used to call him the Cretan wolf. Listening to the distant voice, 'The wolf is howling,' he would say. I never heard the voice raised. I was conscious, though, of an absolute self-confidence in Manolaki. He was reputed to have saved a tidy sum of money in his years as foreman. Certainly he was ambitious for his children. In Greece the professional classes are no more than one step away from the villages; Micky was educated as a lawyer. But at the dig Manolaki kept the look and the manner of a Cretan countryman.

On those July afternoons when I left the cool of the Villa and walked to the excavation I used to find him in cheerful charge of the workmen. Humfry and Alan and James stood by the tomb-chamber where the painted vases with the ashes of the dead had been stacked; sometimes among the objects deposited in the cinerary pithoi small decorative vases would be found, or scarabs, or daggers, or pins of silver or bronze or iron. Since Alan was lame a mule waited to carry him back to the Villa; its long ears added their shadow to the patterns of leaves and branches. Manolaki, smiling under his straw hat, saluted me amiably, then turned back to the job in hand. The afternoons were pale with sun; yet, moving without haste in his heavy clothes, he never looked hot. The scene with the waiting mule and the men shovelling the earth in the shade of the olives had an air of endless peace.

In 1935 we all left for England at the end of July. I had no special ties with Knossos, and though after Humfry's death in the following year I went back to Greece several times before the outbreak of war I did not visit Crete. It was not until 1941 and the airborne invasion that I began thinking again about the people at the Villa.

ii

The Akoumianakis family were deeply involved in the war. Two of the sons were in the armed forces. Micky was serving on the Albanian front. His brother Minos was in the Navy; a prisoner of war for a year, he later escaped from Crete and trained in Southern Rhodesia for the Greek Air Force. Manolaki himself was among the Cretans with whom John Pendlebury was planning the organisation of a guerilla force; so much one knows. But the need for secrecy under which John was working meant that much of the plan and many of the names are not recorded. Manolaki's story I have pieced together as best I could from the memories of his children.

On the day of the invasion the Akoumianakis family saw parachutists dropping in the direction of the Herakleion airfield. It was afternoon. The first attack was concentrated on the Canea district, and through a mysterious failure in communications the defenders of Herakleion had until 3 p.m. no idea that the battle was on and had been on since early morning. No doubt even the ancient masonry, even the restorations of the Palace of Minos looked safer than a house in the village of Knossos. At any rate it was among the pillars and walls of the site that Mrs Akoumianakis and her children spent the first night.

Less than a month went by between the surrender of the Greek armies on the mainland and the airborne attack on Crete, and amidst the confusion of the German advance and the British evacuation there can have been small chance of accurate news about individual soldiers. But somehow the story had seeped back to Knossos: Micky had been killed. It was, then, believing that his cherished, his first-born son was dead that Manolaki prepared to fight. I fancy that like John Pendlebury he did not think of a future; he had committed himself to death. But first he had to see to the safety of his family. In the hills seven or eight miles to the south there was a village called Katalagari where Mrs Akoumianakis had relations; he would send them there. And his daughter Phyllia—she was presently to give proof enough of cool courage—refused to go.

Thirty years later her sister Evangelia described the scene to me. 'My father implored her. "I beg you," he said—he had tears in his eyes—"I beg you, do me this last favour." ' At last she was persuaded. Manolaki despatched his wife and children to Katalagari. Now he could make ready for action.

iii

When the assault on Crete began Greeks who, survivors of the surrendered armies in Epirus and Macedonia, had evaded capture were already straggling homewards. Among them was Micky Akoumianakis.

It was not an easy journey for any of the islanders; especially not for the Cretans. The sea crossing was long. There could be no open transport. Everything had to be done in secret. Nevertheless, when the Battle of Crete was over, singly or in little groups, dangerously, by caïque, some of them were trickling back. Micky reached Knossos in July. He had landed somewhere east of Rethymnon; it was the middle of the night. He had had no news of his parents; in his anxiety he began almost to run towards Knossos. About four hours later he was nearly there. Ahead of him on the path he could see a boy; it was his youngest brother Alex. When the boy saw Micky he burst into tears.

'They have killed father,' he said.

iv

From the Palace of Minos you look east across the valley of the Kairatos to pale chalky heights; climbing, you reach a plateau, dry, featureless, here and there softened by patches of cultivated land. It commands the road from Herakleion southwards; important to the defence of the island, it was the scene of a forlorn skirmish in the Battle of Crete.

It was Phyllia—she was a girl still in her teens—who when the fighting had died down and families were returning to their homes went up the hill to look for her father. She found him lying on his face; he was dead. A little earth from the explosions of battle was scattered over his body and its Cretan clothes. His hands were at his sides, slightly curled, palms upward. One hand still held his summer straw hat.

For some time the Cretans were forbidden by the Germans to bury those civilians who had taken up arms against the invader. Phyllia tried to cover her father's body with earth. Later, a party of Greeks under the direction of Germans from the hospital which had been established in the Villa Ariadne came up the hill, perhaps to search for wounded, perhaps to bury German dead; and they finished what Phyllia had begun. But there was still no question of a proper burial. The days, the weeks went by.

'You know,' Micky, telling the story, said to me, 'that in our church we have a service forty days after the death.' When he came home it was not forty, it was forty-four days after; and as eldest son he felt called on to perform an act of piety. He must attend to the burial.

There had been no rain in the weeks since Manolaki had been killed; so nothing he had carried with him was damaged. His watch and his money were untouched; even the keys of the Villa and its storehouses were there. In the pocket Micky found a letter. It was from John Pendlebury; it was dated May 21, the second day of the airborne assault; John was wounded later that day. The Englishman had recognised the military value of the ridge above the valley, and he asked Manolaki to go to Skalani, a village a mile or two south-east of Knossos; to collect armed supporters; and to hold the plateau against the enemy. But the letter, it seems, came too late. The Germans had already occupied the heights.

The defenders had made one last effort. On the afternoon of May 28 a party of Greeks, led by Manolaki as guide, attempted to storm the enemy position; simultaneously a British group attacked from another direction. Both attempts failed, and disastrously. In any case by May 28 the Battle of Crete was nearly over, and the evacuation of British and Commonwealth troops was already under way. Perhaps Micky was hardened in his resolve to fight on by the point-less sacrifice of his father's life. But first the funeral rites must be observed. Secretly, then, the body was moved; only the family and the priest of Knossos were a party to the exhumation. Half-way down the slope from the plateau there were the ruins of the little Byzantine chapel where Manolaki had dug. The tiny cortege took the body from its shallow grave; carried it down to the chapel; and there reburied it.

Once or twice in Crete I have passed a solitary tomb, the lonely memorial of a fighter, a guerilla. Nearly two decades after the death of Manolaki I was taken to visit his grave by Micky and Spiro Vasilakis. I asked if I might see also the place where he had been killed. We crossed the valley below the Palace, climbed a path through olive trees, and at the top of the ridge turned left along the edge of the plateau. The morning—it was May, but cooler by all accounts than the May of 1941—had been showery, but now the sun shone on the grass of early summer; a field of oats through which to my dismay we boldly marched stood tall, up to my thighs. We passed an S-shaped hollow where German parachutists had posted themselves. If you searched, Micky said, you might find spent bullets and rusty arms. But now flowering shrubs sprawled on the lip of the hollow and on the hillside below.

A little farther on Micky paused. 'It must have been here,' he said to Spiro.

The two men looked around them. At the extreme verge of the ridge on which we stood a tiny slope interrupted the level ground.

'Here it was,' they agreed, 'exactly here.'

Beyond the valley the complex of the Palace of Minos, courtyards and stairways and walls, stood out nobly in the relief of sun and shadow. Manolaki had fallen where he could have looked across to the monument he had helped to recover. And his body, that lay at Hagia Paraskevi, amidst the foundations he had himself excavated. We went down the hillside to the ruins of the little church. At our feet a ravine plunged to the valley; searching for snails after the rain, a child crawled insect-like on the precipitous slopes. There were Byzantine arches of brick in the cliff-face behind us; a slab of stone and a wooden cross marked the grave. The place was enclosed, a temenos with a low wall; and as is proper to a sanctuary it had a spring.

While we stood there in silence Micky offered me some water to drink. Before I handed back the cup I scattered the last drops on the earth. I had the sense of pouring a libation.

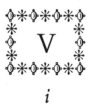

V

i

Folded in its trees, the Villa Ariadne has from the beginning been a haven. Cross the road which skirts the garden wall beyond the Taverna, walk a hundred yards down the hill to where the Palace of Minos offers its subterranean halls and walled pits; there, even on the sunniest day, even amidst the cheerful uncomprehending crowds from the cruise ships berthed at Herakleion, you are aware of violent death. Scores of ancient shrines in Greece are more ferociously situated—clamped to cliffs, shadowed by mountains. Knossos, disposed on its modest shelf of hill, seems pacifically set in a valley beneath bare mild slopes; but you can still smell the blood of the past. Scarcely more than a stone's throw away, the Villa Adriadne has translated the refined savagery of Minos into the stuff of scholarly domestic repose. The Villa means quiet, the Villa means a retreat.

A few miles to the south in a district famed for its dessert grapes there is the big village called Arkhanes; and here in 1941 the German occupying forces established their divisional headquarters. The commander needed living quarters too. No wonder that once the noise of battle had died down, once the house had resigned its place as hospital and let the wounded go, the Villa Ariadne with its reminders of peace should have been chosen.

In this leafy cocoon the German command experienced a certain comfort. Perhaps amidst the constant signs of Cretan hostility they did not feel absolutely safe. Even so it is improbable that they knew what secret tunnels ran beneath the routine of their lives. General Müller, now, Commander from August 1942 to March 1944 of Germany's 22nd Infantry Division, during his occupation of the Villa had a driver whom Micky Akoumianakis knew well. 'I hated the Germans because they killed my father. But then I thought to myself that perhaps all Germans weren't bad—and anyhow why shouldn't I make use of knowing one or two of them?'

Micky was chief British agent in Herakleion. While collecting information about German movements he made friends with the general's driver to such good purpose that he once, while Müller was actually in the house, stayed a night there, ate a hearty meal, drank champagne and slept in one of the basement bedrooms which Evans had thoughtfully provided for himself and his guests. Did the driver, I asked, know what you were up to? He may, Micky said, have had some faint suspicion. But he never betrayed his Cretan acquaintance. He survived the war, went back to Germany and married; for some years he used to write to Micky; once he revisited Crete.

The two men were in fact genuinely friendly. Nevertheless the episode illustrates the traps which surrounded the occupying forces. Sometimes the invaders would be seized by alarm. Nicolas Platon, later the discoverer of the Zakros Palace site, was responsible for the antiquities of the Herakleion district. Fearing, he told me long afterwards, for the Palace of Minos, he covered its precious surfaces with earth, thus preserving the floors and steps from the eroding effect of the 300,000 pairs of German boots which tramped over them during the war.

He also packed away in cellars the treasures of the Museum—but this he was allowed to do only on condition that the contents could at any time be inspected. One day the Germans insisted on opening the cases; it was suspected that arms had been hidden inside. They found nothing; unlikely indeed that Platon would have jeopardised the Minoan inheritance. Still, one can understand the psychological pressures behind the search. Speaking their strange soft dialect, wearing their cloaks and high boots and menacing black headscarves, the Cretans watched with almond-shaped eyes, the eyes of some Minoan fresco. Everybody knew that the villages of the foothills held bands of guerillas. In the far interior the mountains leaned on the intruders. Splitting itself into caves, into ravines, into encircled high plains, the island was mysterious, beautiful—and desperate. There can be something appalling about Crete.

But the island is always ready to welcome its friends. Already in 1941 British officers were being secretly landed; their mission was to organise a resistant fifth column. They came in by the beaches and the inhospitable cliffs of the south coast, progressed to the mountain areas, in the beginning lived for the most part off the country.

One of the first in was C. M. Woodhouse, who afterwards commanded the Allied Military Mission to the Greek guerillas on the mainland. An early arrival was Patrick Leigh Fermor, who in the days of the defence of Crete had been so much impressed by the robust confidence of John Pendlebury. Another was Xan Fielding; another was Tom Dunbabin, who just after the Easter of 1942 came in by the same motor-launch which took Monty Woodhouse out.

Thomas James Dunbabin, the brilliant young Tasmanian-born scholar whom John had seen as a rival for the School Directorship, had indeed settled before the war into a promising position; after Humfry's death and Alan Blakeway's, and on Gerard Mackworth-Young's appointment as Director he had been made Assistant Director. A Fellow of All Souls, in 1937 he married Doreen de Labillière, daughter of the Dean of Westminster. She had been a student in Athens with Tom, she shared his archaeological interests and his enthusiasm for Greek travel; and it was in fact at Knossos, standing on the terrace roof of the Villa Ariadne, that the pair became engaged.

In manner quiet but authoritative, physically he was among the toughest of the tough explorers I met in Athens. One would watch the powerful figure with its cap of shining dark hair bounding up a hillside, not walking; the scholars of that vintage were made ,for endurance—one might say for heroism. As an archaeologist he knew Sicily, and when I saw him in 1941 he was working in the Italian department of the War Office. But it was to be expected that like Pendlebury, like Nicholas Hammond, like so many other young men from the School he should presently be embroiled in the savage adventure of war in Greece.

After he landed in Crete he spent his first days in a cave overlooking the sea; then he set off with his local guides towards the Mount Ida district, where he was to collect information for despatch to Cairo. Presently he saw to it that a wireless set was installed in a cave entered, he says, by 'a hole in the ground just large enough to wriggle through' high on one of the foothills of the mountain; and here or in the shelter of nearby rocks a tenacious British wireless operator lived for months on end. Tom meanwhile, searching for information or establishing contact with colleagues, undertook journeys which even he thought killing; when reinforcements arrived they found at the start, though they were Commando-trained, that the local hill-climbing pace was too much for them. He records one march which lasted for twenty-three hours. Exhausting detours were necessary in order to avoid villages where there were Germans. The alien travellers had to move at night or by difficult mountain tracks. And they had anyway to look like Cretans.

Clothes were an initial problem. Tom had come in dress which 'suggested a dock-labourer rather than a hillman'. However at a village where he spent a week, hiding by day in a kind of eyrie on the hillside and coming down at dusk to a friend's house (it was originally, he says, a Turkish harem), he was fitted out anew. A local tailor equipped with a tape-measure met him privily in a field by a stream and called out the necessary measurements to a friend who wrote them down in a little book; the result made the foreigner, who by now had grown the moustache indispensable to a hill-dweller, inconspicuous at any rate to German eyes, though the Cretans said they could always distinguish the English by the way they walked.

From Doreen Dunbabin I have a story that one day when he was in the Akoumianakis house a German called (it was Micky's friend from the Villa) and of course had to be admitted. Micky showed his usual presence of mind. 'Just sit in the corner,' he said to Tom, 'and don't say anything.' The German came in, sat at the table, had a drink. 'Don't mind that man in the corner,' Micky told him reassuringly, 'he's my cousin, he's not quite right in the head.'

But in the early days Tom and I daresay his colleagues—when possible avoiding the plains, moving secretly along precipitous

paths, sometimes sleeping on naked hillsides or under scrub—
scarcely caught sight of the enemy.

The Germans garrisoned the ports, the beaches, the plains, the roads. In the mountains which form the greater part of Crete they came seldom and unwillingly.

Anyhow by now one of their first reasons for sallying into the hills
had gone. In the first draft of an account of his experiences—an
account which he left unfinished—Tom writes that in the beginning
the mountains of the south held

... well over a thousand men left behind by our evacuation or escaped from the
German prison camps. At first they lived in the villages, sharing the scanty fare of
their Greek friends, or in the monasteries. They moved down to the beaches in
companies a hundred strong under their officers and NCO's, a ragged and footsore
army, for few boots stood up for long to the stony Cretan hillsides. These easy
conditions did not survive the first winter, for the Germans soon heard of the
arrival of submarines (magnified and multiplied by popular rumour) and sent out
patrols and posts to the coast and mountains. They made it a capital offence to
harbour stragglers, and those who remained had to move out of houses and cafés
into caves and holes. A few of them were picked up by accident or treachery. Two
or three died and were reverently buried. One Army doctor who died ... was
buried by the Bishop with half the clergy of the diocese and a crowd of two or
three thousand people, and a year later a song about his life and death was being
sung ...

Myles Hildyard and Michael Parish, born individualists, had
managed their escape by personal initiative, resource and courage
—and the benevolence of the Cretans. The assembly, rescue and
transport to Egypt of the large numbers of which Tom writes—
and to judge from witnesses in Crete there must have been many
more than a thousand stragglers and escapers—were achieved by
co-operation between the Royal Navy, the first arrivals among the
British Intelligence officers, and the undaunted local helpers. Tom
writes of a tiny village in the south, no more than a dozen houses,
said to have fed and sheltered in its olive groves a hundred British
and Commonwealth troops. The Amari district beneath the fierce
slopes of Ida was heroically hospitable from the start. Hospitable
and leafy too; Tom, using one of the code-names adopted by the
British, calls it Lotus-Land. Kokonas, schoolmaster at one of the
villages, Manolaki's birthplace Yerakari, was a leader in organising

an escape route for refugees after the evacuation. Tom writes of him fondly, as he does of friends in other villages of the area—Ano Meros for instance, or Kardhaki where the cobbler kept open house.

There were always in the early days a few of the wandering English sitting in his big kitchen and being served by his lively sisters, or patching their boots in his workshop . . . or even putting in a few days' work in his garden and fields.

Though by the time Tom arrived in 1942 the majority of the stragglers had been taken off they had not all gone, not at any rate according to a story about his first visit to Yerakari. Explaining himself, 'I am an Englishman,' he said. His audience received the information without surprise. 'Ah yes,' they said, 'we have plenty of those. . . .'

Soon he was travelling to make contact with supporters. There was still snow on the high spurs when he went up to Mount Ida and, from the top of a ridge with a shepherd's stone hut and a sheep-pen, 'looked down on to the plain of Nidha, brilliant green and dotted with thousands of sheep'—and saw the sea to both the north and the south. Nidha—the name shortens a Greek phrase meaning 'at Ida'—is one of the big plateaux miraculously cupped in the mountain ranges of Greece and especially Crete; it lies on the track from Anoyia to the summit and a little below the Idaean Cave, the reputed nursery of Zeus, which was first explored by archaeologists nearly a century ago. On this first visit Tom found it choked with snow. Even later its archaeological interest (it had produced some magnificent bronze shields) was not enough to persuade him that the place was more than 'a big comfortless cave, with bats inside it'. But then a cave in occupied Crete was regarded primarily as a refuge, a life-saver. He spent much of his time in caves.

On this occasion, however, he was welcomed in the hills on the other side of the plain. It was an area which from the early days of battle had been the haunt of guerillas. Captain Hamson, Pendlebury's colleague, to whom according to Aristea's statement poor George Drosoulakis had been taking a message before he was killed, had been up in Nidha with an armed band. Now Tom met a party of about forty guerillas, among them such locally famous leaders as Bandouvas, Petrakogiorgis and Satanas—the third, rumour said, at the age of sixteen had carried off his bride; before that had led his village in the last revolt against the Turks; and once in a Herakleion café after a heavy gambling loss had drawn his revolver and shot off the first finger of his right hand, saying, 'You will never roll the dice again.' This initial campaign conference was celebrated by a feast of sheep roasted on the spit and 'the titbits, the liver and the kokoretsi (a long sausage-shape consisting of the entrails wound round on themselves and grilled) handed round on a knife-point to the visitors and the leaders'.

Tom came to know both the group and the area 'in which' he says 'we were later encamped for months'. He came to know also the life of the Cretan shepherds (the salt of the earth, he called them) and to recognise that to hide anything from them, no matter how strict the precautions, was impossible. But they never betrayed him.

I do not remember a shepherd giving us away to the enemy from fear of torture or bribery, and we had them always with us. They would bring us a lamb or a kid, bring up a flask of wine from the village, see what they could get from us in the way of food or boots or pistols (and some of them were not above taking it without asking us).

One can see from these unfinished reminiscences of his, scribbled in pencil which the passage of time has made barely legible, how readily he accepted the way of life of the hill-people. He lived for months in the cheese-houses, the round limestone buildings in the mountains where sheep's cheese is made in the traditional fashion; he ate and drank with the shepherds, sang with them, wore the clothes they wore. Sometimes he was exasperated, as all of us brought up in orderly British ways might have been exasperated, with the country habits of gossip, so dangerous in time of war. But impatience rarely shows itself. Instead there is respect for the people, admiration for their independence, gratitude for their help; there is real liking. The attitude is different from John Pendlebury's. John in his joking paternalistic manner was proud of the Cretans. Tom felt deep affection as well.

But in the summer of 1942 the friendship was only beginning. Rommel in North Africa was driving towards Egypt, and in Crete the members of the tiny British mission found their sea communications

broken. Resources were almost non-existent; the problems of movement and organisation were acute. Cretan helpers there certainly
were. But with the war going, as it seemed, so badly for the Allies
some people were afraid, naturally enough, to see and be seen with
the British. All the more credit, as Tom says, for those who from
the start never doubted. There was always, he adds, the tradition of
Cretan hospitality triumphing over danger; always somebody who
would take the strangers into his house and provide a meal.

Luckily for the mission this difficult period coincided with the
good weather. At least they could sleep out of doors; Tom speaks
gratefully of a threshing-floor near the village of St John. And they
had plenty of grapes to eat. The admirable schoolmaster Kokonas,
for instance, made over the fruit of a vine luxuriant enough to climb
over the branches of three plane-trees. Nevertheless it was a time
of hardship, 'a season of skulking about'. Tom's breeches were out
at knees and seat. And there was the question of Tom's boots.

The last boat to come in before the sea-link with North Africa
and Cairo was cut brought in Patrick (or as he is familiarly called
Paddy) Leigh Fermor, who 'landed characteristically among a
crowd of bewhiskered Cretan patriots foiled in the attempt to leave
the perils of Crete to serve their country in the Middle East'. Tom
adds that the first few days of the new arrival 'were worthy of the
best spy story'. Certainly anybody who travels in Crete will hear
tales of the exploits of Paddy Leigh Fermor; and the name, always
surrounded with the aura of adventure, often recurs in Tom's
memories. For instance in connection with the boots problem.

Soon after Paddy had landed a conference was arranged. It was
to be held at Yerakari—'Lotus-Land was the best place for a conference'; and Xan Fielding (whose name also one can still hear
spoken with respect in Crete, especially in the White Mountains where
he was stationed) 'came gladly from his rugged and hungry western
hills to spend a few days in this leafy valley'. Whether he had durable
footwear of his own the story does not say; boots at that time were
more precious than gold, and the few the British brought in went
nowhere among their helpers. At any rate Tom and Paddy between
them had only one sound pair which they took it in turns to wear. 'I

crippled myself over those boots, marching in a pair too small for me when Paddy borrowed the good pair.'

In spite of the bad news from North Africa the meeting seems to have been a happy occasion. It was the season for Yerakari cherries. The visitors as they went through the orchards were offered handfuls of fruit, and they carried on their discussions sitting under the trees with huge baskets beside them. Only long afterwards did Tom hear what had been going on in the village. The rumour was that the British were meeting to discuss giving themselves up. Had it come to that the schoolmasters of the region were resolved themselves to shelter the three officers, passing them if necessary from village to village, house to house.

No wonder that Tom would always look back with nostalgia on the Amari country and the slopes of Kedros which shaded the valley and 'the hundred and one springs, a hundred known to men and the hundred and first, if one could find it, the water of immortality.' Amusing to note that whatever he may have thought about Zeus's cave on Ida he could not, even in the years of his dangerous wanderings, neglect the antiquities of his lotus-land. Most of the known archaeological sites may have been, as he says, discovered by Pendlebury or by that distinguished native of Yerakari, Manolaki. But long afterwards Tom was to write in a learned periodical:

It is ill gleaning after Pendlebury, but I had the opportunity during the war of seeing a number of unrecorded sites and casual finds. These I put on record as a small contribution to the archaeology of Crete, and as a token of gratitude to my hospitable Amari friends.

And amidst his archaeological preoccupations he was still recalling the cool shade of the villages with their crop of apples and cherries; and 'the cheeses of Ida and Kedros, second to none in Crete'; and the charm of Yerakari and of that Ano Meros of which in his earlier, pencilled account he had written that

... the houses had handsome balconies and vine-covered arbours, and the villagers were so hospitable that they plucked you by the sleeve as you walked down the narrow street, to come in and drink a glass of wine with them. I think it was the most beautiful village in Crete. Certainly it was at sunset on a long summer

167

evening, sitting outside the doctor's house, drinking his wine called Satanas (because it was so insidious) and watching the last rays fade on the bare summit of Ida which rose immediately opposite.

Some months after their first conference in Amari Tom and Paddy and Xan Fielding were together at Yerakari again. It was the Christmas of 1942. The news from North Africa was by now more encouraging. Anyway the Germans were busy celebrating their own Christmas. and the British party could relax some of their security precautions and take a holiday. They made their way 'village by village and house by house' from Yerakari to Ano Meros, where they slept and where by day they went about calling on their friends. The visit turned into a four-day feast which 'called for great strength of digestion' and ended at the priest's house with the singing of the British, Greek and French national anthems, the Red Flag and, in lieu of the American anthem, which nobody knew, 'John Brown's Body' 'with variations'.

That was the best, the gayest, perhaps the most carefree display of Amari hospitality.

Two years later all these beautiful villages were a heap of ruins. The Germans destroyed them a little before they withdrew, and killed many of our friends.

ii

At the time with which Tom's fragmentary manuscript deals life for the British mission in Crete, in spite of occasional feasting, was pretty Spartan. In a country where rumour has wings indeed and may fly into the wrong ears they could not risk staying for long in one place. They had to move often and choose not the well-known hiding places but caves within caves, clefts in the gorges known only to the shepherds.

Once with winter coming they contrived a wall to enclose the space under an overhanging rock. The doorway was just big enough to crawl through, and the last man in shut it by pulling a thorn-bush after him. Snowed up for three days, they were sustained by visits from shepherds and friendly villagers who came to bring gifts of food and drink—and to hear what news there was. The messages over the radio were nearly all the cave had to offer. There was not much the British could do that year. They could collect information about the enemy. And they could spread the news from outside; 'it gave everyone a thrill to handle a forbidden news-sheet, ill-copied through many hands.' But at least the British were there, present.

The mere knowledge that, somewhere in the mountains, there were English in the island was of great encouragement to all good Cretans, whether they saw us or not, whether we did much or little or nothing; we were surely credited with powers and activities which greatly surprised us when we heard of them.

Though life was Spartan it was also quiet, for the British at any rate. There might be an occasional excitement. An enemy search-light, for instance, was installed at Tymbaki, not far from the spot where a British submarine was that very day expected to call; waiting for the rendezvous and eating a picnic lunch brought by the local women, Tom and his party learned that the German commander of Tymbaki airfield had invited himself to a picnic lunch with the mayor (a British supporter) on the other side of the village. But for the time being the mountains, and Tom was chiefly concerned with mountain areas, saw little of the enemy.

The German soldier peopled the high mountains, and many of the mountain villages, with regiments of British and partisans. If he had to go there, he let off a volley to warn these dangerous people to get out of the way.

The terrible punitive expeditions which stained the island with fire and blood came later; Tom's manuscript breaks off before they took place.

Meanwhile the servants of the Villa Ariadne were scattered. Maria was at Katalagari; beyond Arkhanes and the German military headquarters, it was the village to which Manolaki had sent his family for temporary safety. Kosti had withdrawn a few miles farther south to Alagni, where he had property. Manoli had gone to his home in the Lasithi district, which at the start had been mainly Italian-occupied, and there he waited with his wife Ourania for better times. Not that he was inactive. He served as a liaison man. Once, carrying a message to a hide-out in a cave and finding Tom there, he fell on his knees and kissed the well-remembered hands.

He told me long afterwards that he would have joined the guerillas, but he was gently refused. In the mountains, Tom had said to him (and Manoli quoted the phrase), 'You are hunted as the dog hunts the hare.' Ourania, naturally enough, was anyway against the idea. 'What was I to do,' she said, smiling comfortably in the days of peace, 'what was I to do, a woman all alone?'

For three years the Villa surrendered its quiet to the invaders. The German general in residence drove up in the morning to his headquarters, drove back in the evening to dine at home. It is unlikely that he suspected with what curiosity and precision his timetable was noted and checked.

It was in Cairo during the winter of 1943-44 that an impudent plan was hatched by Patrick Leigh Fermor, on leave after eighteen months in the Cretan mountains, and a young captain in the Coldstream Guards who had never been in the island, William Stanley Moss. Obviously it is not for me to write in more than bare outline about the Kreipe episode; the actors themselves have that copyright. Patrick Leigh Fermor, while his books on the mainland are known to everyone concerned with literature about Greece, has not yet told his own Cretan story. Stanley Moss, however, would write in *Ill-Met By Moonlight* a personal account, and on his book I gratefully rely for the main part of my recapitulation.

The story has a peculiar irony: the central figure was not the one originally intended. The character cast by the British for the rôle was that General Müller whose involuntary hospitality Micky Akoumianakis had briefly enjoyed. Much decorated by the Nazi hierarchy, he was hated in Crete; he had been guilty of many of the atrocities inflicted on the population during the Occupation. By the beginning of 1944 the Allies had encouraging news to report, and the Cretans could no longer feel, as they had felt when Tom was making his first contacts, that Hitler was having things all his own way. Still, the Germans were in military control of the island and a successful local uprising was out of the question. In concert, then, with Cretan patriots Leigh Fermor and Moss decided to make a show. They would prove that the enemy hold was weakening. They would abduct General Müller.

Paddy parachuted back into Crete two months before his partner who, having made no fewer than twelve abortive attempts by air, finally came by sea; like nearly all the British and Greeks who came secretly into Crete by water, he landed in the south. Along the coast from Sphakia to Tsoutsoura at the eastern end of the Asterousia Mountains small beaches had been marked down, rocky, isolated, unguarded; Micky Akoumianakis, who with Cretan helpers was involved in the choice, says that about one hundred landings were safely made during the Occupation. 'We never,' he writes of this extraordinary Anglo-Greek co-operation, 'had a failure in that kind of work.' Meanwhile the organisation of Stanley Moss's reception, as of Paddy's, was the responsibility of A. M. Rendel. In civilian life since the war Sandy Rendel has been diplomatic correspondent of *The Times*; but then, with the Lasithi area as his province, he was engaged in the same kind of activities as Tom and Xan Fielding and the rest of the British mission.

A disappointment awaited Stanley Moss. The date was April 4; there had been a change in the enemy dispositions. General Müller had been replaced, and the plan for his capture could not go through. A substitute, however, was available. General Kreipe had just come from the Russian front. He was a regular soldier; he was innocent of the atrocities which marked the career of his predecessor. Otherwise circumstances had not changed. Like Müller, General Kreipe lived in the Villa Ariadne, like him drove up every day to the headquarters in Arkhanes and drove back in the evening to his living quarters. The psychological value of the Leigh Fermor-Moss operation would be to demonstrate that a German general, any German general, could be snatched from the garrison of Hitler's Fortress of Crete.

The operation concerned not only Paddy and Stanley Moss as chief kidnappers, not only Sandy Rendel as reception organiser, but various others among the British in Crete. Xan Fielding, as it happened, was absent from the island at the time. Whether Tom Dunbabin approved of the plan I very much doubt; level-headed, he may have feared the consequences for the Cretans; but his name, at any rate, recurs in the story. Without their Cretan supporters the British would have been helpless; and here the Akoumianakis family come once more into the record.

As British agent in Herakleion Micky was essential to the abduction party; and since he lived at Knossos he could watch at close quarters the comings and goings at the Villa. He provided the disguises—the uniforms of a couple of German military policemen —necessary for the plan; he brought along his second in command, Elias Athanasakis (nephew of Maria from the Villa) with a signalling scheme which made the whole adventure practicable. He was not the only member of the Akoumianakis family to take part. Phyllia, who three years earlier had climbed the hill to find the body of her father, was a courageous observer; gossiping with the German soldiers at the Villa, she gleaned information; she it was who noted the timetable of the General's car. But the catalogue of helpers is too long for this summary. I must keep as far as I can to the names and the stories of people I know.

General Kreipe was usually driven down from Arkhanes between eight and nine o'clock in the evening. Two or three miles south of the Villa Ariadne the Arkhanes road joined another road running north to Herakleion; here embankments and ditches gave cover, and the intersection compelled any driver to slow down.

On April 26, 1944 Paddy and Stanley Moss, both in the uniform of German military police, together with a group of Cretans hid at the junction. A few hundred yards up the Arkhanes road there was rising ground. Here Micky and Elias Athanasakis were posted. They were to signal to the main position with a torch when they saw the General's car coming; to make sure, another man was to pass on the warning by flashing a second torch. It was eight o'clock when the party took up their stations. The spring night was cold; it grew dark. By nine o'clock there was still no sign; anxiety mounted. Then at nine-thirty the torch flashed. Paddy and Stanley Moss climbed out of their hiding-place and stood in the road. The car, headlamps blazing, came down the slope and paused at the junction. Moss held a traffic signal; Paddy, flashing a red lamp, cried Halt!

The car stopped. We walked forward rather slowly, and as we passed the beam of the headlamps we drew our ready-cocked pistols from behind our backs and let fall the life-preservers from our wrists.

As we came level with the doors of the car Paddy asked 'Ist dies das General's Wagen?'

There came a muffled 'Ja, ja' from inside.

In a few minutes it was all over. The doors of the car were pulled open. The struggling General and his chauffeur (who was coshed as he tried to reach his gun) were dragged out. Moss jumped into the driver's seat; the General, with three Cretans holding him, was shoved into the back; Paddy, wearing the General's hat, sat in the passenger's front seat; and off they drove, leaving the rest of the Cretan party in charge of the chauffeur. Micky, not a bloodthirsty man, has more than once told me with an expression of horror that the unfortunate man was killed; how, I have never liked to ask.

For the kidnappers the dangers were only beginning. To get past the Villa Ariadne, where the sentries were starting to open the gates for the General's return, was easy; Moss sounded the horn and without slackening pace drove on amidst startled salutes. But Herakleion itself had to be crossed. It is a fair-sized town, and there were the control posts along the road to be negotiated. Cretans telling me about the exploit have given numbers ranging from thirteen to thirty. Actually, Moss writes, there were twenty-two. He drove up to each slowly to let the sentry recognise the official car, then accelerated. Paddy in the General's hat smoked a cigarette in the front seat; the three Cretans crouched in the back; and the General at critical moments was hidden on the floor. A few times a bar across the road forced a halt. But nobody ventured a challenge; on the contrary, the car was everywhere saluted. There was a tense moment when at the approach to the city exit by the western gate with its anti-tank blocks the man on duty instead of stepping aside stood his ground and came towards the passenger's window. Paddy forestalled him. In German 'The General's car!' he called out. And the kidnappers drove on: out of Herakleion, westward across the coastal plain, uphill through the moonlit night along the twisting highroad towards Rethymnon.

They were about twenty miles from Herakleion when they stopped. It was time for the party to split up. Paddy with one of the Cretans was to drive on, ditch the car and leave in it a letter saying that reprisals would be unjustified since the capture had been carried out by 'a British raiding force'. Moss and the two remaining Cretans set off on foot with the General. Stumbling in the dark, struggling all night across trackless country, they made their way southwards towards their first objective, the village of Anoyia in the northern foothills of Mount Ida.

Moss says that the next stage of the abduction was hampered by ill-luck. Pamphlets in Greek and German were to be dropped in Crete saying, like the letter left in the car, that the General's capture was the work of a British party. The weather was bad and the pamphlets were not dropped.

German threats of reprisals were prompt; if the distinguished victim was not returned in three days all 'rebel villages' in the Herakleion district would be razed to the ground. A few days later, however, Micky, rejoining the main party, was able to report that the villages were still standing; it was two months later that Anoyia was murderously destroyed—as a result, it has been said, of some quite different action. Indeed it has been maintained that the Kreipe kidnapping did not bring retribution on Cretan heads, that it was to that extent innocent. Not all the islanders were convinced. 'Someone had to pay,' a taxi-driver in Herakleion once said to me—though he laughed as he described the exploit itself. 'If such things are done someone must always pay—not those who do the deed, but the women, those who are left behind, they pay. Someone must always pay.'

Micky Akoumianakis has sometimes argued that the burning of villages in that summer of 1944 was done not so much in reprisal as to cover the German retreat from the west and centre of Crete. But perhaps vengeance may have come into it as well. General Müller, whom Kreipe had replaced, after the abduction was brought back as Military Commander of the Fortress of Crete. It is difficult to believe that the hideous massacres which he authorised (and for which after the war he was executed) were a matter of mere tactics.

Official error combined with accident to hinder the kidnappers. The arrangement had been for radio stations to say that the General was 'already on his way to Cairo'. Instead, all broadcasts, including those from the BBC, announced that he 'was being taken off the island'—a different matter and one which failed to discourage a massive search. Three days after the abduction, with Moss and Paddy reunited and welcomed by a guerilla group under the command of one of the most respected of Cretan leaders, Michael

Xylouris, the mishaps began. Tom, who was to have got in touch with Cairo, was nowhere to be found; only later was it learned that he was very ill with malaria. His wireless operator appeared—but suddenly the set packed up. It would take two days for a runner to reach Sandy Rendel in Lasithi or, in the west, another agent with a wireless set. Hastily the runners were despatched.

But now news came that the Germans were preparing a huge man hunt. The British and their Cretan friends had to get to the south coast if they were to escape with their prisoner, and if they were to avoid the hunt they had to move fast and by difficult paths. With guides from another guerilla group (it was commanded by Petrakogiorgis, one of the leaders who had entertained Tom on his first trip into the hills) they set off to cross the barrier of Mount Ida: up the stony foothills, up the fierce naked heights to where in May the snow still lingers, down the merciless southern flank. It rained and they shivered. They took refuge in a shepherd's hut, in a waterlogged ditch, in a cave on the slopes above Nithavris, in a sheepfold near Yerakari. The Germans drew a cordon round the base of Ida, the kidnappers slipped through. Alarms multiplied. Another cordon had been drawn; there is a story (I have it from Doreen Dunbabin) that as the troops searched they hallooed and cried 'Kreipe! Kreipe!' into the unresponsive air. There were more halts in freezing hideouts, more night marches. With the beach from which they had hoped to embark enemy-occupied the party were driven inland and westward.

General Kreipe had been seized on his way to the Villa on April 26. His captors brought him sometimes on foot, sometimes on mule-back, from the Rethymnon road via Anoyia and Mount Ida, via the Amari country and a group of villages—Patsos, Photinou, Vilandredo—south of Rethymnon to a beach at Rodhakino about fifteen miles east of Sphakia; and from there on the night of May 14 they were taken off by motor-launch. They had been on the run for eighteen days.

iii

Elation at the coup of the kidnappers is apt to make one forget the feelings of their prisoner. Sandy Rendel says in his book *Appointment in Crete* that, though he was a party to the exploit, like Tom he never saw Kreipe, but he refers to a message from Paddy during the escape across the island. 'I had,' he writes, 'one gay letter telling me that the General was a charmer.' The General was being a charmer under painful handicaps. His leg had been injured when he was violently snatched from his car. Twice during the eighteen-day trek he had fallen heavily, once from rocks, once, badly hurting his shoulder, from mule-back. Under normal conditions the long marches, as anybody who has walked in Crete must know, would have been tough. In his situation they must have been appalling. But one had never heard his side of the story.

Not that when I went to see him I learned a great deal. Over a quarter of a century had passed since the adventure. No doubt parts of the experience still rankled. But he had put it behind him. He was living in retirement. In agreeing to talk about it at all he showed a kind of stoic generosity.

The house was in a leafy suburb of Hanover. A solid, plum-coloured house in a well-to-do street of solid, plum-coloured houses; a small garden in front, neatly hedged; steps leading up to the front door. I had flown from Berlin, I was early for my appointment; to pass the time I walked down the road, then, misreading the numbers, looked at the wrong house; to my embarrassment I found General Kreipe was standing on the steps of the right one, waiting for me. An elderly man with the look of compact strength; stockily built; the close-cut hair grizzling; the face severe, rectangular, clean-shaven; the expression politely puzzled by my errand. In the room upstairs with its soberly comfortable heavy furnishings Frau Kreipe waited, middle-aged but with a certain elegance; good manners and the well-bred confidence of social position almost but not quite concealed her curiosity. Would I like tea or coffee? And I must certainly not refuse some cake; why, it had been bought specially for me. No, neither of them spoke English. If with his captors, as Stanley Moss wrote, the General had talked French he had abjured the language since. Now it was German or nothing.

But it was not entirely due to the paucity of my German that the details I elicited were scanty. General Kreipe was a professional soldier who by 1944 had been for two years on the Russian front. In Crete he spent only five weeks. He had never been in Greece before; he spoke no Greek. The Villa Ariadne when he was there did not employ Cretan servants, and he had no contact with the local people. The names of villages meant nothing to him. Until that comfortless trek across the island he knew the terrain only from occasional hunting trips. Of the Villa he remembered sleeping in a downstairs bedroom; he remembered that archaeological finds from Knossos were stored, strictly untouched, in a cupboard. Naturally he had visited the Palace of Minos. Did he, I asked, thinking of the measures taken to preserve the site, ever meet Platon?

'Ah, Plato,' he said, for the first time relaxing into pleasurable reminiscence, 'Plato, the Greek Goethe!' With disappointment I realised that he was referring not to the Cretan archaeologist but to a happy acquaintance with the classics.

Recalled to memories of war, he stiffened. I knew that both Stanley Moss's book and a film it had inspired had brought protests from German solicitors. From a friend in the firm of lawyers representing the British film company at this end I knew that the General had complained of errors. The account of his capture, he had said, was inaccurate; he had been beaten up with a rifle butt; and he had certainly never, contrary to the account in the book, given his word of honour not to try to escape. The book, he told me now, had been prevented from appearing in Germany; and naturally, he added curtly, the film had never been allowed in. His resentment at Moss's account extended to Moss himself.

'Paddy,' he said, 'I liked Paddy. But Moss, always with his pistol' (he made a gesture indicative of excessive enthusiasm in a guard addicted to prodding) 'it was childish.' Understandably there was an undercurrent of resentment over his later experiences too. He had spent part of his captivity at Sheffield, then had been sent to Canada; he was not released until 1947, three years after his abduction.

'No, don't say that,' he murmured, warning, to Frau Kreipe. I had not caught what she was saying, but I recognised the indignation of a wife on her husband's behalf and respected it. There was a diversionary move to show me a picture, a view of the Rockies given him by a Canadian officer at the camp. Then I remembered that Moss in his account of the trans-Cretan journey had mentioned an incipient friendship between the prisoner and one of the Cretan guards, Manoli Paterakis. Yes, the General said—there was a shade of gratification in his voice—he remembered Paterakis well. 'In fact he has asked for my address. If he comes to Germany he may come to see me.'

At least, I thought, some tiny element of human warmth has survived from the painful episode.

'It was not worth your journey,' the Kreipes said with solicitous courtesy as I stood up to leave. 'You are flying back to Berlin? Ah, BEA of course; Lufthansa is not allowed.' German planes might not operate from Berlin; once more I recognised, and with sympathy, a legitimate grievance.

The General came to the door with me and pointed to the trees lining the road. 'They are Japanese cherry-trees, beautiful when they come out—the whole street is in blossom.' He limped slightly; he had not had an easy war. And, he told me, he had diabetes. But perhaps, I said, you have been fortunate all the same. If you had stayed on the Russian front, even if you had been left at the Villa Ariadne to the end, you might not have been alive today.

Somehow I do not think he felt lucky.

iv

Twice again the Villa Ariadne was caught up in the current of the war; once before the finale.

Dr Yamalakis, who had spoken so warmly to me about the respect in which Evans had been held, was himself both during and after the war revered in Herakleion. He had a private collection of Minoan and other antiquities which he presented to the Museum. He was a generous and beneficent physician. But his reputation was especially based on his record in the Resistance. He had never failed in help to the British. He had constituted himself their doctor; one heard that if he was needed he would go up to the hills at night—and by day be treating his patients in the Herakleion clinic. Once—it was the Squire who gave me the story—he was among hostages threatened with execution. He was asked whose side he was on. First, he said, the Greeks; second, the British; third, the French. Startled at such effrontery, the Germans let him go.

But when one day in 1960 I found him in his clinic (the waiting-room held a poorly-dressed, ferociously crippled patient who spoke of him with gratitude) he could not be persuaded to talk about himself. It was Tom Dunbabin he talked about—'the best' he said 'of all the British in Crete'. And his own share? Oh, he said, his job had been simply to collect information and pass it on to Tom. At last I elicited something more.

Throughout the Occupation and particularly at the end when the defeat of Germany was certain Tom had made it his aim to prevent the murderous struggles between guerilla bands which had split the mainland. Especially he had fought to avert an extreme left-wing coup. I have been told that it was due more to Tom than to anybody else that Crete did not turn to Communism. When the Germans were evacuating Herakleion in 1944 he had been joined in action by Dr Yamalakis. By this time the Communist bands—and perhaps some of the other groups as well—were more concerned to take over power than to rid the island of enemy troops. It was decided to forestall them in at any rate one area. Yamalakis and Tom with a party of about twenty-five Cretans occupied the Villa Ariadne.

And that, perhaps, made the finale possible.

Herakleion fell to the Allies in October. But the Germans were not done with yet, and in the Canea region, where three and a half years earlier they had first struck, they still held out. They held out for another seven months, in fact to the end of the war. Not until May 1945 did their commander fly to Herakleion to sign the surrender.

It was to Knossos that he was taken, to the Villa Ariadne, then the headquarters of the British. The Allied officers gathered in a room familiar to me from scores of July middays languid with heat when the archaeologists came in to discuss the morning's excavation, when Kosti or Manoli served lunch and Maria flitted noiselessly underground in her black weeds. It was the room where Evans had once held court, where poor Duncan Mackenzie had succumbed at last to infirmity, where generations of British School students had dined and argued and planned the exploration of remote sites.

And there that May evening the German surrender of the Fortress of Crete was signed.

VI

i

ONE WANTS, of course, to find out for oneself. One is curious to know what the terrain is really like—how desperate the distances, how steep the ascents and descents. Imagination alone can never conjure up the sensation of the mountains; you need the aching thighs, the thinning air, the stones under your feet.

Certainly I had a desire to see what ranges Kreipe had crossed. All the same it was less with the idea of tracing the path of the kidnappers than with a fancy to visit one or two places with names which had haunted me that I began an expedition to the Mount Ida district. It was in 1959, the year after my first return to Knossos and the Villa Ariadne. Yerakari, I said to Micky, where your father was born—I should like to see Yerakari; and how do I get to Anoyia, that famous village burned in the war? Almost before I knew what was happening my map was out, a route was planned, and Micky was preparing to write letters of introduction to his relatives and his friends in villages around Mount Ida. Not until I was well on my way did I discover that to one recipient he had written: Never mind about her getting tired, she is used to it.

There was something else I learned later. The Cyprus settlement was still only three months old, and the Cretans, islanders with a long struggle for freedom behind them, were still fiercely pro-Makarios and anti-British. I was probably the first Englishwoman, Micky told me when I got back to Herakleion, who had travelled in the Amari district since the Cyprus problem had been at its gravest. I have always hoped that in sending me on this trial expedition he was relying not only on the generosity of the Cretans but on my unmistakable attachment to his country.

I had a strict timetable. In one day I was to cross Ida, not in the way taken by Paddy and Stanley Moss but in the opposite direction, from Nithavris in Amari, the district so much loved by Tom Dunbabin, to Anoyia, where the abduction party had begun their mountain passage. Innocently I embraced the plan.

First, then, to Rethymnon. I had caught cold: physically I felt wretched; but there was nothing for it but to go ahead. I took the early bus from Herakleion. Before midday I was in Rethymnon with time to spare before the next bus to Yerakari. I strolled through narrow streets, bought food for my trip. In one shop some kind of small private celebration was going on. 'Do you drink?' asked one of the women, and gave me a glass of the local spirits called *tsikoudhiá*. I never found out what we were toasting, but I left in a glow of friendship. Later, lunching in what a stranger whom I consulted described as the best restaurant in the place, I ate grilled red mullet, hot, with the customary cold oil-and-lemon dressing, and watched a magnificent hawk-faced Cretan in patched riding breeches and black headscarf wandering into the kitchen to choose his fish, then sitting down to eat it from his fingers. The man in town clothes at his table smiled at me conspiratorially.

Finally I delivered one of Micky's letters. It was to the director of an orphanage, Theocharis Saridhakis. I crossed a hall dense with the curiosity of little boys in dark blue school uniforms. 'Ah, my dear!' cried Mr Saridhakis, greeting me enthusiastically in English. Smiling gaily, he left his lunch to congeal while I was served with cake and the traditional spoonful of preserve in a glass of water. He had been a journalist before the war. When the invasion of Crete began he was at his desk.

'I left it, I never went back. Except during my military service I had never held a gun before. But now I was asked to carry some arms to a certain position, so I took a rifle and joined in the battle. I was lucky in the war, three times captured, three times I escaped, once without my shoes. Yes, I was lucky. See this amulet? I am never without it . . .'

Somebody, I said, ought to write the story of Crete in the war; it is a great story.

'I have written it,' cried Saridhakis, 'thousands of pages of it, but it isn't published yet.' Familiar names echoed through his talk, Paddy, Tom, Pendlebury. We walked together to the bus station.

'She is a foreigner,' I heard him saying, 'you must look after her.' And though I have often been embarrassed by the hospitality which offers a stranger this courtesy, for once I was glad enough to sit by the driver. The inland roads in those years could be excruciating, and in a front seat one suffered less from the jagged chunks of unrolled stone.

You must be tired, I said to the driver as we bounced round huge potholes. Not really, he said philosophically; he knew villages with worse roads. There had been rain. The valley dipped southward between glittering banks of broom and bell-flower and mallow. The hillsides were still bright, though dark rays of shadow lay across precipices and gorges. But when we reached Yerakari the sun had gone. The passengers got out of the bus, collected their luggage and dispersed towards their homes. I waited. I had Micky's letter to a cousin; the driver volunteered to find him while I sat outside a café in the darkening, deserted little square. Moss and his prisoner, I remembered, had sheltered for the night in a sheepfold above Yerakari. Now the village, burned and rebuilt, had a bleak, naked, new-born look. In the dusk it was cold; I began to shiver. Presently a figure in riding breeches, boots and dark jacket approached: black hair and moustache, the face long, melancholy—George Akoumianakis, Micky's cousin, president of the village. He took my letters (I had one from Saridhakis too). Standing, he read them impassively. Then gravely, 'Let us go,' he said, 'I will show you the village.'

Up steep paths, past the wreck of the church, past the house, rebuilt now, where Manolaki had been born. A woman rushed out of a doorway to greet me in English. She and her husband had been in the Middle East, they loved the British, would I sleep in her house? Awkwardly, for I did not yet know what was planned for me, I thanked her; but as her welcome gained impetus George Akoumianakis interrupted.

'You are making a show for us,' he said ironically.

We moved on. At a café the schoolmaster—white hair, white pointed beard, humorous falcon face—came out to talk of Paddy and Tom and the organisation of the escape route after the British surrender; it was Tom's friend Kokonas. At last I was shown a blank open space, grey in the vanishing light, with a memorial. It was the place of execution.

'When the Germans burned a village,' said Akoumianakis (he had been a policeman during the Occupation, had heard he was about to be arrested and had fled to the mountains), 'they took twenty men and shot them. Once a man escaped and reached another village in Amari. But the Germans came and burned that one too— only they couldn't find twenty men. Anyway they took him to make up the number. Somehow he wasn't killed. When he came to himself he was wounded and buried under a pile of dead bodies. But he was alive, he dragged himself away, he survived. The women? The women were usually taken to Rethymnon and kept there for a fortnight, then released. But some were killed. In Yerakari two women were killed. People who were blind or ill died in their houses.'

Pierced by the chill of the burned, murdered, resurrected village, I was thankful to be taken at last to the Akoumianakis house; thankful, though I had to force myself to eat, for wine and the supper of eggs and potatoes cooked over a fire of sticks by Mrs Akoumianakis; thankful for the warmth and laughter of the café where I was taken for a post-prandial peppermint; most thankful of all to go to bed. I slept in the main room, my hosts in a room leading off it; the door between was left open. In the corner there was a symbolical picture of Liberty; an oil lamp hung on the wall. 'I will come,' said Mrs Akoumianakis, 'and turn down the light.' I undressed and scrambled unwashed into bed. I was too sleepy to worry about the consensus of opinion that for me to walk from Nithavris over Mount Ida to Anoyia in a single day was out of the question.

Only vaguely, as in a dream, was I conscious of a figure putting out the lamp and tucking me in for the night.

ii

With her indulgent, faintly motherly air my hostess woke me

up at seven. It was late, she said, and I must get up, for I had a long trip to Nithavris ahead of me. Yerakari was buzzing with life, and an old man—it was Mrs Akoumianakis's uncle—was already waiting with a donkey to take me on the next stretch. I had letters to deliver, and every few miles along the valley we halted, sometimes at a ruined settlement, sometimes at a hamlet gradually reviving. Once I was reproached by a country policeman, a ragged poverty-stricken representative of a burned tumbledown village.

'The English forget us—don't they know the sacrifices we made?'

We know, I said, we know. But I rode on sad and ashamed. And once—it was in the village of Vryses—I was reminded of the British involvement in Cyprus.

The place was tiny, but in August 1944 it had lost thirty-nine dead, the church had been destroyed and the local spring had vanished. 'We found it again later,' said my informant, who had been in the Middle East in the war; and he went on to describe an example of what I could not help regarding as unusual attention to detail on the part of the German Government.

'When the President of West Germany heard about the village he asked if the church had really been burned, and when he was told that was true he sent some money for rebuilding it. . . . Would you like to see the new school?'

The schoolmaster was already at the door, and when I went in the room, large and airy, was full of children watching me with unquenchable interest. Without a pause I was guided round the pictures on the wall. 'Here we have the Saints . . . and here are the heroes of the War of Independence.' I expressed admiration of the proud whiskered figures in klephtic dress and the fiery churchmen preaching revolution. 'And these' (it was said wholly without malice or intention to embarrass an English visitor) 'these are the heroes of Cyprus, here is Makarios.' I recognized the continuity of history. The men of 1821 might have been the guerillas of 1941. The portrait of Makarios might have been the portrait of that Archbishop Germanos reputed to have raised the flag of rebellion at Hagia Lavra more than a century earlier.

'Very fine,' I said; and the schoolmaster led me into his house for a drink.

As we moved farther into the Amari country the echoes of war deepened. At Kardhaki, in 1959 still a scatter of half-repaired shacks, I was led to the home of one Sotiri (long afterwards I learned that he was the brave cobbler of Tom Dunbabin's diary). He looked politely puzzled until I said I was a friend of Micky's; then he rushed me excitedly into his house, called his wife and children and burst into anecdotes about Tom and Paddy. Especially Tom.

'When he came here for the first time I said to him: How do you know I am not pro-German? How can you be sure I shall not betray you? Bah, he said, I know you won't. He had a little book with the names of all the good men, the reliable men written in it.'

It is perhaps unlikely that Tom, dedicated as he was to his job, would have carried about with him quite so incriminating a document. Nevertheless the story testifies to the trust which existed between him and the Cretans; I was sorry that I had no personal messages for this good friend.

But my guide, stumping along and talking with great sweetness as I rode his affable donkey, distracted me from melancholy reflections: 'It is a good donkey, six years old, quiet. Its name? I don't know; it hasn't got a name. I was afraid you wouldn't know how to ride, it is difficult going up and down hill, but I see you are used to it, I am relieved. In other parts of Greece do you see the man riding or the woman? Ah, in Crete the woman must always be the one who rides. I think that is beautiful, don't you. . . . I never had time to learn much reading and writing, I was always a soldier, always fighting, ten years I was in the army . . .' (Breaking off to address a group of men working on the road) 'Good morning, this is an Englishwoman, she is a writer, she has come to see Crete.'

I began to feel a sense of detachment from my normal life. Everything I saw, everyone I met belonged to another world. The valley had died, the valley was being born again. Today Tom's 'most beautiful village in Crete,' Ano Meros, had no 'handsome balconies' and no 'vine-covered arbours'. But it was stirring in the early summer air. I had brought a letter from Saridhakis to his wife Calliope, the schoolmistress here, and at midday she came out of the school and took me home for a lunch of mince cooked in vine leaves, fried eggs, salad, olives, wine. The food was delicious, but my head buzzed with my cold and again I had to force myself to eat.

From the window I could see my hostess's children playing in the lane outside. Their voices came high and faint as the cry of young birds, the sun blanched the soil at their feet. There was something reviving, too, in the atmosphere of the little house and in my hostess's pleasant eager manner. Nevertheless the past still murmured in my ears. Saridhakis had told me he had barely escaped with his life from Ano Meros. His aunt had not been as lucky. After lunch Mrs Saridhakis took me across the lane into a tiny orchard overgrown with grass and flowers.

'There was a tree,' she said, 'it has been cut down now. Here we found the body of our aunt. She had been killed, she was lying just here.'

A little girl, one of her children, stood listening.

'Do you like quinces?' Mrs Saridhakis asked. 'They aren't quite ripe yet, though.' She picked one from a tree. It was sour, like the presence of death in that quiet sunny orchard.

But triumph too, that was present.

Ano Meros was the parish of Kyriakos Katsandonis, a priest famous in the war and the Resistance; hunted by the Nazis, evacuated to the Middle East, he had worked for the British and for the Greek Government in exile: the warrior-priest, Tom called him. I waited for him to wake from his midday rest, then I went up the steep little track to his house. A tall imposing presence, a brilliant glance; his wife brought coffee. On the wall I saw a photograph of Paddy in Cretan dress, heroic with a dagger. Philadem, said Katsandonis, beaming, Philadem. The old Cretan song with that refrain was a favourite with Paddy; he sang it often, and the name stuck; in Crete you will still hear him called Philadem. I remembered the legendary tales: Paddy in his Cretan disguise going up to a German sergeant at a village café near Knossos and clapping him on the shoulder with the greeting 'Servus, Kamarad!'—and Micky, seeing the man putting his hand on his revolver, dragging his friend away; Paddy on the same evening, still elated with wine, pushing between two drunken German soldiers, embracing them and walking a quarter of a mile arm-in-arm with them towards Herakleion, singing German songs and exchanging expressions of warm regard while poor Micky, distraught, followed on the other side of the road. Now the warrior-priest told me how after some lucky escape from danger Philadem had begun softly singing 'sto psilo vouno'—'on the high mountain'; the eagle perched on a rock and drenched with snow calls on the sun (the sun of liberty is intended) to rise and dry his plumage.

I took my leave, reluctantly said goodbye to my gentle old guide and set off with a stouter, bouncier donkey on the last stage of the day. My new guide, a man of about thirty, tall, lean, cheeks slightly hollowed, eyes intent, the manner respectful but self-respecting with the air of inherent independence characteristic of the Cretans, walked behind, silent unless addressed. I had a letter from Saridhakis to one Karapanos at Khordhaki. I found him sitting outside his tumbledown hut in a cloud of flies which I was hospitably invited to share. But I learned little, despite my companion's help in questioning, except that Karapanos had spent the Occupation in his village, collecting information for the British, instead of going to the mountains. The afternoon deepened as I bounced on up stony slopes, down hills ferociously stepped with rocks between the olives.

Once we crossed a fine old stone bridge over the River Platis. 'Are you afraid, would you like to get down?' 'I feel fine', I said, thankfully at ease on level ground. Once my guide gave me an opportunity only too rarely offered to a woman travelling alone in the remoter districts of Greece. 'Soon we shall be coming to a village—would you like to urinate?' Then as we turned away from the embryo road and took a short cut the landscape expanded. The leafy slopes were left behind. From Rethymnon I had almost crossed the island; there ahead was the southern sea. The hills were naked. In the hollow beneath us, a village: at last Nithavris. Behind it, a steep bare mountain-side. With apprehension I looked at the range I was to traverse next day. In the sinking afternoon sunlight the view was menacing.

We came down into Nithavris about six o'clock. I am looking, I said, for Elias Voskakis, I have letters for him. He will be back, a woman said, he has gone to Rethymnon, he will come by the bus. My luggage—a knapsack and an air-bag—was deposited in his house with injunctions from my guide that the children were not to touch it. Then I waited.

The café tables were set on a verandah. After a few minutes a Voskakis cousin appeared, and with him I went up the wooden stairs and sat watching the business of the evening. Men and women were coming home from the fields, leading flocks and herds to the spring. Young calves pranced gaily to drink; the soft-moving cattle were a frieze of bronze and gold in the last of the light. Around me the village elders sat talking. One old man had a shepherd's staff with a metal crook. It was examined, fingered, pronounced useless: too small, everybody said, it won't hold the fleece of a sheep. I offered cigarettes and asked about the walk to Anoyia. Across Ida? People shook their heads; impossible in one day.

'It would be all right if you found somewhere on the way to sleep for the night.'

Remembering that this was the opinion at Yerakari too, I was discouraged but obstinate. I must, I said, get to Anoyia tomorrow night, for I have to be in Herakleion by the next day. Well, they retorted, you can't go over Ida, then.

The company grew. The scene was gentle, friendly, pastoral; I alone with my suffocated cold felt chill. People came politely to shake hands. Presently the schoolmaster arrived, a handsome young man in smart black trousers and a white open-necked shirt: bright dark eyes, a moustache close-trimmed, pink cheeks. Had I been to Gortyna? With graceful courtesy he talked about the famous inscription which runs forwards and doubles back. *Boustrophedon*, he said, using the classical word and illustrating with a gesture of his hands, it is like oxen ploughing a field.

Then a moment of social embarrassment. Did I speak French? Yes, I said, then, in French, do you? Everybody stopped talking and listened. And as he smiled in silence, I realised with self-reproach that I had humiliated him. He could neither speak nor understand a word of French.

Time crept, my stock of conversation dwindled. I began to doubt that bus from Rethymnon. At last as dusk fell there was a murmur in the square below us; then wheels, voices, the clatter of arrival. A short, strong-set man of about forty with dark round head and curly hair came up the steps; it was Elias Voskakis. Silently he handed me an envelope. It came from the Director of the Rethymnon orphanage, it brought me the poem, elaboration of the Pendlebury legend, which I have already quoted. 'You sleep with the smile of triumph on your lips'—my visit had stirred Anglophile memories of war in my friend Saridhakis of two days earlier, and he could not wait to share them. Chilled as I was, half-dazed from my journey, I felt a kind of amused, grateful warmth as I read his verses on the life and death of John Pendlebury.

Recovering myself, I gave Elias my letters of introduction. Deliberately he read them. Then gravely, and in the words and the tone used twenty-four hours earlier by George Akoumianakis, 'Let us go', he said. I bade the company goodnight and gratefully followed him across the square, past the stable at the foot of the outside staircase and into the house. In the main room, a cloth-covered table, a sideboard and a big photograph of Elias, with hair standing out in two defiant wings, as a young man. And again a good simple supper—eggs, cheese, black bread. But you must eat, cried his wife, her young cheeks red with welcome, you will need strength for tomorrow. My reluctance to take more than one hard-boiled egg was incomprehensible to them all. Relatives appeared; everybody joined in the discussion about the chances of getting to Anoyia in a day. The cousin suggested that I might do it if I rode a mule. A mule, said Elias darkly, couldn't do it. Perhaps, somebody hinted, if you arrive at night—at least there is a moon. The opinion was still that the trip was impossible for me. Only Elias, looking grimly at me, was for trying, and that, I knew, only because the letters from Micky and Saridhakis had placed me in his charge.

At last the cousin and the other visitors went home. My bed was made, and Elias and his wife withdrew up a few steps to an inner room. But first she suggested that I might wish to use the lavatory. Enthusiastically agreeing, I was given a lamp and led to the stable at the foot of the outside stairs.

'There,' she said, pointing genially to a corner in the straw, 'there you will sit.' And delicately she left me. A few pigs grunted, and in the pale lamplight I could see a trio of sheep looking at me with mild astonishment.

That night I scarcely bothered to undress before I crawled into bed. I was surrounded by solicitude, and Kreipe himself could not have felt a stronger inclination to bolt.

iii

When I woke Elias was standing in the room holding the lamp in one hand and pulling his trousers over his shirt with the other. He had a cold; I had heard him coughing in the night. 'What time is it?' he asked. The children had broken the clock; 'they break everything,' he grumbled. Four o'clock, I said. It was not yet light. I put on a skirt and combed my hair. Would I like to wash? I stood on the stairs outside the house while Mrs Voskakis poured a mug of water over my hands and I splashed my face. 'A little over your hair too,' she said encouragingly.

There was no breakfast. I had forgotten that you cannot expect breakfast in a remote Cretan village. In Rethymnon I had bought some sweet biscuits, but improvidently, thinking with justice that we already had too much to carry, I had offered to leave them for the family, and I could hardly take them back now.

'You must give some to the children yourself,' said Mrs Voskakis. I handed one to a little boy. 'Do you like it?' I asked.

He ate it. 'No' he said.

Then I remembered something in my skirt pocket—a gift of a handful of almonds from the schoolmaster and his wife at Vryses— and surreptitiously in the grey half-light outside the house I munched a few. Why we were waiting I had no idea. A shepherd came out of a cottage, and I could hear Elias asking him about the possibility of riding a donkey over Ida.

'Certainly,' the shepherd said, 'the animal could go up and it could come down, so long as you don't mind its coming down' (his hands made a roly-poly gesture) 'head over heels.'

He gave me a measuring look; only too clearly I did not pass the test. About the details of the expedition ahead I knew that I was to be shown a cave where General Kreipe had been hidden. Nothing more. I felt hungry and a trifle faint. We went on waiting.

Presently Mrs Voskakis came panting up the hill, leading a donkey; perhaps suspecting what might be in store, the creature had escaped but been recaptured. For a few mad seconds I almost thought of making a run for it myself. Too late. My luggage was loaded. I bundled on. And off we went, Elias in front and two little boys, his son and a friend, trotting behind. It was a little after five o'clock.

For an hour I was in a fool's paradise. The grey sky was only thinly patterned with blue. But the donkey was comfortable, the slope was easy, and we climbed through woods which exhaled an agreeable morning damp. After half-an-hour one of the boys made off up a hill; 'he has work to do.' We climbed on. What, I thought, is all the fuss about?

At that moment I was told to dismount. The second little boy, the son, was sent back with the donkey. 'Let us go,' said Elias.

One learns by experience what a Cretan means by a walk; even Tom Dunbabin had to learn. Elias, who had generously lumbered himself with my airplane bag, my coat, everything except my knapsack, set off uphill at a pace which no doubt was moderated for my benefit but which in three minutes left me breathless. He was wearing riding breeches, high black leather boots, a light shirt, a dark blue jacket, no hat; all that day I saw in front of me his round dark head, his neat, burdened shoulders and those boots marching briskly, inexorably forwards. The first stretch was mercifully short. At the top of the slope we turned and doubled back a few yards. The trees were dense; not until we were standing directly above it could I see the fissure in the hillside.

'Here it is,' said Elias, 'here we hid Kreipe.'

We clambered down. Branches of holm-oak overhung the entrance. The floor was a bed of leaves, deep, soft, dead; one staggered, waded, sank in it. Farther back, a steep drop into a dark hole —the inner cave, invisible from the hillside.

How long, I asked, cautiously inspecting, were they here with Kreipe? Like the number of Herakleion guard-posts passed by the abduction party, this, I suspected, had become a matter not of fact but of legend. Nevertheless Elias replied with absolute certainty. 'Eight days,' he said.

Eight minutes in that musty gloom seemed to me as I scrambled back into the air more than enough.

There was a short respite. There was even breakfast. At the top of the slope a shepherds' encampment welcomed us with milk and a huge domed sheep's cheese. A shame to cut it, we said. But they insisted, and Elias produced bread from his striped shoulder-bag. The bread was not merely hard, it had the consistency of cold lava. Even dipped in the faintly warm sheep's milk it was rock-like. No matter, I was glad of it, and for a moment I felt optimistic about the whole enterprise. At midday, said one of the shepherds, you will be at the top, at three o'clock you will be at Anoyia.

Then he destroyed the effect. The weather, he went on, looks like rain. I turned towards the mountain range ahead; clouds darkened the heights.

'It will rain,' I heard him saying, 'if the clouds come down you won't be able to move.'

For the second time that morning I took fright. Pusillanimously I tried to shift the responsibility. You have a cold, I said to Elias, you mustn't get wet through—if it is going to rain wouldn't it be better not to go on? My failure was ignominious.

'You are thinking of me, are you?' He laughed. 'We will go on, we will try.'

From the next few hours I recall a mixture of despair and exhilaration, a walking nightmare shot with gleams of delight. As we climbed out of the wooded hillside and emerged on slopes too high for trees the island stretched its length behind us. To the southwest the curve of the plain at Tymbaki; then gradually the entire south coast, clear, coloured, sunlit as far as the eastern tip. But ahead I saw a huge concave cliff like the back of an amphitheatre. That, I knew, we had to negotiate.

'We have an hour, an hour and a half uphill,' said Elias consolingly, 'then it is all downhill.'

Credulous enough to believe him, I staggered on, zigzagging upwards, gasping for breath. When I was allowed a rest I dropped to the ground without the energy to take off my knapsack. No water, no springs anywhere, only ridge upon ridge. The cliff was behind us now, but in front I saw only the surge of the mountains,

like a sea of petrified waves. Yet, in this wilderness, arid, trackless—
without a guide one would be irretrievably lost—there were obstinate blossoms: pale dwarf tulips flushed with pink, their petals
curling open to show a golden heart; and, its greenish-white
trumpet crumpling round the yellow pistil, the tiny arum which
grows on Mount Ida.

Patches of snow on the northward-looking slopes were dripping
into reddish-brown pools; Elias filled his water-bottle. The way
led through a pass. In the snow-watered level soil yellow heartsease
grew; the ground was starred with tiny blue flowers; and pin-
cushions of green thorn had put out blossoms of white and pink. But
soon I had no time for botany. We were climbing, toiling diagonally
up the naked slope; more and more often I flopped down to get
my breath, and I could read restiveness in Elias's look.

At last we stood on the ridge. We had come to the lower end of
a col which swung up to a crenellated height; we must climb almost
to the crag before we could begin the descent. Probably, I reflected,
we are near the Idaean cave. But the thought of walking even a few
yards out of our way was intolerable, and I refrained from enquiring.
Eager for the descent, for that unbroken descent which hours earlier
I had been promised, I dragged myself up the incline and looked
over the edge.

At the foot of the crag the ground plunged away to the left in a
long, boulder-strewn, near-precipitous drop.

'That,' said Elias, 'is the way. Now you see why you couldn't ride
a mule.' And he set off down.

I could indeed see why no mule, no donkey could take a rider
down that cliffside. Without the example of Elias I could hardly
have believed the slope negotiable by normal human legs. But
there he was, bounding, leaping, almost running down. Gingerly I
began to creep after him. The angle seemed to me appalling. I felt
with the stick he had lent me, I clung to boulders, I crawled.

'Come faster!' he shouted from far below. Knees weak with
the downhill strain, I picked my ant-like way. 'Don't be afraid, let
yourself go!' I dropped to all fours; life was reduced to the necessity
of getting down that unspeakable slope. When I came to the end
my knees were trembling uncontrollably.

But it was still not the end.

The descent led to a dry ravine. First on one side, then on the other I tottered on down; the cliff reared at our backs, sharp stones slipped underfoot.

'Nidha!' cried Elias, encouraging. 'There it is!'

I looked where he pointed. Remote, the huge plain, green, beatifically flat, stretched below, the plain Tom Dunbabin had seen from, perhaps, the very spine of Ida we had crossed.

'There! See the little white chapel!'

I shall never reach it, I thought. And on again, over the brow of a hill, on along a goat-track; on down a slope following the curve of the plain. Would I like to drink? I gulped snow-water from Elias's water-bottle. Then on again, past a friendly shepherd's hut, on through spiny scrub, on with legs torn and scratched, interminably on. No, I shall just fall down where I am, I said to myself when Elias called me. We had reached the chapel, and that was enough. But somehow I dragged myself over to find him standing by a rough gravemark. It was, I saw, a relic of the war. I did not copy the inscription. Later, I thought; I am too tired now. But at least, looking at the grave in that mountainous solitude, I was reminded that there are worse things than being tired after a walk.

'Here is the spring,' said Elias, 'come and eat.'

Hard-boiled eggs, salt cheese, hard bread, oranges—our lunch would have been a feast for those who passed that way between 1941 and 1945. Elias had been one of them—a runner in the war, carrying messages over Ida. Every week he had crossed from Nithavris to Nidha where we were now sitting, or from Nidha to Anoyia where we were now bound. He had not made the trip since 1944, but he remembered the way well enough. Once, he said, one Easter he had crossed four times in a week and finished with a bullet-wound in his hand.

It was three o'clock when we sat down to eat. The shepherds above the cave at Nithavris, he pointed out, had said we should be at Anoyia at three. How much farther? Four hours: we must hurry lest night overtook us. A drink first? We were sitting by a round stone bowl which caught the spring water and channelled it into a cattle-trough. I took a long swig from the bowl. Then I noticed round the rim numbers of black worm-like creatures. Were they perhaps leeches? They live in the water, said Elias. Yes, I said, I can see that, but what are they?

'We call them,' (I recognised the root of the word which has given us dipsomaniac) '*dipsítes* because they live in the water.'

No time to be fussy. I had another drink.

At 3.45 we set off again. Relieved that my legs had not given out altogether, I was feeling better, though not well enough to go back to the grave-mark and copy the inscription. I was even torn, when we came to a shepherds' encampment on the plain and Elias asked if we could hire a donkey or a mule, between on the one hand exhaustion and the desire to ride and on the other vanity and the desire to be able to say I had walked the whole way. There was anyhow no animal available, and rejecting what from Elias's black looks I suspected was a ribald invitation to stay the night we hurried on, across the plain, up the slopes on the far side, on to fairly level ground with late asphodels still in flower, even on to a recognisable track running round a valley. We saw an old man on the path.

'How far to Anoyia?'

'You are nearly there.'

A few minutes later we met a solitary shepherd.

'How far to Anoyia?'

'The rate you are going' (looking at me) 'seven hours.'

I had flattered myself that I was keeping up a fair pace. Cretans, though, have other standards, and with the fear of being benighted I put on a feeble spurt. The going was not so rough now, and the late afternoon air was refreshing. I grew over-confident. And you were afraid, I said to Elias, that we might have to spend the night on the mountain! He turned on me angrily.

'Of course I was afraid. If the clouds come down on Ida you can't see where you are, you can't see a thing in front of you, you just have to sit where you are and wait!'

But seeing me properly dashed at this he added, 'Soon we shall have a good road, a carriage road.'

At six o'clock I ventured to ask how much farther it was—an hour? He smiled sardonically. 'I am afraid it is farther than that.' We were dropping down into a ravine; between the cliffs the evening shadows were gloomy. But when the valley widened we were in sunlight again and following a wide grassy track. There were trees, there were fields with people working; after the naked wilderness the sense of human life once more. Elias called to a young man and made a final attempt to get a donkey for me. In vain; and anyway by now I meant to finish on foot, though I could not resist reminding him of the promised carriage road.

'She doesn't like the path,' he said to the young man; and they laughed. This path is all right, I said irritably.

I ought to have known better. At the top of a rise the grass turned to sharp rock and boulders where the feet balanced precariously.

'There is Anoyia,' said Elias, pointing to scattered lights far below.

And at that moment the sun set. It was in blue and purple summer twilight burnished by a moon mercifully at the full that we began the last descent, steep, rocky, beset with jagged shifting stones. It was by night and moonlight that at last we reached the outskirts of the village through which Kreipe fifteen years earlier had been led by his captors.

We had left Nithavris just after five in the morning, we had begun to walk just after six. When after what seemed hours of trudging village streets we went in to a café in Anoyia and ordered a drink it was half-past nine at night. Stupefied I sat while talk went on over my head. Who is she? She is a journalist . . . she understands Greek . . . she is very tired. Once, offered a newspaper with a cartoon showing a two-headed British lion, one tongue licking Khrushchev, the other licking Uncle Sam, I roused myself. The British, I said furiously, were right, right to try for peace in the world; hadn't the Cretans seen enough of war? Then, too tired for even the friendliest inquisition, I sank back into silence while Elias went to seek hospitality from a cousin in the local police. He came back with the news that the cousin was away. But he had found a room.

The hotel was of the most unassuming. But it was clean, it was welcome. We sat at a bare table and opened our bundles of food. 'I am hungry,' he said, though by now he had a streaming, roaring cold. I could eat nothing but an orange. And he too was tired. Do you know, he asked, why I am tired? To me it seemed natural enough, but I tried a few guesses. Because you have been carrying my air-bag all day? Because you have carried my coat as well? Because you have a bad cold?

'You remember,' he said, 'what the shepherds told us this morning? We ought to have been here at three this afternoon, and we got here at half-past nine. I am tired because we walked so slowly.'

The bedroom had a tin basin to wash in and three beds; a man's jacket was hanging over the back of the nearest one. I took the farthest, removed my skirt and blouse and put on pyjamas over what was left. I could see Elias sitting modestly on the far side of the middle bed and taking off his coat and waistcoat before he turned down the lamp. Presently in the sleepy dark I heard quiet footsteps. It was the third visitor, the one with the jacket, coming in and going to bed.

No more than a minute later, as it seemed, Elias was waking me. It was a quarter to five: time to get up and catch the bus to Herakleion.

iv

Elias had been out of luck with mechanical objects. Not only was his clock broken; his cigarette lighter had let him down, and as on our walk we paused for a few minutes in the dwindling afternoon he had jabbed again and again with his thumb, struck no spark, kindled no flame and at last thrown the thing furiously across a gorge brimming with shadow. I did not think of replacing his clock, but irrationally, though of course he had been paid for acting as guide, I felt responsible for the lighter. I sent him a new one from Athens. Then I put his name out of my mind until a year later, in the summer of 1960, I was back in Crete.

I knew I should not have enough time to go to Nithavris that year. I hoped, though, to get as far as Yerakari and Ano Meros; meanwhile I had an errand. The monastery at Arkadhi, about fifteen miles to the south-east of Rethymnon, is celebrated for its role in the Cretan struggle for liberty. Here during the uprising of 1866 (the date is commemorated in Herakleion's 1866 Street) a force of revolutionaries collected. They were surrounded and outnumbered.

But with the active support of the Abbot and the monks they refused to surrender. The story says that the Abbot himself, in a move which slaughtered both defenders and besiegers, gave the order to blow up the powder magazine.

The name of Arkadhi was to be a symbol of Cretan independence. Like many Greek monasteries the place was a centre of resistance in the 1941-45 period, and there had been a plan to set up on its walls a plaque with the names of both the Cretans and the British who had fought against the Occupation. As a result of the Cyprus situation the plan had been dropped. But Paddy Leigh Fermor, when I asked him for advice about Crete, suggested that I might go to Arkhadi and see whether, since relations with the British were improving, the idea of the plaque might not now become a reality.

My trip turned out to be one of the fruitless errands common in Greek travel. The people you want to find have gone to visit their families in another village; they are seeing to property on the other side of the mountains; they are occupied with the marriage of a daughter—anyhow like Elias's cousin at Anoyia they are away, and why shouldn't they be? In this case not only the Abbot of Arkadhi was away. His second in command was away, all the dignitaries were away attending some distant ecclesiastical ceremony; only the monks were there, and I could hardly ask to see them. A boy of about eighteen came out into the deserted courtyard; he was helping while he waited to get a job, he would show me round. I looked at the church with its fine façade; at the historical relics—arms used by the monks in the famous defence; at a building like a dovecot with steps up and a circular pit in the middle—crouching, I peered down to see, piled up, what I was told were the bones of the heroic suicides.

In a shady court there was a plaque. The flame of liberty, said the inscription, the sacrifices for freedom—but they were sacrifices a century ago; no plaque for the fighters of 1941-45. Dejected, for I began to wonder if the damage to Anglo-Greek relations was worse than I had imagined. I took back the letter of introduction which Micky had written for me and got into the car which had brought me up from Rethymnon.

The failure of my errand left me with time enough, if I spent the night in Rethymnon, to go to the Amari villages. I found a hotel. Potted palms in the entrance, nobody in the office; at last a girl showed me to a modest room. In Greek we chatted, in Greek we conducted the negotiations, in Greek I filled in the usual visitors' form. She looked at it.

'Do you speak Greek?' she asked.

It is a question which has been put to me often enough after a long talk in what I know is elementary but I flatter myself is comprehensible Greek. But I still find it disconcerting.

My driver, I was glad to note, did not ask it when after a lunch of over-oiled fish I said I wanted to go to Yerakari. The road had been improved since my bus ride to the village, and we bowled along briskly until we were held up by a lorry. It had been used for work on the surface, it had broken down and now was stuck out at right angles. Beyond it a car full of German tourists waited; a pile of stones prevented anything from passing in either direction. My driver put his car into low gear and tried pushing. The lorry, heavily loaded, was immovable. Nothing could be done until another lorry was fetched. Fuming, we all waited. I offered a cigarette to a man working on the road. Where was I going? To Yerakari, I said; last year I was at Nithavris, I walked over Mount Ida with somebody called Elias Voskakis.

'But I know him! I am Voskakis too, George Voskakis, we are related.' Again Tom Dunbabin's name was my passport. Tom? Of course he knew Tom. Why, he himself had worked with the British in the war, he had helped with a wireless set hidden in the hills above the Amari valley. And he told me the story of Tom in the disguise of a Cretan shepherd walking unrecognised past a German archaeologist who had once been a colleague. Philadem? Certainly, George Voskakis said, he knew Philadem. Then he mentioned another name, Monty; yes, he said, Monty Woodhouse. And I thought of Tom's laconic account of a first solitary landing in Crete: 'A few hasty words with Monty, who left in the ship which brought me, and I was left in my new kingdom.'

By the time the road was cleared I felt more hopeful about Anglo-Greek relations. And in Yerakari all my doubts vanished.

The village was sleepy in the afternoon sun. But under the

presidency of George Akoumianakis some kind of prosperity was returning—the new church almost finished, a new road built to Ano Meros. I asked first for Tom's schoolmaster friend Kokonas, and a little girl was found to lead me to his house. Smiling, his wife received me. 'You look much better than last time,' she said, and remembering how ill I had felt then I could well believe it. Her husband was sent for. A year earlier he had been polite; now I was startled by the warmth of his welcome. When I reached the Akoumianakis household I was overwhelmed. On my first visit they had been formally kind. This time I might have been a long-lost, close member of the family. No doubt the cooling of tempers in Cyprus helped. But behind the change there was something else —the historic attitude to the stranger. It is always hospitable. But it is especially responsive to the extended hand.

The first time I went to Yerakari I was a visitor; by going back I won acceptance as a friend. George Akoumianakis's sad dark face was illumined, his wife rushed to greet me; every detail of our first meeting was recalled, and my account of my walk over Ida was laughed at and applauded as if it had been the March of the Ten Thousand. I was taken to the orchard. The family filled hands and aprons with cherries; and like Tom, like the other British officers who in the war had been entertained I was loaded with fruit.

But your uncle, I asked, where is your uncle who took me on his donkey to Ano Meros? The old man was waiting outside a café. 'Why didn't you ask for me?' he said reproachfully. But I did, I did! I cried as we clasped hands; how could I forget you?

'I saw you go by when you arrived,' he said proudly, 'I knew you at once.'

He speaks, Mrs Akoumianakis said afterwards, very highly of you because you knew how to ride his donkey.

At Kardhaki I stopped to ask for Sotiri who had told me about Tom's little book with its list of good men. He was not at home; and at Ano Meros I learned that Mrs Saridhakis had gone to Rethymnon. But Tom's warrior-priest, Kyriakos Katsandonis, he was there, a benignly commanding figure sitting outside a café.

It was late evening, and in the pale light I did not recognise his companions. Teasing, he asked me where I had last met them;

then, amused and quizzical, he told me. One was the muleteer who had taken me from Ano Meros to Nithavris; the other was Karapanos, the man I had last seen in a drone of flies at Khordhaki. We sat together for a while, talking. The village murmured in the dusk, men's voices ricocheted in the crowded café behind us. Passers greeted their priest respectfully, and once a young couple came up to kiss his hand. We talked about Philadem, we talked about the song of the eagle; once again Kyriakos repeated the words for me. At last I made a move to leave.

'Let us go,' he said, standing up. In his priest's tall hat and long skirts, his beard streaked with grey, he looked immensely powerful. Stifling an instinct to make some gesture of obeisance, I put out a hand in farewell.

'But aren't you staying the night?' he said, startled. My car was hidden from view by the bus which he thought had brought me. No, I said, I have to get back to Rethymnon, I must go now.

'But you can't go!' he said angrily. 'We have killed a chicken, you can't go yet!'

Clearly there was no gainsaying him. We went up the lane past the house where Mrs Saridhakis had entertained me for lunch. We were a party of four, Kyriakos, Karapanos from Khordhaki, my driver and myself. Mrs Katsandonis was cooking the chicken and presently would serve it.

Photographs on the walls: not only Paddy in his Cretan panoply ('he was very handsome,' said Kyriakos) but our host himself—with the British in Cairo, with the King of the Hellenes. The church's treasure, the heavy sacerdotal cross with its chain was brought out of a drawer for us to admire. The scene was easy, domestic, contented. There was a bowl of honeysuckle on the table. A kitten stalked round the priestly ankles; Kyriakos looked at it with indulgent liking. Chicken fried in good Greek oil, cheese, wine, coffee—the dinner was delicious. Lamplight shone on elated faces. Grateful to feel myself admitted, I listened to the talk about the war, about Cairo, about life in the mountains. The echoes of the terrible past grew convivial.

Churchill, said Kyriakos, ah, Churchill, a great man, a saviour. 'Eviva!' we cried. More wine was poured. 'Eviva!' we cried again.

Philadem, said Kyriakos, and the other two repeated the word. 'Philadem!' The name was a kind of talisman, and this time it was to Paddy that we drank.

v

At Yerakari and Ano Meros I had debts of gratitude to pay. But the slopes of Ida, those I did not think of revisiting. In England I had sometimes remembered the grave on the mountain overlooking the plain of Nidha. Surely, I said to myself (one forgets, in sedentary comfort, what it is like to be tired out), surely you could have noted down the inscription. But when I arrived in Crete that following year I certainly had no intention of climbing again.

I went up to Knossos and installed myself in the Taverna, where by the courtesy of the British School I was to stay. On the other side of the road there was a petrol station now. And that very evening a *kentron* was to be opened, a little eating-place (called, of course, the Ariadne) with dancing at night; and next afternoon, so Ourania told me, there would be a Festival, an entertainment in celebration of some local anniversary with a show in the Villa gardens and schoolgirls performing what was described as a Minoan play.

Startled by these marks of sophistication, I climbed the outside stairs to the terrace roof of the Taverna. The air was cool and soft, and already in the late afternoon the owls were calling from the pines. Droves of tomorrow's performers were leaving after rehearsal, and when I took the Herakleion bus I found myself in the middle of a party of schoolgirls. They were singing *Samiotissa* with the lover's promise of roses and golden sails for his Samian girl, and I could not resist joining in.

'Are you a journalist?' a woman next to me asked. 'Perhaps you will write about our Festival.'

In search of a new place to dine I walked through familiar streets —Evans Street, 1866 Street, through the market and past the banks of fruit and the hens sitting silent with tied feet, past the butchers' open stalls with bloody hunks of lamb, beef, veal, pork, liver and pigs' trotters hanging from brutal hooks, up into Liberty Square with the big cafés and the cinemas, down again into Lion Fountain

Square, now a confusion of rebuilding with the Morosini fountain temporarily dusty and dry.

There was a crowd where a man lay inert on the pavement, a policeman holding his legs and a woman nursing his head and rubbing his chest. Supposing him ill and not wishing to add to the watchers, I walked on. I dined in a taverna looking across the ramparts; oily fish, beer, small stony black cherries, a woman's voice singing on the radio, youths in jeans, a faintly homosexual look about the customers.

On my way back to the bus stop a voice hailed me. 'Kyria Dilys!' It was Micky Akoumianakis, sitting having a drink with his wife. 'Why don't you come up to the cave on Ida tomorrow?' he said. 'Mr Hurst—he used to be Vice-Consul—is here on holiday. He has been spending four days in the White Mountains, now he wants to see the Cave of Zeus, the Idaean cave. Why don't you come?'

I hesitated. I should straggle behind, I said, I have just arrived and I am out of practice, and anyway I am terribly slow at the best of times. Then I thought of the cave and my failure the year before to go out of my way to see it. Here was a chance I might never have again.

Well, if you are sure Mr Hurst won't mind, I said, and I sat down to make arrangements about a car to fetch me in the morning.

Did you know, Micky remarked conversationally, that we had a murder here this evening?

'It was where you saw the crowd and the man on the pavement. A girl shot him. She had been what she called engaged to him for months but he wouldn't marry her, so she just took a pistol out of her bag and shot him then and there in front of everybody. When she was arrested she said she had done the right thing. She was glad, she said.'

One learns, I thought as I went home by bus, about the sudden violent passions of the Cretans. At that moment the driver, though I had said nothing about the Villa Ariadne, made a special stop there for me. Afterwards I saw the bus swinging on over the bridge towards Arkhanes as I made my way through the dark garden, past the dog barking and bouncing on his chain, to tell Manoli and

Ourania that I must be up at five o'clock and that I should have to miss the Minoan play.

Michael Xylouris, I found, was to join the expedition. I had never met him, but I knew his name from accounts of the Kreipe episode when he and his guerilla group had received the kidnappers on their way up to Mount Ida; several people, among them the Squire, had recommended me to try to get in touch with him.

We must start, Micky had said, at six o'clock, and at six o'clock I presented myself at Mr Hurst's hotel. Nobody, of course, was to be seen. Nobody ever is ready at the hour planned for the start of a Cretan expedition, but I cannot break myself of the habit of credulity. Presently an elderly gentleman with obviously English aquiline features emerged from the interior of the hotel. I knew that Mr Hurst was an experienced climber. He had been Vice-Consul at a tricky moment in the Cyprus troubles, but his taste for the mountains, Micky said, had won him the respect of the Cretans. Anyhow here he was in climbing clothes—fawn jacket, shorts, stockings, heavy boots, green felt hat, large knapsack; to my alarm he was carrying an ice-axe. But while he ate his breakfast he reassured me. He had no walking-stick and used the axe instead. Comfortingly, too, and with enviable courtesy, for I could see that nobody had warned him that I should be gate-crashing his party, he said he no longer cared to walk fast and would insist that the rest must take their pace from him.

At last Micky Akoumianakis arrived, bringing with him a good-looking young man who was introduced as George. He was Michael Xylouris's nephew; and in a large stout car we set off to find his uncle. After an honourable career in the Resistance Michael had settled down to civil life; he had a butcher's shop in Herakleion. White hair, white military moustache, the sturdy figure putting on a little weight, he wielded a kind of authority, and not only in the Xylouris clan. Certainly his presence that day, as well as Micky's, gave the trip a special quality, and it was with an ambassadorial air that we drove to Anoyia. We drank coffee under a plane tree in a part of the village I had not seen on my first visit. Then we jolted up a track first of stones, next of grass. The driver was told to come back for us at six o'clock. It was half-past eight, and we started to walk.

'I shan't come with you, I can't walk so far.' Michael was reluctant. Then, drawn perhaps by memories of the war and the passage of Kreipe and the kidnappers 'along this very path', as he put it, he relented. At first the climb was gradual and interrupted by patches of level walking. Low on the ground, the minute yellow globes of some creeping plant; ahead, the crests of Ida were streaked with white, though there was less snow, I think, than when Paddy and Stanley Moss had gone this way with their prisoner.

At a shepherd's hut we were invited to rest. A curve of stone half-enclosed a stone table; above it, a flypaper and a ceaseless buzz of flies. A boy fetched cheese. It was the first, the pure, fresh cheese, soft, warm, delicious; sitting in bars of shade and sun, we ate it with a little dark bread. 'Why don't you stay here with us?' the shepherds cried. But we excused ourselves and hurried on—downhill, through a little pass, across a small plain. The place, Michael Xylouris told me, was called Hagios Mamas.

'The Germans camped here when they were looking for Kreipe, fourteen battalions of them. And all round up there' (he pointed to the surrounding heights) 'we had look-outs watching what they were doing.'

Last year, I said, I crossed in the opposite direction, from Nithavris. I described the walk which should have taken nine hours and which I had ignominiously completed in fifteen and a half. Everybody laughed. But which way did you come, from Nithavris to Nidha which way? I tried to identify the paths which Elias and I had followed. But I knew none of the names. We climbed, I said, over the mountain till we were high over Nidha, then we came down by a steep slope to the spring; it was terribly steep, I insisted, shuddering, almost like a cliff. Heads were shaken, faces were blank; nobody could understand. It really was terribly steep, I repeated.

At a second shepherds' encampment there was a chapel by a spring, there were offers of hospitality. We will stop, we promised, on our way back. A little farther, and we were in sight of the fierce north-looking slopes above the Nidha plain.

'I shan't go any farther,' said Michael. 'I will wait for you here.'

Once again he pointed to the heights. 'Over there we took Kreipe.'

In my turn I pointed to a savage descent a little to the left. 'That is where Elias and I came down.'

There was a general cry of recognition.

'Eh!' Michael exclaimed. 'Now I see. From what you said I couldn't understand where you crossed.'

'But it really is very steep, isn't it?'

'Oh yes, of course, very steep,' said Michael and Micky in unison, with the indulgent smiles one offers to a boastful child.

Down through the folds of the hills, across the huge green expanse of Nidha, up to the chapel and the spring where Elias and I had eaten lunch. I had forgotten how far it was above the plain; the Cave is higher still. I dragged myself up the last yards of the path; gratefully I noted that Mr Hurst had kept his promise about pace. All the same Micky and George Xylouris were already at the top, grinning. Inky birds flapped and scattered. The huge arched mouth in the cliff belittled the visitors. Striated, the rocks showed their teeth; patches of scrub and a clump of stunted trees grew in front. 'A big comfortless cave, with bats inside it,' Tom Dunbabin had written. Black in the grey face of the mountain, the mouth had a dead, empty look; only in the cracks of the lips there was life where flowers grew, white, virginal, springing from brilliant green leaves. Oozing and slippery, the entrance sloped down sharply. George lent me his stick, but I was disinclined to explore far. I was not sorry when we turned and went down once more towards the sunny plain.

This time I wrote down the epitaph on the grave. 'Michael Basil Brentsos,' it said in touchingly mis-spelt Greek, 'was executed here by the barbarous conqueror on September 3, 1943.' In the enormity of the landscape death took on a new dimension of loneliness. But to the Cretans, inured both to violent ends and to the silence of the mountains, the memorial seemed less dramatic. 'Ah, 1943, h'm,' said Micky, casually reading. We tried the door of the chapel. It was locked, and we went to join the others at the spring.

The *dipsítes* were still there. But nobody noticed them; only when I asked again what they were somebody brushed a little of the water out of the bowl with his hand. We all drank from the cup which the infallible Mr Hurst had brought; we ate frugally and fortified ourselves with a nip of Micky's *tsikoudhiá* We could hear in the distance the sound of sheep-bells, like clear water trickling over pebbles. It grew louder; then there was the quiet thunder of feet as a pale, solid, walking cloud, forming and re-forming, moved up the hill. The cloud stretched, lengthened, wound on the path towards us. At last the flock, jostling and crying, came to file along the line of troughs watered by the spring; and embraced by the sense of pastoral company we sat and watched until it was time to set off for our rendezvous with Michael Xylouris and the shepherds.

It was three o'clock and more when, after crossing the plain and climbing through the surrounding hills, we arrived at the encampment by the chapel. The sun was hot, and I was beginning to flag, but the beaming faces of the shepherds showed that this was no time to be unsociable. Immediately we were pressed to make a night of it, to eat, drink, stay till morning. Michael himself backed the invitation. I was thankful that the decision lay with Mr Hurst, and that he firmly said No; left to myself, I might not have had the moral courage to refuse. As it was we were in for a beano. Secretly Micky called me to look behind the chapel wall. One of the shepherds was there. He was standing by a fire of sticks, roasting the spitted carcase of a lamb.

When I went back to the party a large round sheep's cheese was on exhibition; there was joking competition, since Mr Hurst had a camera, to be photographed holding it. Our hosts were all smoking. In the mountains a shepherd soon runs out of cigarettes; by the end of the afternoon Mr Hurst had given away five packets. So had Micky. 'They are *thirsty*,' he said, 'for cigarettes.' Timidly, for I was conscious of the robust masculinity of the company, I asked George Xylouris to distribute the few I had brought.

'But no,' he said, smiling, 'you must offer them yourself.' And with my single packet I went along the line of unshaven, fiercely friendly faces. When we were called to eat I looked at the building by which we sat. It was one of the cheese-houses of which Tom Dunbabin had written and in which he had again and again been given food and shelter. Then once more I heard his name. Tom, said one of the shepherds, Tom often came here. It was Charalambos, yet another member of the Xylouris family, speaking.

'Tom was in the hills above here, he had a radio in a cave. Many of the English came this way. Bill—yes, Moss, that's the one— Bill slept here many times. And Philadem—as you know, they brought Kreipe this way. . . .'

And laughing he talked of the abduction and the time when Paddy had absented himself for several days from the party. He was in fact, as Moss's book makes clear, trying to get in touch with one of the British wireless operators. But for the Cretans his trip, far from being practical and necessary, had an impudence which they admired. Of course it is possible that for reasons of security they were deliberately kept in the dark. But in the story which Charalambos told there was no hint of secrecy. Paddy, it said, 'never apologised, just came back and said he had been on a binge somewhere.'

The tales multiplied. Michael, too, had adventures to describe. 'Once I spent forty-eight hours hiding in a cave on Psiloriti' (Psiloriti is the Cretan name for Mount Ida). And to the listener something of the mood of the mountain people during the Occupation was communicated, something in their temper which had responded to the deadly times. As with the priest and his friends at Ano Meros, distance and memory had transformed hardships and dangers into a kind of pleasure.

Something else, too, I recognised. We ate sitting on stone benches round a flat circular stone. The roasted carcase of the lamb was hacked up, the joints were laid on the stone; everybody took a piece with his fingers and gnawed it. We threw the bones over our shoulders; we drank water from the spring and wine from the shepherds' own stock; we finished up with slices of sheep's cheese and the last of Micky's *tsikoudhiá*. Freshly killed, the lamb was as tough as it was skinny; I had a struggle to hide how little I could get down. But everybody else ate heartily. We laughed, we toasted one another, and George Xylouris explained and I fancy refined for my benefit a joke I had not understood.

I had heard of the welcome of the Cretan mountains, I had read about the generosity with which the British in the war had been sheltered and entertained. Now I saw for myself something of what it must have been like. I thought of Tom on his first reconnaissance trip over Ida and the meeting with the guerilla leaders celebrated, high on the mountain, with wine and the roasting of a sheep. I thought of him with Paddy and Xan Fielding on their four-day Christmas feast in the Amari villages. There was no longer the background of danger. But the food was the same, the rough gaiety was the same. Even the faces were the same. A passage from the past was being re-created.

Then the moment of illumination passed. We were saying goodbye and taking messages which in England we should forget to deliver; we were stumbling downhill towards the place where our driver of the morning was to meet us. Michael had been called aside to advise in an argument. Two young people wanted to marry, but their parents had quarrelled; he was needed to arbitrate. He caught us up as we were passing a flock of sheep; half their number looked mournfully out from under red-branded foreheads. What, somebody asked, does the red mark mean?

'Those,' said Michael, 'are the ones to be slaughtered.'

One needed, perhaps, the reminder that life is rarely romantic for long.

vi

At Anoyia, after a drink under the plane tree with village elders and sociable citizens in dark suits, we shook hands all round, at his request left Michael behind, and drove homewards; George and a younger Xylouris, one of the ubiquitous cousins, crammed into the front, Mr Hurst, Micky and I sat thoughtful at the back.

Why are you so silent? George asked, turning round, is something wrong? No, no, nothing wrong. But you *are* silent! We are tired, we said, after our walk. To relieve the tedium he set the car's record-player going. 'Get up, get up and dance!' the disc urged. George is a very good dancer, said Micky, he is a champion.

It was nine o'clock when we reached Herakleion. Disinclined, after the long exhausting day, to eat, I had a welcome glass of whisky with Mr Hurst at his hotel; paid, though he civilly demurred, my share of the car; and caught the bus back to Knossos. I made my way to the Villa to find Manoli and Ourania sitting up in the kitchen. What a pity, they lamented, that I had missed the show. Many visitors had come, many foreigners, and the Minoan play was beautiful; it had been a great day for the Villa. Then I arranged for an early breakfast, said goodnight and went down the dark garden to the Taverna. A solitary visitor, I unlocked the door and went in to the stealthy house. The owls were still calling in the pines as I plummeted into sleep.

VII

i

THERE WAS SOMETHING dream-like in those few days spent at the Taverna. Before the war it had always been in the Villa itself that we stayed. The Taverna was for the Curator to live in, and though in the summers when Humfry and Alan Blakeway and James Brock were digging nothing stopped me from visiting the house at the end of the garden I always thought of it as strictly an archaeologist's preserve. I suppose I must have looked in at some time or other. It no longer held for me the mystery which, enveloping the whole of the Evans domain in Crete, had made the very word Taverna enigmatic. In the lethargic summer days I walked past it every afternoon. But it still kept its distance. I was never on familiar terms with it.

Now it was handed over entirely to me. At night amidst the scent of honeysuckle I climbed the steps to the verandah and took the key from its hiding-place. In my bedroom, two beds, a cupboard, shelves, a chair, a table, a wash-hand stand, a bit of carpet, an electric lamp by the bed. On the floor beneath, the kitchen and another room; there at ground level one went out to the courtyard and the door to the road. The whitewashed wall with its drapery of morning glory deflected the sound of traffic, and I slept without hearing the buses or the occasional lorry from Herakleion.

In the morning Ourania brought a tray with tea, bread, butter and (mistakenly supposing that no English visitor could begin the day without it) a large, freshly opened jar of marmalade; everything was tranquil, orderly. In the library I recognised the archaeological books I had seen on shelves for half my life. On the walls, Arthur Evans as a young man, holding a vase; a photograph of his friend the American archaeologist Seager; a replica of a splendid steatite head of a Minoan bull. On the verandah where one looked out to the wire-enclosed patch of garden with the tall dry grass, the fading hollyhocks and the pithoi half-nourishing a few dark crimson geraniums there were the baskets of sherds inseparable from all archaeological residences. A little way beyond, a broken statue, the draped figure of a woman, stood in front of an outhouse, a workshop. Yes, it was an archaeologist's preserve all right.

But its status, and the status of the Villa of which it was an appendage, had changed.

ii

The signing of the German surrender did not quite end the rôle of the Villa Ariadne in the story of the war. Tom Dunbabin, having with Dr Yamalakis and the faithful band of Cretans checked less amiable elements in the guerilla movement by occupying the house, was presently installed there; he was among the officers appointed, in the aftermath of battle, for the protection of ancient monuments. The Palace, he reported to the Committee of the British School, needed 'some repairs'. As for the Villa itself, though one could hardly have expected it to be immaculate there was general agreement that the German military had been careful enough tenants. Later on Piet de Jong told me that they had behaved with the utmost correctness, avoiding disturbance and, if they commandeered furniture from the village, scrupulously giving receipts—of which when the war was over the Cretans, he said, took full advantage. And between April 1946 and September 1947 the house was lived in by the Liaison Officer to the British Military Mission in Crete, and room was found also for a number of other Army and Air Force officers.

The Squire, whose departure from Crete with his mother had been so reluctant and so precipitate, was kept late on war service in Egypt. He was still Curator of Knossos, he was longing to get back. At last he was allowed to make the trip; it was not long before his report on finds made 'during agricultural operations in 1940' bore witness to the tenacity of archaeological preoccupations. His appointment was extended; from the autumn of 1946 he was to be Curator for another three years. But a year later he resigned. In his final season at Knossos (it was six years since at Herakleion harbour John Pendlebury had taken farewell of the Hutchinsons) he showed himself a steadfast friend to Hilda Pendlebury on her one and only return to Crete. He was with her in her search for witnesses; he was with her at the enquiries into her husband's last living days and at the memorial service on the hillside at Kaminia. Then he too left the island, retired to Cambridge—or rather to Harston, a few miles outside the city—and settled in the house which had been his home since childhood.

When I visited him there his mother—a formidable woman by all accounts—was dead, and he was living alone in a state of academic disorder as endearing as it was incurable. The gate of the tangled front garden stood open; one had the sense of an abandoned orchard somewhere behind the slatey Victorian cube of the house. There was a damp breath of ice as one crossed the threshold. But the Squire exuded the warmth of a man who felt he was cushioned in comfort. Remote in the farther of two rooms opening to make one a tiny electric fire burned; when we moved in its direction for lunch I should not have been surprised if he had suggested turning the thing off to spare me from over-heating. We ate from a table half of which was laid with a doubled cloth. The other half was piled with books and papers; around us shelves, chairs, tops of furniture were stacked with periodicals, their edges brown with dust.

'She cooks' (that invisible She of the scholar's bachelor establishment) 'she cooks a joint for me sometimes,' he said contentedly. 'I think' (sawing at a warmed-up disc) 'this is veal.'

And perhaps it was. I would not have risked judgment. But I knew that he was opening for me a treasured bottle of retsina. And as with enjoyment and a sense of drama he talked about Crete and the Villa and the approach of war, as his long serious face was illuminated by memory, I was affected myself. I began to feel happily warm. In fact I nearly missed my bus back to Cambridge, and should have missed it had he not rushed into the road, elbows and knees working in the action of a runner out of practice, to stop it for me. I could see that his long legs would have been at ease on those mountain walks with John Pendlebury.

The Squire's retirement to Cambridge had left the Villa Ariadne without superintendence. But another figure from the past history of the domain reappeared. Though Piet de Jong had worked with many archaeological enterprises, his distinguished work linked him especially with Knossos. Now he was appointed Curator. And to Piet and his resourceful wife Effie fell the job of restoring to order not only the Palace but the whole estate.

In the 1930s anybody from England who spent any time in Athens was bound to hear of Effie de Jong. Piet I knew from the start of my days in Greece, and his amused ironic presence was one of the sociable pleasures when Humfry was excavating on the mainland at Perachora. And from report and talk one was aware of his wife as somebody to be reckoned with in the British colony. Ah, Effie de Jong, people would say, she speaks Greek so well, you know; yes, you'll be seeing her. But it was a little time before I met her. For a whole season, perhaps, instead of coming out to Greece she would stay alone at the cottage in the Norwich neighbourhood which was her home base. The de Jongs were unruffled by the long separations enforced by work which took Piet to quarters in Corinth, or Crete, or Turkey, or the expedition tents near the Perachora lighthouse.

Nevertheless they were in some ways the most married couple I can remember. Avid observers of human eccentricities, they complemented one another. Piet, describing in the unwavering tones of his Yorkshire upbringing some incident, some character, was a spellbinder; his eyes behind the studious-looking spectacles would glint with mischievous pleasure in his own performance. And when he was with Effie he still described and enjoyed the remembered absurdity. But subtly he deferred to her reminiscences and anecdotes. One felt that he was proud of her and that she relied on his enjoyment; the pair of them glimmered quietly together.

She looked like a homely little Scottish body; fading brown hair, short bunchy figure. But she could be formidably cynical, and the soft, precise, deliberate Scottish voice emanating from that unspectacular figure sometimes made her comments all the more appalling. 'Oh,' she said once, listening, after the Battle of Crete, to a romanticised account of some local hero's honoured grave, 'oh, I thought the dogs ate him.' And from Piet, looking down his long, delicate, enquiring nose, came a subterranean murmur of laughter.

In spite of this unsentimental turn of mind the de Jongs were kind. They were good friends; I think with gratitude of a cossetted week-end spent, at a time when I badly needed it, in their Norfolk cottage. It was an occasion which displayed their self-sufficiency. I will not swear that they actually drew water from a well, but I recall two people living quiet, solitary, economical, completely contented lives. Effie in the kitchen and the garden, Piet in his garage-workroom at a treasured lathe—I had the impression of a devoted practicality.

It was a quality they were going to need at Knossos. The estate which Evans had bestowed on the School had understandably deteriorated. The olives were in fair shape, so was one of the two vineyards, but the other, neglected, had been given over to barley. Though structurally the buildings and, largely no doubt as a result of Professor Platon's foresight, the Palace itself had survived the war, everything needed cleaning, tidying, rehabilitating. A start had been made. Recovery, though, needed time. Piet and Effie took up the job in the December of 1947. The house, the fields and the garden began to revive. As early as 1948 things were far enough advanced for the King and Queen of the Hellenes to visit Knossos, where they 'took tea', as the Report of the School reverently records, 'at the Villa Ariadne'. The Palace was repaired, the routine of archaeological life was restored. Each year small-scale excavations were carried out.

But changes were taking place in the outside world. Archaeology, once regarded with suspicion by a strict academic society which preferred textual evidence to the testimony and the aesthetics of excavation, was becoming fashionable. The number of students applying for admission to the British School swelled. Financially it was growing difficult to keep up a large establishment in Crete as well as in Athens. Most disquieting of all was the responsibility for the Palace. The fees charged for entrance went to the Greek authorities while the British School paid for keeping the site in order. Evans's restorations were stoutly built, but there was always the fear—one had felt it before the war, in Humfry's day as Director—that the walls and the handsome columns of painted cement would come crashing down in an earthquake. By 1951 the Committee had made a painful decision. They offered the Villa, the Taverna, the Palace site and the estate to the Greek Archaeological Service.

The Greeks could hardly refuse the gift of a bit of Greece. The offer was accepted. The British would be allowed to use the Taverna indefinitely as a house where their students and their excavators could stay. But the Palace of Minos on its rounded hill, that soil wrested from obstructive Mahometans half a century earlier, would be surrendered. There would be no Curator haunted by the fear of a disease of the vines or a failure of the olive crop. The Villa would cease to be a foreign enclave.

The de Jongs had the task of dismantling—a task likely in any country, and especially in Crete with its genius for fabrication, to stir rumour. As I had been told, Effie spoke Greek with enviable assurance and with none of the fumbling for a gender or a case-ending which affects less confident foreigners. Whether or not she spoke with absolute correctness she was immediately understood. But she did not like the Cretans. And though they liked Piet they did not like her. Perhaps they were conscious of her feelings. She was, they said, using a colloquial Greek word, very nervy.

The de Jongs set about clearing the Villa. The library was moved into the Taverna; so was some of the furniture. A few pieces were sent to Athens, a few were left in the house. The tedious and thankless job was done with the efficiency which characterised both Piet and Effie. But nothing prevented the birth of a malevolent local myth, and one or two of the more cantankerous among the Villa hangers-on insisted that the de Jongs were selling up the place. A decade later I was to hear the story—and with embellishments.

In 1952 the keys of the Villa were handed over, and Effie was included in the Committee's acknowledgment of its debt to the Curator, as a result of whose 'energy, perseverance and careful husbandry' the neglected estate and the buildings had been transformed and the Palace recovered from the traces of war. 'Proud to hand over to the Greek Archaeological Service a site which bears such evidence of skilled administration and scholarly care'—the School's expressions of gratitude read like a citation. And indeed the end of a famous campaign had been reached. At last the deed of transfer was formally signed, and the house and the land where the great Evans had celebrated so many triumphs passed out of the hands of his countrymen. It was 1955—almost half a century since he had planned and built and named the Villa Ariadne.

iii

Melancholy shadowed the surrender of the outpost of adventurous scholarship. The School felt it. Many of the Cretans felt it, in particular those who had known Evans and had been connected, in however modest a capacity, with his work at Knossos. A great mistake, several of them remarked glumly to me when in 1958 I first went back to the Villa, to part with the place. Naturally the former servants of the estate were especially despondent. They had worked all their lives at the Villa. Why should they stop now? After all, they said stubbornly, the British School had not stopped digging.

Manoli, as a matter of fact, was still in employment. Whenever the British carried out excavations at Knossos he now worked as foreman. And with their two children he and Ourania, who acted as cook, were allowed to go on living in the servants' quarters. He was not consoled. I thought of him as I had known him before the war, a good-looking dark boy in black trousers and white shirt serving, deftly enough, at table. Reappearing at Knossos after more than two decades, I saw a middle-aged man with blunted features, a moustache, deep wrinkles round the eyes; the grey check shirt dusty and torn by work on the site; on his head a peasant's straw hat, the wide brim saucer-shaped, frayed. I was hailed, of course, as belonging to the glorious past of the Villa. I was 'one of the old ones'; I would understand. And though I knew well enough that the School Committee with cramped funds had done what it felt possible, giving each retiring employee a lump sum, I found it hard not to be affected by the laments of the Knossos dependents.

The absence of a pension was the first complaint. Manoli had others. For many of the people who had helped during the war, he said, Tom Dunbabin had found jobs. There had been jobs in banks, jobs in Athens or Herakleion, and he would have done better to snatch at such a chance. Instead he had remained at the Villa. Tom had said someone was needed who knew the place, Tom had asked him to stay; and he had stayed. Had he taken a job elsewhere he might have been entitled to a State pension. Now he had no pension, nobody to look after him.

'The golden years of my life are spent!' he cried. 'Where can I go now, what can I do?'

Difficult to harden one's heart against a man who talks about the golden years of his life, even when one knows that he has in fact been found a perfectly good job. Emotionally I was trapped.

'People say,' he went on, 'that the servants at the Villa were able to save money. But a man has expenses; I have educated my children, I have a son, I have a daughter; there was the war; it was all expenses.'

People, I fancy, were not far wrong when they believed that the Villa servants had saved money. All the same private savings have nothing to do with the hope of a pension, and I could not help admiring the dramatic conclusion. 'After forty years,' Manoli said in a fine burst of righteous exaggeration, 'a man should not be thrown out to die like a dog.'

Anyway I felt I should like to talk to the older servants, those who, unlike Manoli, were no longer working. I found Maria, that flittering household moth who decades earlier had cleaned sherds on the Evans excavations, at her village of Katalagari. Bunched together in skirts and scarves, hooded in black, she came at the rumour of an English visitor to hobble along the narrow street, where to my surprise she recognised me instantly. I was glad to get out of the airless little staircase of her house to a balcony which smelt sweet with flowers in pots; a boy was sent running to fetch *loukoúmia*; a bottle of *tsikoudhiá* was brought; and I sat drinking and holding Maria's arthritic old hand while a crowd of friends and relations pressed in. Are you from London, from London are you? Where are you staying, where are you staying? How many days, how many days? Slowly and with piercing clarity for the benefit of a foreigner the women duplicated every question. A party of little boys stood watching from a rooftop across the street. One of my audience—it was a daughter, a handsome woman with no headscarf, the hair severely parted and drawn back—spoke bitterly about the lack of a pension from the School. And completely reduced by gentle old Maria's welcome, I will do, I said, what I can. It won't be every month or even every year, it won't be much, but something I will do; I won't forget. I left carrying a bunch of scarlet lilies cut from one of the balcony pots. Maria herself had complained of nothing, asked for nothing.

Kosti, the former steward, was in a different mood. His village, Alagni, is about twenty miles from Herakleion; I was driven up in a hired car which half-filled the tiny square, the plateia, I sat in the café, ordered a drink and asked the man who served if he knew Kostis Khronakis. A messenger was despatched, a young man with bright lively manners and an incipient moustache appeared—Kosti's son Minos. A few minutes later a well-remembered figure came stumping into the plateia, a battered coat thrown over the shoulders, a wisp of black worn round the head. The once-fair moustache was grey; the chin was stubbly; but the eyes peering out of the wrinkles still blazed a mad bright blue. He had no memory of me until I mentioned Humfry. But then he sat down and without pause ran through his repertoire of anecdotes, beginning with the one in which, according to some of my friends, the central figure is Hogarth ('Hoggeris' in Cretan). For me, though, it has always been Evans. Anyway Kosti himself, no matter who is being rescued, invariably plays the part of the rescuer. 'I carried him out of the waves on my shoulders, on my shoulders I carried him.' The story was once well known among his Cretan acquaintances. 'Has he told you,' they would say, 'about carrying Evans on his shoulders?'

When I went into his house Kosti, surrounded by wife, son and a variety of relations and neighbours, got on to a more urgent subject. He had worked for the School and the Villa for forty-seven years: 'Now they have thrown me out.' Making a personal bid for my sympathy, he recalled a letter he had written to me after Humfry's death; he had been to Mycenae, the letter said, and there had put flowers on the grave. Yes, I said. I remember; that was kind of you.

'Shall I write to the School Committee in London about my pension? Forty-seven years I have worked. I have been very ill, I have had three operations, my legs have gone black, would you like to see them?'

I made a hasty diversion. How did you get on, I asked, in the war? Did you ever see any of the British officers? Did you hear about General Kreipe?

'Once Mr Dunbabin, you know, Tom, came to the house. His clothes were all in rags—I gave him some of mine. Yes, we had four Germans billeted here, they slept in this room. One was a bad lot, he killed two Greeks in the next village. Two of the others were good men, anyhow none of them ever gave us any trouble. Then one day they came in and told us: "They have stolen our general, it is the end of the war!" Not long after that they went off hanging their heads with the Greeks laughing at them. . . . Shall I write to your Prime Minister about my pension? I am strong, I can still work. Why' (the blue eyes glittered with mischief) 'I will come to the Stadium in Athens and wrestle to show you. . . .'

Incautiously I described conditions at the Villa; there was no work. The place was shut up. I had forgotten the myth about the de Jongs.

'It is all the fault of Mrs de Jong, all her fault. When she and her husband left they took things from the Villa, they left it bare. It is all her fault.'

Nonsense, I said, what things?

'Furniture, all sorts of things. Forty-seven years I worked, I know how to cook, how to do everything, now they have thrown me out. . . .'

Well, I said, stop telling these silly stories about Mr and Mrs de Jong and when I get back to England I will see what can be done. As I was driven away Kosti with his family and a small crowd of fascinated observers stood waving in the plateia. That, I thought, is that until another year.

Next morning I walked from the Herakleion hotel up to the Museum. At the entrance desk an official stopped me. Kosti Khronakis, he said, is looking for you; he is still somewhere about. There was a search. Upstairs among the strange formidable faces of the frescoes (so different from the faces of the replicas in the Palace), downstairs among the double axes and the jewellery and the decorated pots—not a trace of Kosti. But when I went back to the

Astir Hotel there in the street, a coat thrown over his shoulders, was a figure waving frantically with a stick; he had come down by bus from his village.

'Since I went to the grave at Mycenae and strewed flowers' he began as we sat on the hotel terrace; the waiter bringing drinks grinned delightedly. 'After forty-seven years I have been thrown out. Will you take a letter to the Committee for me when you go back to England?'

All right, I said. But I am going to Athens tomorrow, so get the letter written, leave it at the hotel and I will take it. He demurred. Today (for such a letter has to be professionally composed in high-class Greek) was too soon. Never mind, I said, I will give you my address in London; write to me there. And now we must leave, for I am going to Mallia.

'To Mallia? I will come with you!'

At last with repeated promises I detached myself. Once more I looked back from the car to see the stubborn old figure standing in the sun, waving. 'Shall I,' he had said again as we parted, 'send a letter to your Prime Minister too?' He thought for a moment. 'And shall I put in a little one for the Queen?'

It was indeed true that there was no place for Kosti at the Villa any more. Long after the hand-over conditions at the property were anomalous. In 1958 when, making my first nostalgic return, I had crept down the stairs and peered into a bathroom with dripping tap and a bedroom where creepers were beginning to thrust fingers through the window-hinges, the British School was apparently still authorised to use the house as overflow accommodation for students working on excavations, and the Director came up from the Taverna to join them for meals. A year later I found the Taverna unoccupied, but Piet and Effie were living in the Villa—living a picnic life in one room with camp-beds, a stove, a table, a couple of broken-down chairs, a threadbare carpet and a cupboard which they said was a relic of the Evans furniture.

Piet had been making exquisite drawings, 1,400 of them, for a German publication of the Cretan seals in the Herakleion Museum. He had been allowed to take trays of the impressions up to the Villa to work from, and he was now waiting for Professor Platon, who was at Rethymnon, to come back to Herakleion and approve the work. The Museum's professional mender occupied a next-door room and sometimes slept there. Manoli and Ourania still had the servants' quarters. For the rest the house was a shell, and at the sound of footsteps in the garden tiger-striped, long-eared cats shrank into the thirsty tangle of mullein and wild poppy. As late as 1960, five years after the Greek Archaeological Service had taken over the estate, there was still no change. The little Taverna seemed to me when I was staying there that year to have assumed the modest comfort, the self-sufficiency, the calm cloistral air which had once belonged to the Villa itself. But the big squat stone house still slept.

In 1962 I was again briefly in Herakleion. On the bus to Knossos I asked for Evans's house. The conductor made no difficulty; that at least was the same. Stealthily, for I wanted to look by myself before I was overwhelmed with the commonplaces of news, I made my way past the Taverna courtyard and up through a garden still matted with dry weeds. The Villa was silent. The silence, though, was of a new kind. The house was closed. But the dark green shutters were fastened back, and through basement windows I could see bedrooms freshly equipped—mattresses tidily rolled on the beds, lamps on the bed-tables, basins with running water.

'Yes,' said Ourania, when the uproar of the dog brought her out, 'they have had archaeologists here, Greek, English, I don't know who else. They have turned the dining-room into a drawing-room.'

And now I remembered that in the previous autumn an archaeological conference had been held in Crete. Delegates had stayed at the Villa Ariadne, and the house had been put to the purpose for which Evans intended it. Once more it had served as a quiet meeting-place, a retreat for researchers and scholars.

Or perhaps not so quiet, for in the preceding decade the underground skirmishing which is the daily life of archaeology had burst out into the open.

iv

The battle had begun in the early 1950s with a revolutionary philological study. Or perhaps one should look back to the start of

223

the century and that fabulous first season at Knossos when Evans had unearthed hundreds of clay tablets, some of them with hieroglyphs but most bearing linear inscriptions of two kinds, to be known as Linear A and Linear B. The second of these scripts was the more sophisticated and the later in date. There was also much more of it; and though scholars threw themselves enthusiastically into the task of trying to decipher anything that turned up the chances with Linear B seemed the more promising.

Evans immediately recognised that the tablets represented inventories, lists of people, animals, goods. But in what language? Etruscan? Hittite? He believed it to be an unknown tongue, in fact Minoan, so that even if it could be deciphered it might still be incomprehensible. Since he had begun his explorations with the idea of finding an early system of writing the hope of reading the script was dear. A few of the tablets were illustrated in his 1900 report in the British School Annual. In 1909 his *Scripta Minoa I* included the hieroglyphs, the Linear A and another handful of the Linear B inscriptions from Knossos. In 1935 came Volume IV of *The Palace of Minos* with more Linear B. But exhausted by the creation of the enormous book the ageing giant never managed to publish the great mass of the tablets. Six years later he was dead. The riddle was still unsolved; and his old friend Myres was left to grapple with editing the collected material.

For half a century after Evans's first triumphs Linear B remained, in spite of numerous scholarly theories, an enigma. In 1939, however, there was another of the discoveries which translate myth into history. It was the discovery described by John Pendlebury in that letter to his father: 'Blegen has got a Palace apparently of the Homeric period. . . .'

The American archaeologist the late Carl Blegen had been digging on the west coast of the Peloponnese at Pylos, reputed domain of Nestor, wisest of the Greeks who sailed against Troy. And like Schliemann proving the truth of Troy, like Evans verifying the golden tales of Minos, Blegen brought archaeology to the defence of legend. There, a few miles from Pylos, were the remains of a Palace which the evidence marked as Nestor's. He found not only the Palace of Nestor. He found, as John Pendlebury reported, large numbers of inscribed clay tablets (there were in fact hundreds of pieces): and though at the time John thought they differed from the Palace of Minos finds the seven photographs which were immediately published showed clearly, according to later and more fully informed experts, 'that the Pylos tablets were identical in script, layout and language with the Linear B documents which Evans had found at Knossos'.

But the war delayed fuller publication, and more than a decade went by before the Pylos material could be made generally accessible. Then suddenly a rush of evidence. In 1952 Blegen, once again excavating, found more tablets. That same season Evans's old adversary Wace brought to light at Mycenae a number of Linear B pieces. And Myres now published in *Scripta Minoa II* the Knossos material. Or a great part of it; authorities maintain that various factors—the difficulty of dealing with Evans's notes, interruption by the war—combined to make the book incomplete. Not that there was blame for Myres, who at an advanced age had been faced with so difficult a problem. Two years later he was dead. He was eighty-four; and another towering figure from the romantic era of archaeology had vanished.

That summer the British School was digging in the island of Chios. The *Sunday Times*, benevolently encouraging an experiment in underwater archaeological exploration, had presented the School with skin-diving equipment; an indolent, un-athletic, ignorant bystander, I swam about, ignominiously failed in an attempt to skin-dive, rambled over the hills and by the kindness of the Director, Sinclair Hood, shared the life of the expedition. The party included a reserved young man with dark hair and serious refined features, Michael Ventris. He was the team's draughtsman-surveyor; his wife Betty worked with him; and the industrious pair would be seen setting off with their notebooks in the long shadows of early morning or the stunning heat of afternoon towards the foundations of an archaic temple high in a hollow of the hills.

I had been sent to Chios as an observer. I observed, I asked questions. Who was Michael Ventris? He had won a certain fame, somebody said. Philologists were still arguing; too early for general acceptance; but it really seemed that Ventris had deciphered Linear

B. In the interval, nearly twenty years, since my last visit to Crete I had forgotten the existence of Linear B. Nevertheless, recognising that interpretation of the script was likely to cause an outbreak of scholarly sniping, I looked across the table with a new curiosity at the grave, concentrated young face—which at that moment was probably grumbling about the vegetable stew which sometimes provided our main dish. Meat was scarce in Chios.

Michael Ventris had been a schoolboy when he began to think about Linear B. In 1936 he was in the audience at Burlington House when during the exhibition celebrating the British School's fiftieth anniversary Evans lectured on the Minoan discoveries. That was the start. Ventris says that four years later he 'tested the theory of an Etruscan relationship on the Knossos tablets in an adolescent article.' Trained as an architect, he did not lose interest in the problem of Linear B. But there was always a major obstacle—the impossibility of getting a proper look at the script.

At last by 1952 the cryptologists got their chance. Not only was *Scripta Minoa II* at their disposal, not only Blegen's 1939 material, which was published in 1951; Wace generously let two decipherers have an early look at photographs of the tablets newly found at Mycenae. One of the two was John Chadwick, a Cambridge philologist and classical scholar. The other was Michael Ventris. And in 1953, mainly as the result of 'an idea suggested' by Ventris, an article jointly written appeared in 'The Journal of Hellenic Studies'. The idea was that Linear B represented not Etruscan or Hittite, not, as Evans had believed, Minoan, but an early form of Greek. Some archaeologists had already suggested this. Ventris and Chadwick set to work to prove it by transliteration.

Not to be expected that everybody would be immediately convinced. But the next year or two brought more material and more evidence, and in 1956 Ventris and Chadwick were able to publish *Documents in Mycenaean Greek*, a solid book with interpretations of three hundred tablets from Knossos, Pylos and Mycenae. The authors admitted that their translation was sometimes tentative. But they felt confident that in principle they were right—and by then most scholars felt so too. Linear A remained mysterious. Earlier, more primitive, it possibly represented a really unknown language, perhaps the Minoan tongue which Evans thought was expressed also in Linear B. In detail, indeed, the whole subject, A and B alike, is impenetrable except to the serious student, and I risk referring to it only in so far as it concerns the Knossos story.

But one need not be a student to see what it meant if the Knossos Linear B tablets really were written in a form of Greek. Artistic and archaeological evidence had shown that in its great creative period Knossos was closely linked with Mycenae. Evans maintained that Mycenae was a colony, 'a Minoan plantation'; and in *The Archaeology of Crete* John Pendlebury, describing Crete as 'a world power', wrote of 'the extension of her empire to the North, over the Mainland and islands' and of 'the Minoanization of the Mainland'. But if Linear B was Greek then at the time the script was being written on those famous clay tablets the language of the educated, the ruling class in Knossos would have been Greek. And then the situation is reversed: Mycenae, Greek Mycenae would, as some archaeologists had for years been arguing, have been the dominant power; a Mycenaean, a Greek Mycenaean could have held the throne of Minos. Evans believed that Knossos was wrecked by an earthquake. Pendlebury suggested that the disaster came with invasion from the mainland, 'a deliberate sacking' by rebellious dominions of the Cretan empire. The deciphering by Michael Ventris and John Chadwick of the Linear B script strengthened a third theory: that on the spring day, evoked by Pendlebury in a dramatic phrase, 'when a strong South wind was blowing which carried the flames of the burning beams almost horizontally northwards', it might have been the Minoans themselves, the subject people, who rebelled against their Greek overlords and set fire to the Palace.

v

The general public may have been little more than mildly concerned about the archaeological excitement generated by the Ventris-Chadwick reading of Linear B. They were certainly not allowed to ignore the next outbreak of hostilities.

In the summer of 1960 a distinguished Oxford philologist, Professor L. R. Palmer, published in *The Observer* an article which claimed to demolish Evans's system of Cretan dating. Evans believed that Knossos was destroyed in 1400 B.C.; that with 'squatters' in occupation the civilisation of the place fell into decay; and that the Linear B inscriptions belonged to the period before the catastrophe. But if the language was Greek, Mycenaean Greek as Ventris and Chadwick called it, some new thinking was called for. Pylos, a Mycenaean-age city, fell about 1200 B.C.—and Blegen had found Linear B in the ruins. Could the tablets belong to a period much later than Evans had maintained? And was it possible that the great days of Knossos came to an end not in 1400 B.C. but two centuries later when the Mycenaean palaces of the mainland were destroyed?

The theory had already been advanced by archaeologists who questioned Evans's dating; and excited by the encouragement given by Blegen's discoveries and the Ventris-Chadwick decipherment Professor Palmer set to work to provide supporting evidence. In the Ashmolean Museum at Oxford he found the excavation Day Book kept by Evans's assistant Duncan Mackenzie. The Day Book, with entries from the beginning of the Knossos exploration in 1900, showed certain discrepancies between its on-the-spot record and the exposition in *The Palace of Minos*—discrepancies in details of stratification. They hardened Professor Palmer's suspicion that Evans had got his dates wrong by a couple of hundred years.

Observers of an excavation in progress might think it possible for the notes of the first days to be modified by later reflection or indeed by later discoveries. But it is not for me to risk an opinion; one tries to avoid a minefield. The newspaper which published the Palmer article was less inhibited. Perhaps, it suggested, Evans 'carried away by the splendour of his discoveries', had 'unconsciously mis-reported the evidence'. Alternatively, had Professor Palmer 'exposed a conscious misrepresentation, reminiscent of the Piltdown Man fraud'?

Hastily Professor Palmer repudiated the notion of fraud or deliberate misrepresentation on Evans's part. He dissociated himself, he said, from 'the mischievous suggestion' which had been made not in his own article but 'in a news column'. The repudiation was prompt. But one can never be prompt enough; anyway the fight was on. Professor Palmer had said he had 'discovered' the Mackenzie reports. No question, came a retort, of discovery. The existence of the Day Books was known to many Minoan scholars. He had not found the Mackenzie reports, he had asked for them. He had been provided with them by officials of the Ashmolean Museum who had long been classifying and using them. There were cries of 'mischief' and 'unnecessary personal attack'. Even the palaeontologists were affronted. They jibbed at being lumped in with archaeologists: the experts in the Piltdown case, they said, were all honourable men, incapable of hanky-panky with the evidence.

In the mêlée Professor Palmer showed that he was very well able to take care of himself. Some of his opponents admitted that Evans might have been mistaken about the history of Knossos after 1400 B.C. Sinclair Hood, who as Director of the British School at Athens had for the previous three years been in charge of exploration at Knossos, was among those who accepted the possibility that the dates could do with reconsidering. He agreed, he said, with the Palmer theory of a Palatial period after what had long been widely accepted as the final destruction at the end of the fifteenth century B.C. Why, at one time Evans himself, he pointed out, had thought that the Linear B script was still in use in the later period. But now the British School had a fact to offer. In those three years of excavation fragments of tablets had been found in a deposit which belonged to the period before 1400, before the destruction of what Evans had called the Last Palace. In this case at least, Mr Hood wrote, 'the date given by Evans for the Linear B tablets of Knossos is confirmed'.

On this foundation of theory and counter-theory, evidence and counter-evidence Herakleion held its 1961 Cretological Congress, and the Villa Ariadne once again housed visiting archaeologists. It was not only from Ourania that I heard about the meeting. It had been an international affair with representatives of more than a dozen countries; among the British were Sinclair Hood, John Boardman, Reader in Classical Archaeology at Oxford (he had been working on the Chios dig when Ventris was there), and the formidable Palmer himself. Dr Yamalakis was among the listeners. Like a good many Cretans he shrank from any thought of dethroning Evans, Crete's great benefactor. The audience, he said, was shocked when Palmer lectured; they didn't, they couldn't applaud. Perhaps he was speaking out of loyalty. There were others, though, who felt that the conference went to support, except in matters of detail, Evans's basic conclusions. John Boardman, for instance, felt it. At the start of the controversy there had been a plan for him to collaborate with Professor Palmer in a book presenting the evidence on the Linear B material. Now he found that he disagreed not only on the evidence but on the way it should be used. The way out chosen was to publish two independent studies, and in 1963 under the title *On the Knossos Tablets* they appeared looking, askance at one another under the same covers.

The exchange of academic civilities went on. Professor Palmer found and published a letter to Evans in which Mackenzie, writing in 1905, testily insisted that the evidence for stratification in the Early Minoan period was totally inadequate. Why had he never made his disagreement public? Perhaps he had not been a free agent, Professor Palmer hinted, quoting a reproachful passage in which Mackenzie speaks of financial straits and asks for six months' overdue fees. But, somebody replied, there was no question of reluctance on the part of Mackenzie to speak out; what about looking up what he had said on that very matter of stratification in the 'Journal of Hellenic Studies' in 1903, two years before the letter?

Explorers in lands of shifting uncertainties, driven by a desperate curiosity, the archaeologists and the philologists struggled on. At Thebes, the Thebes of Oedipus and Cadmus, in the deposit of a Mycenaean palace were found not only fragments of Linear B clay tablets but Babylonian cylinder seals one of which could with as much assurance as learning affords be assigned to round about the second quarter of the fourteenth century B.C.—and that anchored the tablets to the same date. It was not perhaps as late as Professor Palmer would have liked. But it was later than Evans's system of chronology strictly demanded.

The excavator in this case was that Professor Platon whose resource had done so much during the war to preserve the Palace of Minos. Soon his name was to become internationally famous.

At the beginning of the century when Evans was making his first discoveries at Knossos Hogarth carried out a dig at Kato Zakros on the shores of the extreme eastern end of Crete. He discovered house foundations, pottery, fine seal impressions. But he concluded that Zakros was a Minoan, or rather, for the word Minoan was not yet in use, a Mycenaean trading settlement; he did not persist in his search. John Pendlebury of course passed that way. In 1938 he was in Eastern Crete with Hilda. There are two villages at Zakros. The Pendleburys stayed in Ano Zakros, the upper of the two, then had 'a short quiet day' at Kato or Lower Zakros, where they 'heard stories of Hogarth . . . and Evans in the old days'. His letter to his father says nothing more of the antiquities. A few days later he writes from Knossos about a visit to a private collection belonging to 'a very nice Dr Yamalakis'. The doctor, whose name was to be so closely linked with the Resistance in Crete, just before the war possessed some gold objects believed to have come from Zakros. Whether he owned them at the time of the Pendlebury visit one cannot tell; though Zakros is several times mentioned in *The Archaeology of Crete* John makes no reference to finds of gold. Kato Zakros in fact remained obscure. Then after the war the Greek archaeological authorities took a hand. Professor Platon, investigating, suspected that the site had been something more than a port. A liberal American patron, Leon Pomerance, offered funds. In 1962 digging began in earnest. And there in the coastal plain were the foundations not simply of houses but of a Minoan palace, two-storeyed, with a central courtyard, a throne-room, a banqueting-hall, a kitchen, perhaps two hundred and fifty rooms in all; and everywhere the relics, the decorations, the vases, the storerooms of an advanced civilisation.

Up to that time the great palace sites in Crete had been discovered and explored chiefly by foreigners, British, Italian, French. Now the Greeks had a fourth palace to set beside Knossos, Phaistos and Mallia. It was still, when I went there in 1966, a remote place, a four-hour drive from Hagios Nikolaos along roads often ferociously pot-holed or blocked by boulders. We skirted the Gulf of Mirabello. Along hairpin bends we came down to Sitia, where Cumberlege and Nicholas Hammond, hurrying back to Herakleion to meet Pendlebury on that desperate day in 1941, had put in and found a mysterious break in telephone communications. Arid empty landscapes led us to the upper village of Zakros and the road down to the sea and the plain. On the left of the descent a ravine split the hillside. Even in the morning light it was a cavern of darkness. But the sea blazed, a fringe of reeds glowed emerald at the shore; where on the level ground the foundations were exposed a cluster of men worked peacefully. The rulers of Zakros, perhaps, had felt safe in their valley.

It was with a commendable lack of malice that Professor Platon, leading me round, pointed to the spot where the British explorers had dug sixty years earlier; Hogarth missed the Palace by a few yards. As for the Pendleburys, 'We must,' Hilda said to me once, 'have been sitting on the very site—and we saw nothing.' But John may be forgiven. Generations of men had failed to re-discover the Palace; alone among the great Minoan sites it had never been plundered.

Professor Platon believes with Professor Marinatos that it was destroyed as the result of an eruption on the volcanic island of Thera to the north and that earthquake rather than invasion or revolution wrecked the great Cretan palaces in about 1450 B.C. All but Knossos, which he thinks survived until 1380 B.C. (a date close to that suggested by the Babylonian cylinder seal found at Thebes). And perhaps indeed Thera, where Marinatos has lately been uncovering beneath volcanic ash the frescoed houses of a rich city, is a key to the enigmas of Crete. The outsider can do no more than record the views of the insiders—noting as he does it that there is precious little finality in the affairs of archaeology.

vi

In 1962 the rebuilding in the centre of Herakleion was finished, and as, reflecting on the rôle of the Villa in the Cretological Congress, I sat at dinner I watched groups of little girls in red or white dresses dancing on spider legs round the Lion Fountain. Before I went back to the hotel I walked through the market. In the dark it was shuttered and blind; outside the deserted butchers' stalls the terrible drum-shaped chopping-blocks, white-splashed, might have been execution blocks. A solitary cat glided past as if on castors and vanished up a side-alley. Russian cosmonauts might be circling the moon, and indeed the Cretan papers were full of the story. But here in Herakleion nothing much had altered.

At Knossos, however, there were changes.

Michael Vlakhakis at the kiosk had taken a wife. The bridegroom was over fifty while the bride was only twenty-nine; it was a great joke in the village. But Michael was delighted with himself. 'I left it late,' he said, 'but still . . .'; and unasked he told me all over again the story of the exhumation of John Pendlebury. Up at the Villa Manoli and Ourania continued to reflect gloomily on the action of the School in handing the house over to the Greek Archaeological Service. 'The rooms have been closed,' they reported, 'since the Conference last summer; it is a terrible waste.'

It was a relief to find the Palace of Minos in livelier shape. A day of blistering white sun; the heat was stunning on the lower slopes where one or two buildings had been roofed in with a kind of ribbed plastic; but visitors went stubbornly round, crossing the shadowless courts, peering into the light-wells, examining the fresco reproductions. While I sat on a bench eating a lunch of grapes and figs and biscuits I saw with pleasure party after party stopping to look at the Evans bust and to read the inscription. When I went out I bought a few postcards.

'Where,' the man at the desk asked, 'did you learn Greek?'

'Here, in Athens, in the country.'

'Did you ever know Evans's foreman?'

'Why, yes, Manolaki who was killed fighting in the Battle of Crete—of course I knew him.'

'I am Akoumianakis too—he was my uncle.'

Warmly we shook hands. We talked of Micky, and I reflected that in Crete nearly all men are if not brothers at any rate cousins.

That year I did not go to see Kosti, for by him at least I had, I felt, already done my duty. After his obstinate pleading—and after my visit to Maria, whose silence had affected me more deeply—I knew in my bones that words were not enough; something had to be done. I was not under the impression that Kosti needed the money. He owned land, probably a vineyard or two; one of the friends to whom I wrote for help remarked that she was possibly much worse off than he was. She stumped up all the same. I think she felt, as I believe all those who joined in felt, that British prestige was involved, that it was not fitting for old retainers of the School to be left regarding themselves, no matter how unreasonably, as shabbily treated. Perhaps we were subscribing not so much to a gift for Kosti and Maria as to a tribute to the great past of the estate which they had served and to which we were all indebted. We could not let down the name of the house. We might have called ourselves Friends of the Villa Ariadne.

Archaeologists are not often rich. But in the ready response to my appeal for subscriptions there was generosity as well as a grateful and perhaps an amused recognition of the part played by Kosti and Maria in the Knossos legend; one friend, I remember, a phonetician whose connection with the School was remote, actually asked to be included. In the end there was £175 to distribute. The list of donors had a special link not only with the Villa but with its founder. Evans's half-sister Joan subscribed; that was not surprising. What one could hardly have counted on was that she should be in Crete in 1960. In 1935 she had come out to meet Evans. But it was the troubled time of the Venizelist revolt, and she got no farther than Athens. Perhaps—for in the last year or two of the 1950s illness had prevented her from travelling—she had not thought to see Crete again. But in 1960 something decided her. She felt better; and with two friends, the Dyneley Husseys, exactly a quarter of a century since her brother's last visit, she arrived in Herakleion.

For the purposes of the Kosti and Maria fund the timing could not have been better. The money was waiting. I was in the offing to make any necessary arrangements. After the tranquil nights of sleeping in the Taverna I could move to the Hotel Astir to meet Joan and her party.

Not that I could altogether stifle my anxiety. There was the question of place—whether to bring Kosti and Maria down to Knossos for the presentation and thus make sure that both were available at the right moment, or to ask of Joan, who in England some months earlier had been hardly able to walk, to go by car and endure the exhaustion of a rustic excursion. I took local advice. At last the village trip was elected; we must risk finding that Kosti was visiting a cousin at the other end of the island.

Luckily by the late afternoon of the chosen day the brilliant Cretan sky dimmed; it was cool enough when the four of us, Joan, the Husseys and I were being driven in a large hired car towards the hills. I can still feel the relief I felt then when on our arrival at Alagni Kosti's son Minos appeared to say that his father was at hand and should be promptly fetched. He was, I need hardly say, in his vineyard.

The appearance of a member of the Evans family gave the occasion a flourish even more splendid than I had hoped. I was well aware that without Joan the presentation would be wanting in authority. Even so I had not realised quite what distinction her presence would confer on the function. She played up with something which I can describe only as majesty. To begin with she wore a hat, a formal hat with a wide brim and a swathe of veiling. The people of Alagni had not seen an English lady in an English lady's hat for two generations, and as with a sweep of skirts she alighted from the car a susurration ran through the village. Immediately—the Evans magic was at work—Kosti was there; and he ran, legs turning black or not he ran to kneel and kiss her hand. It was with the air of a royal procession that we moved off to his house for refreshment. It was in the royal tradition that Joan, whose doctor had forbidden her to drink alcohol, made as she held her glass the gesture of one taking a swig of rakí.

The formalities were at first hampered by Kosti's insistence on displaying a small bundle of letters and testimonials from Sir Arthur. I myself may have contributed to the delay. Seeing an aged woman in black come into the house and sit resolutely down I made a move to greet her. I was hurriedly brushed away.

'No, no,' said Vasiliki, Kosti's wife, 'she is nobody, she is a neighbour. She has just come to look.'

But at last we got under way. Joan made a speech in English, I offered a translation sadly lacking in the elegance of the original; then, using the correct Greek phrases which I owed to a friend and which I had committed to memory. 'A few of your well-wishers in England,' I said, 'wanted to make you a small present as an acknowledgment of your friendship and of the happy days at the Villa.'

I had written on the envelope containing the money a rough transliteration of the subscribers' names, and for the benefit of Kosti I read them out as Joan made the presentation. Several times he stopped me to make an identification. Once a name (it belonged to one of the most generous donors) was greeted with disapproval. When I came to Piet and Effie 'How much,' Kosti asked sourly 'did she give?' 'Plenty,' I snapped back. My mood was not improved when after a sum of money handsome enough in the circumstances had been handed over Vasiliki turned to me with a request. 'Can't you,' she said, 'get a job for our son Minos?'

But my thankfulness at the general success of the occasion outweighed everything else, and when after riding a short distance with us on the running-board (in the direction, naturally, of his vineyard) Kosti stood at the curve of the road, once again waving till we were out of sight, I felt a shade of sadness—the chill, perhaps, of a farewell which might not be repeated.

The money had been divided between the two beneficiaries in the proportion, according to their respective wages at the Villa, of three for Kosti and two for Maria. The old lady, however, was grateful enough for the pair of them. The news of our arrival spread quickly through Katalagari, and from nowhere a figure appeared who turned out to be her son. Maria herself, we were told when we had climbed the stairs and settled, all four of us, among the flowering plants on the balcony, was dressing. Meanwhile the family, beaming now that their grievances were to be redressed, crowded in on us; the handsome daughter, so bitter at our earlier encounter, smiled among the anonymous press of excited women, and a curiosity of little boys peered from behind skirts or edged, whispering loudly, up the wooden stairs. Presently Maria, engulfed in black skirts and shawls, emerged from some inner darkness. She appeared to be chuckling; she remembered, apparently, an earlier meeting with Joan Evans. But when? For in 1935, after all, the visitor had not reached Crete. Ah, much earlier than that; and amid general applause it was disclosed that she recalled seeing Joan as a girl when with her mother—Arthur Evans's step-mother—she had come out to the island before the First War.

With this background of reminiscence the function went famously. Once again I was frequently stopped as I read out the list of donors. But this time it was for a different reason. Maria would listen attentively. Then 'How are Mrs Pendlebury's children?' she would ask: or 'Mr Hutchinson, is he well?' And the old creased face looked out from its black headscarf with infinite goodwill. Saying Thank You is not a matter of instinct. It has to be learned. Rustic society does not always learn, and sometimes in country districts of Greece one is uncertain whether or not a gift has been welcomed. This family left us in no doubt; and in a celebratory mood and with a happy conviction of having done the right thing we went back to the car, Joan and I each carrying a bottle of Maria's home-grown *tsikoudhiá*.

It was in character that Joan Evans should not forget a third faithful servant of the Villa Ariadne. Manoli was, as she rightly put it, a bit in danger of being left out, and when I had been enquiring about Kosti and Maria I had intercepted some meaning looks between him and Ourania. He still had his job. But he must not be allowed to feel neglected; she would go and see him. In the gathering dusk we drove to Knossos. I had been able to give warning of her visit, and we were expected in the Villa kitchen. Ourania had tidied the room, Manoli had shaved and put on a clean white shirt. Hands were kissed, refreshments offered; at once gratified and self-respecting, in conversation and bearing our hosts gave a display of faultless manners.

'I feel,' Joan said as we were on our way back to Herakleion, 'that Manoli will be our next responsibility.'

For the moment, however, it seemed that he was safe.

There was one more name for her to remember—Akoumianakis. That evening the square outside the Astir Hotel and the neighbouring church was crowded. Thinly cheered, a Deputy, a former Minister, was visiting Herakleion. Half a dozen black saloon cars drove round in a circle, and I could see huge rings of bread, ritually tied with ribbon, changing hands. A gathering less formal but perhaps livelier and friendlier was held when Joan and her party entertained to dinner Micky, son of that brave steward who had died fighting in the Battle of Crete.

vii

When in 1962 I was hearing about the excitements of the Cretological Congress there were workmen in the Villa garden. They were digging foundations—digging them, I saw, where once John and Hilda Pendlebury had fondly laid out their hard tennis court. I asked what was going on. A museum, I was told; we are building a museum. Munificent help from Joan Evans and from another Philhellene and friend of British archaeology, Marc Fitch, had enabled the School at last to afford a Stratigraphic Museum. And four years later Joan, with Marc Fitch in support, was once again in Crete to declare the Museum open.

A letter from her written next day describes an occasion both ceremonial and celebratory—exorcism by the village priest with 'no bell, but book, candle, icon, live coal, holy water and an aspergil of rosemary'; speeches; the ritual cutting of a garland; holy water sprinkled throughout the Museum; and a feast with champagne for the visitors and the traditional sheep for the villagers. Sinclair Hood, defender of the Evans name in the Linear B controversy, was there; so were a number of Greek archaeological officials and such local personalities as the Chief of Police. Peter Megaw, who now with his wife Elektra had succeeded Sinclair in occupation of the Director's house in Athens, translated the English speeches into Greek. The great days of Evans were represented as well as mortality would allow. Piet de Jong came to recall them, and the company included, Joan said, more of her brother's former workmen than one would have believed possible. Even Kosti had survived; a car was sent for him and, tottering a bit, he arrived with bunches of flowers, wild Cretan tulips and scarlet anemones, for his benefactress; Micky too was there, a representative for his dead father.

The Greek Archaeological Service had equipped and furnished the Museum; it was an agreeably Anglo-Greek day. And at last the Knossos collection of sherds—among them those which John Pendlebury had found 'labelled in pencil on worm-eaten wood . . .

by a Greek foreman'—had been taken from their storage place in the magazines beneath the Palace of Minos and properly housed. It was sixty-six years from the day when Evans had begun digging. It was sixty years since he had built his house. Another stage had been reached in the life of the Villa Ariadne.

VIII

i

CERTAINLY HERAKLEION had changed in the five years since I had last seen it. Now in 1971 concrete buildings were going up along the road from the airport. Olympic Airways had a new terminal in Liberty Square, and the Square itself had assumed the air of the centre of a provincial capital. In King Constantine Avenue the shops were a good deal more productive than I remembered, and enquiring tentatively about a replacement for a raincoat I had lost I was rushed into a store-room from which I emerged with some kind of protective covering in hideous blue nylon. On August 25 Street tourism had left pockmarks. Rent A Car, said the notices over the travel and shipping agencies on the way down to the harbour, Rent A Boat, Take A Tour, Buy Greek Popular Art.

From the friendly Astir Hotel I went up the hill, past the Lion Fountain and the traffic policeman at the junction, and into the market. It looked neater and cleaner. Perhaps it was, or perhaps the impression was due to the introduction of such doubtful amenities as detergents and plastic buckets. Perhaps also there were more shirts and shoes, hats, spectacles and sweaters. The rest, though the variety seemed greater, offered the traditional kaleidoscope, bank after bank of cherries, apricots, oranges, beetroot, cucumbers, strawberries, beans, courgettes, olives, melons, almonds, peppers, carrots, aubergines, medlars and apples, with here and there a basket of eggs, a pile of cheeses, hunks of raw meat dangling in a row from hooks, and a shop-counter loaded with bread; everywhere the warm smell of coffee from the beans roasting on the turning machines. The wealth of the earth: no supermarket has such a look of plenty. The succession of stalls had scarcely altered. The colour of the evening air was the colour I had seen in Herakleion year after year;

nowhere else is dusk as blue. To my relief—for a moment as I turned a corner I could not see the name—something else was unchanged. Evans Street was still Evans Street.

Next day when I went to the Museum I saw a handsome boulevard where I remembered only chaos, and as I crossed the road to the entrance I was nearly run over by an unexpected rush of traffic. My visit had coincided with the arrival in the harbour of a couple of cruise ships, and I struggled in on the tail of parties of Americans and Germans. Polyglot, the voices of the lecturers battled for a hearing. With a great sliding and clopping of shoes and sandals one party would trail on to another room and re-form in front of another show-case; and dodging between the groups I edged in to look at an ivory; a bull's head with inlaid eyes; a vase from Zakros, its handle a curve of rock-crystal beads; or the huge photographic enlargement of some Minoan seal. A group of watercolours, too, I remembered, Piet de Jong's vision of the Palace of Minos before its ruin, with pillars and stairways unbroken and unblotched and the frescoes—the flying fish, the figure-of-eight shields—bright and new on the walls.

The bus station in a turning off August 25 Street was new to me, though the waiting-room with its bundles of luggage and the counter for coffee was of the familiar kind. The bus westward towards Rethymnon and Canea was due to start and indeed did start at eight in the morning. But the man at the ticket-desk advised me to wait until eight-fifteen and take the express bus.

'You will get there first,' he urged.

Perhaps we did. At any rate one was spared numerous stops at villages. We scurried at a great pace along the way out of Herakleion taken by the captors of General Kreipe; and with the new road-surface and an up-to-date machine we reached Canea in less time than it had once taken a private car. Souda Bay was empty; not so much as a caïque in sight where the battered British ships had burned and sunk in 1941; and Canea itself, once the last stronghold of the German garrison, was a dusty, commercial town busy with traffic.

An hour's drive away on the high plain of Omalos a cold wind ruffled green crops. A Greek Alpine Society sign pointed the way to the crests of the encircling White Mountains. At the far end of the plain a little Tourist Pavilion was plastered against the cliffs where the long descent began to the Samaria Gorge and the pass to Hagia Roumeli and the sea. Chance had brought me there on the anniversary of the Allied evacuation of Crete. Next morning as I went down the Gorge, airless and damp with the threat of rain, I thought how thirty years earlier to the very day the last of the British and Commonwealth troops had been struggling over hot waterless hillsides to Sphakia, a little to the east of Hagia Roumeli, some of them to embark for Egypt, others to find no room in the ships, only the order to surrender—and to begin next afternoon under guard the penitential march back.

Myles Hildyard was in that company, and the Omalos plain it was which after his escape sheltered and fed him. But now the pastoral life went on undisturbed. Only a plaque set in the rock-face on the road down to Canea commemorated the death of a Greek and a New Zealander, members of the Resistance who were killed in a fight with German troops in February 1944; and at Alikianos people will show you a memorial chapel with a glass case full of terrible relics—the bones of massacred Cretans whose bodies were found in a field behind its border of trees.

In the Amari valley peace had settled still more gratefully than at Omalos. I could not afford the time for the slow perambulation of my first visit, twelve years earlier, so I hired a car with a driver at Rethymnon. Anyway I could not have recognised the stopping-places. Smooth roads curled round the flanks of the hills. Villages once no more than a few hovels were now tidy groups of tidy houses. The soft leafy beauty which had enchanted Tom Dunbabin had long gone. Even the ramshackle charm which I remembered— the occasional patches of overgrown garden, the vine coiling up the outside stairway—was missing; everything was characterless, or so it seemed at first under the fringed clouds of that overcast day. For the visitor there was a shade of melancholy. But I wrenched my thoughts back to the condition of the inhabitants. They, wherever I talked, were content.

I had no luck at Yerakari, where I had slept in the house of the village President. Poor George Akoumianakis himself, I knew, was dead, and the gentle old uncle who had taken me on his donkey to Ano Meros, he too was gone, and the schoolmaster Kokonas, friend of the British in the war. But I had hoped to find Mrs Akoumianakis. In vain: a little bunch of women collected to give me the news.

'Ah, Evangelia—she has been ill, she has gone to Athens for a cure. She entertained you long ago? What a pity you have missed her. And her husband, you know about her husband—he did, you know, a great deal for the village. It is sad for her without him.'

At Ano Meros I was more fortunate. In another village I had heard news of the warrior-priest. He is ageing, somebody said. No, no, said somebody else, he is still tough. I told my driver to pull up at a café. The priest, I said, Kyriakos Katsandonis, where is his house? Then I remembered the track up the hill. A fine house, said one of the bystanders. Certainly it looked grander than the picture in my mind from my first visit twelve years ago; and when I was entertained there on my second visit it was too dark to see.

This time a dog was grumbling amiably from a verandah at the top of the flight of wooden steps. A woman came out: Mrs Katsandonis; then an imposing bearded figure in tall priest's hat. He did not recognise me. But when I mentioned my talisman, Tom, he remembered. Thank you, I said as I sat down in the room where we had drunk toasts to Churchill and Paddy Leigh Fermor, thank you, I will not eat anything, I have a long way to go and I can't stay; I came only to greet you and to bring you a book. In that distant past—though to me it seemed like yesterday—I had promised one of Paddy's books, and now I laid it on the table. He looked puzzled. Then 'Ah, Philadem!' he cried, pleased—though I suspect that reading English was a lost accomplishment. The dog sat at my feet, beaming. From the kitchen Mrs Katsandonis called to it not to worry me.

'Leave him,' said her husband, 'she is stroking him.' Then to me: 'He is a Bulgarian dog, my son sent him to me from Bulgaria.'

Once more I went round the photographs on the walls—Kyriakos in the Middle East in the war, Kyriakos with the King of the Hellenes, Kyriakos on some recent ecclesiastical occasion with a proud-looking hieratic group. The room had a self-satisfied air.

When I made to leave Mrs Katsandonis came in with a plate of almonds. I took one. No, no, you must take them all, she said.

'All, all,' said Kyriakos. 'You have eaten nothing, they are for you. They come from the woods up the hill at the back, they have a very special flavour.'

As I went down the track again he stood with his wife on the verandah. They raised their hands in gestures of farewell, and beside them the dog waved a valedictory tail. Looking back at the powerful, Michelangelesque figure in the high black hat, I had the feeling that I had received a plate of almonds from the hands of the Almighty.

We drove to Nithavris under skies softly threatening rain, not like that crystal evening when I had first looked down on the village and taken fright at the thought of crossing Mount Ida the next day. There was a tarred road where I had once toiled along on the back of a donkey. The café where we pulled up might have been the one where I waited, shivering and listening to the talk about a shepherd's crook, but I should not have known it. Elias Voskakis, I said, not very hopefully, to a trio of men sitting at a table, do you know where I can find Elias Voskakis? They turned towards the slope behind them.

'Voskakis!' they shouted. 'Elias Voskakis! Somebody is looking for you!' And to me: 'He is coming, he is coming.'

I looked where they pointed. Coming down the slope with its rough stone steps was a man with a neat round head, the cropped dark hair turning grey. He wore a waistcoat over shirt-sleeves, a stud at the collarless neck, trousers in place of the breeches and high boots I remembered. By the hand he led a tiny boy with neat round dark head, a miniature of himself.

'I knew you as soon as I saw you,' he said. Then, proudly and lovingly, 'This is my grandson.'

In his house we held a reunion—his children, his grandchild, the cousin who on that first anxious evening had joined in the discussion about the chances of reaching Anoyia in a day; only Elias's wife was away, working in the fields, and I had without seeing her to leave the present I had brought. It was a sweater in a colour not, I trusted, too bright for life in an Amari village. I hope it will suit her, I said.

'It will suit her, it will suit her.' The cousin brushed aside feminine doubts. It would, he implied, have to suit her, and that was the end of the matter. And he urged me to eat more of the cheese and the slices of cucumber which had been brought, while Elias poured *tsikoudhiá* from an enormous bottle.

'You sent me,' he remarked placidly, 'a lighter to replace the one which I threw away on the walk. I thank you.'

It was the first I had heard of its arrival; I had forgotten all about sending the thing. Now I remembered something else. His daughter, a pretty girl, dark like him, fresh-faced like her mother, was married, she was a mother herself. Was it you, I asked, who broke the clock that night I stayed in this house?

She had not forgotten. 'Yes,' she said, laughing, 'Father was very angry.' I myself could recognise the furniture in the room where we were sitting. Something, though, was missing—the photograph of Elias with wings of fiery, frizzy hair. 'I don't know,' he said, a little abashed by the reminder of youthful vanity, 'what has happened to it.' The family was still hospitable, still solicitous. But the past was fading. Once proud of his own strength, Elias was proud now of the strength to come. The boy who had climbed week after week over Mount Ida, who had carried dangerous messages, run under fire, suffered a bullet-wound in his hand, was a village elder now, gentle, quiet, living in the promise of his children. The hazards and the heroics were blurred. The Amari valley was reverting to its position as a refuge from a harsh outside world. Perhaps it was still Lotus Land.

All the same I was glad not to be setting off again over Ida; glad to be travelling back to Herakleion with its bustle and its warmth and its urban lights piercing the cobalt blue haze of evening.

ii

The bus journey to Knossos was familiar as ever. True, the way out of Herakleion had a touch of sophistication now—more houses, an occasional public building along the road. But one still looked out on vineyards, and fig and olive and eucalyptus still bordered the fields. At Knossos itself, a few concessions to the tourist—a waiter, for instance, at the open air tables, and a general air of expecting foreigners and cars which had not been detectable when I first went back to Crete in 1958. But there was still the same sense of a moment in time trapped between enormous dramas.

It was a sunny morning when I set out to walk to the road fork where Paddy Leigh Fermor and Stanley Moss had held up General Kreipe's car. Lorries on their way to Arkhanes thudded past me; they lifted puffs of dust which settled on the drying grass and the herbs on the verges. A little way beyond the Palace entrance, at the point where an antique aqueduct spans a gorge on the right, I was hailed from a house. Two girls were working on the verandah. Come up and rest, they said, you will be tired. Later, I promised; I have an errand to do first. Here and there a neat villa, whitewashed behind its terrace wall, looked down on the road. The way was farther than I had thought, and surprised that I had not yet reached the junction (I began to think of it as something like the Schiste where Oedipus challenged the passage of his father) I stopped to ask if I was on the right track. A policeman was talking to the driver of a truck which had pulled up.

'Yes,' he said, 'keep on up the hill and bear right. Would you,' he added, offering a packet, 'like a biscuit?'

A triangle of grass and a wide road, a main road, going back towards Knossos; a driver coming down the hill would have had to slow down. To make sure I was not mistaken I asked a girl who was passing, and a man came out of a field to join in. Delightedly he confirmed. Yes, yes, this was the very spot; why, he had been in the game himself, I must come to his home, it was just down the road. On my way up I had noticed a small workshop and factory. He had a job there, he had a house; and in the nakedly new living-room his wife made coffee and brought *loukóumia* and the summer hospitality of wedges of cucumber.

He had known the British in the war, he and his brother had worked with them and had decorations to show for it. Enthusiastically appearing, the brother brought out for my admiration an enormous round medal. The scene of the Kreipe adventure was still a landmark. I had unfolded the map in their minds.

But only for a moment. Time was blunting the sharp edges of history. When I passed the house by the aqueduct again I accepted the invitation to go up the steps and drink a glass of cold water. Yes, certainly the two girls knew the Akoumianakis family, Micky, Phyllia, all of them. And Manolaki who had been killed in the war? Their father—did I perhaps remember him?—would have known Manolaki better than they did. We sat looking over the plain, gold in the summer weather; down the road where at the bridge the Cretans, forbidden, had rebelliously brought flowers to lay on the graves of two British soldiers; across the valley to the green verge of the river beyond the slopes where generations of Minoans had built their fantastic palaces. Above the river the hills, pale and dry, ran in diminishing curves towards Herakleion and the sea. It was a landscape which through the centuries had been soaked in blood and veiled by the smoke of burning houses. The two girls were contentedly busy setting plants of basil in tiny pots. The verandah, shady, framed in leaves, smelt of peace.

iii

Thirteen years since I had first seen Crete after the war. It was with the feeling that I was retracing my own life that I went down the road and into the Palace of Minos.

The site looked more disciplined than before. More of the restored buildings and stairways, it seemed to me, had been roofed in with plastic. The fresco copies were all under glass and the swallows no longer nested behind them. Signboards in English and Greek made the labyrinth more manageable. All the same I still pulled up short on the edge of high walls. The summer flowers, mocking the schemes of the scholars, flaunted over the evidence so carefully left for future generations. Summer chrysanthemums, sprawling across the great central court, softened its severe rectangle. Plumbago trailed candid blue blossoms. Stonecrop rooted in the interstices of crumbling cement, and purple mallow and dusty white umbelliferous flowers crowded in forgotten pits. A sweet musky scent drifted from slopes dotted with spires of acanthus, spiny as a hedgehog.

There were no troops of tourists with guides that morning, but every hall, every corridor, every flight of steps had its visitors with their maps and plans and cameras. On my way out I passed an obviously more experienced group. One of them, scratching at the powdering walls of the deep cutting where they stood, was demonstrating some archaeological point. They were talking English, and I guessed, rightly as I learned later, that they were from the British School at Athens and living in the Taverna.

I stopped at the souvenir stall in the courtyard to greet the representative of the Akoumianakis clan. Yes, he said, Professor Platon was now in Salonika, but he would presently be back and exploring Zakros. Tourists? Not so many English this year, but crowds of Germans. And Knossos—yes, the British were digging this year; I should see them up at the Villa. Then I crossed the highroad and went to the kiosk to find my old friend.

'Michael,' I asked a waiter, 'is Michael here today, Michael Vlakhakis?'

The man stared at me.

'Michael is dead,' he said.

Somehow I had counted on the twisted figure with the incongruously welcoming grin. If his injuries had not killed him surely nothing else could; I had looked forward to hearing more about the marriage so long delayed and the young wife whose capture had so much elated him. Too late, I thought, one leaves things too late.

'His widow has the kiosk now,' said the waiter. 'Look, she is coming now.'

I looked round to see the young wife. A lean, rangy woman was galloping towards me. The rook-black hair was strained back over deep dark-rimmed eyes; the cheek-bones high, the face long, bony, the whole body in its black lustreless widow's dress full of a desperate energy.

'I knew you,' she cried, taking my hands, 'at once I knew you, he told me about you. A month ago he died, tomorrow I have the service, you know that after forty days we have a service for the dead. . . . He was in hospital, a month ago it was.' The sharp-edged voice gave a gulp of melancholy, then quickly recovered itself. 'A month ago it was, only a month.'

He was very happy when he married you, I said. I am so sorry for you, he was such a good man.

'A good man, a very good man. The war it was which killed him, you saw how badly he was wounded. He was with Blebbery, as you know well. He suffered, terribly he suffered, but what could we do? That is life. Yes, I have two children, a boy and a girl, they are both at school. Fortunately I have the kiosk, otherwise how could I manage?'

Seeing the display of friendship, the waiter refused to let me pay for the coffee we were drinking. Presently the children, neat, well-dressed, under the instruction of their mother well-mannered, arrived from school. Lucky that she had a boy; he would work, no dowry would have to be found for him.

'Next time'—even her gestures of farewell were angular—'next time you come you must stay in my house. I have a house in the village, you must stay there.' She darted to the kiosk, seized two coloured postcards and pressed them into my hands. 'A week you will stay.'

When I walked up the road I saw, pinned to a tree, the black-bordered notice of the service for Michael.

The morning glory was in flower on the wall of the Taverna, but I did not try the door by the whitewashed courtyard. The main gate was open, and I went through it and up the drive.

From the Annual Reports of the School I knew that there had been changes in the buildings, that the Taverna had been enlarged and that a house for the caretaker and foreman had been provided. I did not stop to look. Instead I made my way straight to the Stratigraphic Museum. That too, I had heard, had been extended. Not that I should have noticed the change. In 1966, a few months after the formal opening, I had walked round the outside. The building itself, Joan Evans had written, was simple, efficient, not ugly. 'I think Arthur would like it.' But that day everything had been closed, the approaches were ragged, and I retained no more than the impression of a square building impossible to see into. Now in

1971 I knew at least the name of the extension. Piet had seen the Museum opened. But he had seen it without his Effie; he had not bothered to last out much longer after her death. The extension was called the Piet de Jong Building.

On my way through the garden I met some uninvited English tourists with cameras and jocular comments. Do you live here? they asked, a little uncertain of their ground after my curt responses. Uninvited myself, I could hardly blame them for taking a look. But the encounter made me pause at the doorway of the Museum. Anybody there? I called in Greek. A Greek girl appeared, muttered nervously, disappeared; then an Englishman, one of the group I had seen in the Palace. It was Dr Peter Warren, the School's Assistant Director.

I had not expected to find anybody working. Memories rushed back from the distant past—the chance, inquisitive, uninstructed visitor, the exasperation of the archaeologist interrupted on the job. Apologetically I introduced myself. And again the memories: three people at work, Dr Warren, his wife, another girl; a table covered with sherds; stacked shelves; the sense of concentration on identifying, piecing together, tabulating, noting. The functional building with its storage space and its workrooms enclosing a central courtyard—the amenities were beyond the dreams of the generation I had known. But the dedication was the same.

Abashed by the kindness of my reception, protesting, truthfully enough, my ignorance of the work in hand, I withdrew in haste and made off towards the Villa. The garden had come to life again. Where trees and shrubs once drooped thirsty and neglected, the palms, the olives, the pines now shone green. The leaves of the blossoming pink oleanders glittered. Bougainvillea swarmed irrepressibly over walls and woodwork, geraniums exhaled from rich damp earth. In the light wind sunlight wavered through the trees and freckled the statue of Hadrian. Everything was sweet, cool, gentle.

I circled the Villa. It was the same—but to me it was foreign. Poor Manoli had not lived to become the 'next responsibility' which Joan Evans had foreseen; he was dead these four years. Ourania had retired to a place of her own; no dog barked and bounced on his chain. The new caretaker-foreman and his wife lived in the new house; anyway I did not know them. Fifty times I had walked in that garden or sat listening while Humfry and Alan and James happily talked about the day's exploration. Now James too was dead. Hilda Pendlebury would never read what I had written about her life at the Villa with John. The Squire, who so reluctantly had left Knossos in 1941 and so eagerly returned to it after the war, would never again run to stop a Cambridge bus for me. Tom Dunbabin had survived the fearful risks of the caves and the mountains only, little more than ten years later, to fall fatally ill in Oxford. Dr Yamalakis, defender of Evans, was dead. Michael Ventris, solver of the Linear B riddle, had been killed in an accident. Kosti and Maria, the indestructible ones, they too had vanished.

A stranger, I walked past walls heavy with creepers, past dark basement windows. A bed, a bath—the frugal furnishings of an archaeological establishment were as before. At the top of the stone steps the front door was open. The hall was bare as ever; only the plaque recording the ownership still hung on the wall by the replica of the head of the charging bull. All around, the dogged presence of the British diffused a scholarly energy. But the working life of the Villa seemed to have withdrawn. Temporarily at any rate it had taken up residence in the extended Taverna and the Stratigraphic Museum.

And yet, half-naked though it was, Evans's house looked immortal.

iv

Ghosts walked with me that afternoon when I went up the hills on the opposite side of the valley. Irrigation work was going on by the stream, and the path I had once taken with Micky and Spiro was barred; I missed the way and, scrambling through scrub and thorn, I went straight up the steep slope. In the distance the valley widened into the glitter of the sea. The plateau with its memories of battle stretched featurelessly, and I could not see the ravine where I had watched the child climbing in search of snails. Women were reaping in a field. Hagia Paraskevi? One of them thought she knew the way, and with a tawny dog who suspiciously rejected my advances and gambolled ahead we hurried over the bristly earth with its bleached thistles until we came to a sudden drop.

'There,' she said, 'I think Hagia Paraskevi is somewhere down there.'

We were looking down over a split in the line of the hills. I could see nothing familiar, but I began to clamber round the head of the gorge. My guide and her dog watched until I reached the other side. Opposite, the cliff hesitated and put out a ledge. And there was Hagia Paraskevi, tiny against its backdrop, solitary—I had not realised how solitary—in the enormity of the ravine. My guide waved and turned back; the dog bounded away; and I crawled down the spiny terraces of the slope and crossed to the shrine.

Metal votives hung on the wall under the arches of brick—miniature hands, legs, an ear; an ikon showed the holy one, the saintly Paraskevi, carrying a plate with, staring from it, a pair of eyes. On their spiked stands the candles drooped and melted in the sun. The low wall of the temenos was overgrown. The flowers of summer, mullein and sage, thyme, lucerne and carrot, scrambled and seeded; fig trees, grown tall, leaned over cracking masonry. Wasps clung luxuriating to the rim of the stone basin where the spring oozed and trickled. From the valley came a faint whisper of life. Once I heard the voice of a frog from the pit of the ravine; nothing else, only the sun shining on olive groves and vineyards, the dark belt of trees which hid the Villa, the curve of the road towards Arkhanes.

I looked at the inscription on the stone slab with the cross which marked the grave of Manolaki. Name, age, date; he was killed on May 28, 1941; he was fifty-eight. I reflected on the chance by which John Pendlebury and Manolaki Akoumianakis and Arthur Evans had all died within a few weeks of one another. But even the memory of death could not disturb the serenity of the still afternoon.